A YEAR OF WATCHING WILDLIFE

A GUIDE TO THE WORLD'S BEST ANIMAL ENCOUNTERS

01.   02.   03.   04.   05.   06.

DAVID LUKAS

MELBOURNE | LONDON | OAKLAND

CONTENTS ↗

Whether you encounter a pride of lions exploding out of the African bush to chase a wildebeest, or find yourself wandering amid a colony of 250,000 penguins on the coast of Antarctica, wildlife-watching is one of the most exciting reasons to travel.

This is a great moment in history to go on a wildlife expedition. Never before have there been more wildlife destinations opening up or as many people travelling in search of wildlife, and in response many countries are developing new access points, accommodation and tours

SEEING THE
SPLENDOUR OF NATURE

in areas that were previously difficult to reach. Even better, in response to the growing threats to the earth's ecosystems, many countries are setting aside vast swathes of wilderness faster than they can be explored or documented, providing travellers with numerous opportunities to venture into brand-new national parks or nature reserves that are practically unheard-of and see almost no visitors.

Here, then, are our choices for the world's top wildlife-watching events and destinations as a guide for travellers in search of wildlife. These range from mind-boggling displays of abundance such as the powerful image of 30 million seabirds on South Georgia Island, to subtle displays of remarkable behaviour by a single animal such as the utterly charming spectral tarsier of Sulawesi. Included in this book are trips to see giant colonies of fruit bats, to swim with migrating rays, to seek out untouched tropical islands, and to wander into vast mountain ranges in search of snow leopards.

These events and destinations are arranged chronologically, week-by-week through the year, with four weeks per month. Each week leads off with a profiled destination that offers some of the best, and most unexpected, wildlife gatherings in the world. The profile destination is followed by three special feature animals from other sites around the world.

Obviously, animal behaviours and events don't always fit neatly into a weekly calendar (though a few events are remarkably predictable), so in these cases every attempt has been made to suggest an ideal time to plan your journeys based on weather, best conditions for travelling, and peak windows of opportunity for trying to catch an animal's behaviour. Each event is also given a difficulty ranking. Because of the explosion in traveller-oriented services and guided tours, very few events received a 'hard' ranking, though if you wanted to arrange your own expeditions instead of joining a tour, many 'easy' or 'medium' sites could become much harder to access.

What you have here is a chronological catalogue, or a wish-book, of amazing places to go and intriguing animals to see. These are places and animals to dream about, to tell your friends about, and to inspire you to come up with your own future travel plans. You will come away with both a renewed sense of the shimmering splendour of nature, and an awareness of the ways in which the growing crush of humanity is deeply impacting wild places and wild animals all over the world. We hope that your travels inspire you to get involved and to tell others about what you've learned.

A YEAR OF ↗ WATCHING WILDLIFE

A GUIDE TO THE WORLD'S BEST ANIMAL ENCOUNTERS

⬇ ARCTIC NATIONAL WILDLIFE REFUGE (ALASKA)

↘ NO

↘ CAPE

⬇ YELLOWSTONE NATIONAL PARK (USA)

↘ HIGH ISLAND (USA)

↘ EVERGLADES NATIONAL PARK (USA)

↘ CIÉNAGA DE ZAPATA NATIONAL PARK (CUBA)

↘ PAPAH NAUMOKU KEA MARINE NATIONAL MONUMENT (HAWAII, USA)

↘ BANC D'ARG•

↘ BELIZE (CENTRAL AMERICA)

↘ ASA WRIGHT NATURE CENTRE (TRINIDAD)

↘ CORCOVADO NATIONAL PARK (COSTA RICA)

↘ GALÁPAGOS ISLANDS (ECUADOR)

↘ ANAVILHANAS ARCHIPELAGO (BRAZIL)

↗ MANU NATIONAL PARK (PERU)

↘ PANTANAL NATIONAL PARK (BRAZIL)

↘ FALKLAND ISLANDS (SOUTH ATLANTIC OCEAN)

↘ SOUTH GEORGIA ISLAND (SOUTH A

↘ JANUARY, FEBRUARY, MARCH

↘ APRIL, MAY, JUNE

↘ JULY, AUGUST, SEPTEMBER

↘ OCTOBER, NOVEMBER, DECEMBER

WRANGEL ISLAND
RESERVE (RUSSIA)

LAPLAND (NORTHERN EUROPE)

BIRDWATCHING (FINLAND)

ANTIC SEABIRDS (GREAT BRITAIN)

KRONOTSKY NATURE RESERVE (RUSSIA)

SLAND (IRELAND)   BIALOWIEZA NATIONAL PARK (POLAND)

KORGALZHYN STATE NATURE RESERVE (KAZAKHSTAN)

KAVKAZSKIY NATURE RESERVE (RUSSIA)

BHUTAN (EASTERN HIMALAYAS)

TANG NATURE RESERVE (TIBET, CHINA)

KEOLADEO GHANA NATIONAL PARK (INDIA)

KAZIRANGA NATIONAL PARK (INDIA)

TIONAL PARK (MAURITANIA)

AÏR & TÉNÉRÉ NATURAL RESERVES (NIGER)

TAMAN NEGARA NATIONAL PARK (MALAYSIA)

SINHARAJA NATIONAL PARK (SRI LANKA)

GUNUNG LEUSER NATIONAL PARK (INDONESIA)

NOUABALÉ-NDOKI NATIONAL PARK (CONGO)   DANUM VALLEY CONSERVATION AREA (MALAYSIAN BORNEO)

NGORONGORO CRATER (TANZANIA)

BWINDI IMPENETRABLE NATIONAL PARK (UGANDA)   RAJA AMPAT ISLANDS (INDONESIA)

WILDEBEEST MIGRATION (TANZANIA & KENYA)

KAKADU NATIONAL PARK (AUSTRALIA)

MADAGASCAR (INDIAN OCEAN)   GREAT BARRIER REEF MARINE PARK (AUSTRALIA)

NINGALOO MARINE PARK (AUSTRALIA)

KGALAGADI TRANSFRONTIER PARK (AFRICA)   SHARK BAY WORLD HERITAGE SITE (AUSTRALIA)

SARDINE RUN (SOUTH AFRICA)

KANGAROO ISLAND (AUSTRALIA)

TIC OCEAN)

SARDINE RUN, SOUTH AFRICA

↗ OCEANS

THE MASSIVE BODY OF SALTY WATER THAT COVERS 70% OF THE PLANET'S SURFACE IS ONE OF EARTH'S GREATEST DEFINING FEATURES AND ALSO ONE OF ITS MOST SIGNIFICANT HABITATS. Fortunately for wildlife-watchers, the ocean's many spectacular animals are mainly concentrated along shorelines where upwellings of nutrient-rich waters feed phenomenally productive food chains that include seabird colonies with millions of birds and sardine runs that number in the billions. The most active periods for wildlife generally occur during summer, when the sun's rays are at their peak and fuel massive plankton blooms. During these times, the abundance of food attracts predators big and small, from 12,000kg whale sharks eating tiny krill to 2000kg great white sharks slamming into helpless seals.

The sheer number of animals and open habitats along the ocean's edge makes for some dramatic viewing. Here you can watch birds and seals breeding in noisy colonies on precarious cliff ledges or isolated beaches; you can watch animals lunge, dive and chase after food; and you can witness the sheer exuberance of life in its fullest abundance. You might find yourself snorkelling in a tropical paradise among colourful reef fish or clinging desperately to a ship's railing as it sails between icebergs with albatross hovering effortlessly off the bow. Many such adventures await you in your year of watching wildlife, but we've covered five of the very best choices opposite.

RAJA AMPAT ISLANDS INDONESIA

CORALS & REEF FISH, FEBRUARY (P46-7)

This newly discovered tropical paradise off western New Guinea appears to host the most diverse underwater ecosystems on the planet. Surveys in 2002 found unbelievable numbers of marine organisms including the highest counts of tropical fish of any site in the world – 284 species of fish on a single dive alone.

VALDÉS PENINSULA ARGENTINA

KILLER WHALES, MARCH (P60)

Ranked by wildlife experts as one of the most dramatic wildlife events in the world, the annual gathering of killer whales off the coast of Argentina is a real eye-opener. The killer whales arrive to eat baby seals, but they catch them by leaping onto the beach and dragging the seals back across the sand.

NINGALOO MARINE PARK AUSTRALIA

WHALE SHARKS & CORALS, MARCH (P62-3)

Although it rivals the legendary Great Barrier Reef on the opposite side of Australia, Ningaloo Reef attracts a fraction of visitors. Ningaloo's charm is that it's a fringing coral reef, which means that you can swim from the shore for some of the most beautiful snorkelling you'll experience in your life.

EAST COAST SOUTH AFRICA

SARDINE RUN, JUNE (P102-3)

When sardines make their 'run' up South Africa's east coast there is sheer pandemonium as hundreds of dolphins, seals and sharks, along with thousands of gannets, pile in to feed on billions of schooling fish. Dive or snorkel in water literally boiling with a frenzy of fish and predators.

AVALON PENINSULA CANADA

HUMPBACK WHALES, JULY (P116)

Seeing some of the world's great whales is one of the premier wildlife-watching experiences, and there are many places you can snorkel with whales or watch them from a boat. However, there are very few places where you can watch them so close to the beach that you can almost touch them, and observing them at Avalon Peninsula is best of all.

AVALON PENINSULA (CANADA)

RAJA AMPAT ISLANDS (INDONESIA)

NINGALOO MARINE PARK (AUSTRALIA)

EAST COAST (SOUTH AFRICA)

VALDÉS PENINSULA (ARGENTINA)

TOP LOCATIONS

↗ RAINFORESTS

RAINFORESTS ARE THE RICHEST AND MOST COMPLEX ECOSYSTEMS ON EARTH. With hundreds of thousands of plant species found on every square kilometre, there are countless niches for impossibly diverse ecological webs. But what the visitor notices most is the profusion of life, from screaming and squawking birds hidden in the dense foliage to the ceaseless hum of insects buzzing all around. These are places of mystery, where animals dart furtively among the shadows, where you lose all sense of direction and time, and where any animal you see might be unknown to science.

Located in tropical zones near the equator, rainforests escaped the ravages of the Ice Ages and in some areas have remained unchanged for millions of years, serving as natural laboratories for the evolution of many unique species. Despite their status as some of the world's most ancient and stable habitats, rainforests are also remarkably fragile. We have learned only recently that rainforests dry out and burn easily in a changing climate, and that once cleared they may never grow back. Sadly, our world's diverse and highly evolved rainforests are being cleared at a phenomenal rate, sometimes for exploding human populations but sometimes for pure greed and profit. You can almost forget this legacy when you stand amidst the splendour of a pristine rainforest, but one of the great questions of our time is how we'll protect these areas from extinction.

DANUM VALLEY CONSERVATION AREA
MALAYSIAN BORNEO

 ORANG-UTANS & BARBETS, MARCH (P54-5)
There was great excitement in the scientific community when word of Danum Valley's riches started surfacing in the 1980s. This pristine lowland rainforest offers hope for some of Borneo's rarest and nearly extinct animals. You're not likely to see the rarest of the rare, the Sumatran rhino, but there's so much more to see here.

BHUTAN EASTERN HIMALAYAS

EAST HIMALAYAN WILDLIFE, MAY (P82-3)
If you had to pick one bright spot in the whole world, it would be Bhutan. This secretive and largely closed nation is run according to a set of Buddhist principles that include respecting the natural world and causing no harm. he result is the most exceptional mix of pristine habitats (including rainforests) and intact wildlife populations on earth.

MANU NATIONAL PARK PERU

MACAWS & GIANT OTTERS, SEPTEMBER (P158-9)
It is said that Manu has the greatest biodiversity of any protected area on earth, but it's hard to say for sure because this vast area has so much life that it's almost impossible to measure. One tree alone could have 43 species of ant, while the park is home to 10% of the world's bird species.

NOUABALÉ-NDOKI NATIONAL PARK CONGO

LOWLAND GORILLAS & FOREST ELEPHANTS, DECEMBER (P198-9)
Few stories in the world are as sad as that of the destruction of the Congo basin and the killing of its wildlife for the bushmeat trade. If any hope remains for the Congo, it's in this vast and unspoiled wilderness heart where animals have no fear because they've never encountered humans in a negative way.

CORCOVADO NATIONAL PARK COSTA RICA

TAPIRS & MONKEYS, DECEMBER (P206-7)
The rainforests of Corcovado present some of the best wildlife-viewing opportunities in a country long famous for its successful conservation work. This is a particularly fun and accessible place to learn about rainforest ecology for travellers willing to hike in and camp out. You'll see an endless pageant of tropical mammals and birds here.

TOP LOCATIONS

 # DESERTS & GRASSLANDS

AT THE OTHER END OF THE SCALE FROM RAINFORESTS WE FIND THE CLEAN LINES AND OPEN SPACES OF THE WORLD'S DESERTS AND GRASSLANDS. For anyone who thinks these places are barren and bereft of wildlife, we offer up the following top five picks to change your mind. Admittedly, life in these habitats is a little different because there are few hiding places, and food and water may be in scarce supply, but animals have somehow found unique solutions to these dilemmas, resulting in some remarkable adaptations and lifestyles. In some cases the animals that have solved these problems occur in great numbers; in other cases they are spread thinly across great distances.

One of the joys of visiting these deserts and grasslands is to encounter the sheer openness and lack of human interference in such enormous spaces. Almost without exception, you may pretty much have these places to yourself, which can be immensely satisfying or completely terrifying. Sit quietly here and let your imagination run to the horizon. You may not see large numbers of animals, but every sighting will be as sharply etched in your memory as the lines of shade and sunlight. If you arrive during the brief rainy season you may see a landscape transformed with an abundance you can scarcely comprehend.

KORGALYZHYN STATE NATURE RESERVE
KAZAKHSTAN

SAIGAS & CRANES, MAY (P90-1)
Sadly the vast Central Asian steppes are nearly gone, but this hidden jewel in northern Kazakhstan has been overlooked, and even within the country Korgalyzhyn is scarcely known, so you're likely to have this 2589 sq km of unbroken grasslands and wetlands all to yourself.

AÏR & TÉNÉRÉ NATURAL RESERVES NIGER

DORCAS GAZELLES & SAND CATS, AUGUST (P130-1)
This immense and fabulously desolate region of rugged mountains and Saharan sand dunes is one of the largest and most spectacular wild areas in the world, yet only a handful of people visit each year. It takes a serious expedition to see the surprising mix of wildlife in this arid landscape.

CHANG TANG NATURE RESERVE TIBET, CHINA

TIBETAN WILDLIFE, SEPTEMBER (P146-7)
The 700,000 sq km Tibetan Plateau in the rain shadow of the Himalayan Mountains is one of the harshest and least accessible places on earth, but it is also home to newly discovered wild yaks, wild asses, gazelles, antelope and snow leopards. About 130,000 people live in this area that sees almost no visitors.

EMAS NATIONAL PARK BRAZIL

GIANT ANTEATERS & TERMITES, SEPTEMBER (P156)
The sprawling grasslands of southern Brazil are home to a handful of giant scattered ranches and little else, freeing up lots of space for maned wolves, greater rheas, giant anteaters and other animals that aren't used to seeing people. One interesting highlight is the hundreds of thousands of 2m-tall termite mounds dotting the plains as far as you can see.

KALAHARI DESERT NAMIBIA

DESERT BIG GAME, NOVEMBER (P42-3)
The most surprising thing about the Kalahari Desert is that it is not a desert at all – arrive after the first sprinkles of rain in November to see the sand dunes transform into grasslands teeming with abundant elephants, wildebeests, lions and antelope. Even the arid coastline is brimming with giant seal colonies and huge numbers of migrating birds.

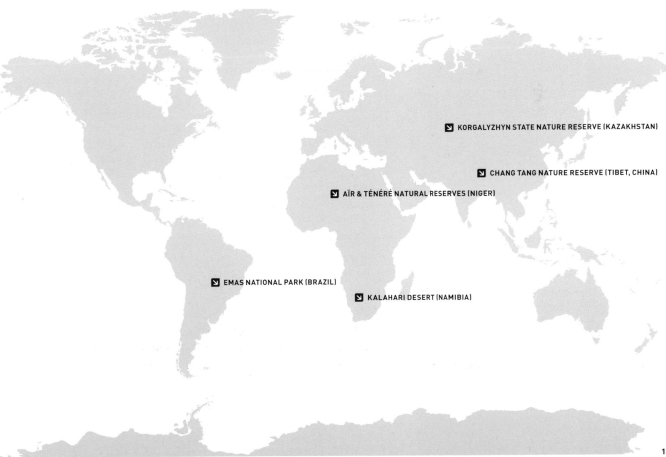

KORGALYZHYN STATE NATURE RESERVE (KAZAKHSTAN)

CHANG TANG NATURE RESERVE (TIBET, CHINA)

AÏR & TÉNÉRÉ NATURAL RESERVES (NIGER)

EMAS NATIONAL PARK (BRAZIL)

KALAHARI DESERT (NAMIBIA)

TOP LOCATIONS

↗ MOUNTAINS

BY THEIR VERY NATURE, MOUNTAINS ARE RUGGED, HOSTILE ENVIRONMENTS THAT HUMANS ONLY RARELY VENTURE INTO. Although they lack the huge numbers of animals that other great habitats attract, the premier mountain ranges of the world have maintained their wild character and continue to safeguard relatively intact wildlife populations. Even in this day and age, it is amazing that there are still mountain ranges that are scarcely known and almost never visited by travellers, despite their stunning mix of jagged mountain peaks, snow fields, lush alpine meadows and crashing streams. You might also stumble across traditional mountain villages where the way of life hasn't changed in centuries and the people are as friendly as ever.

Don't limit yourself to thinking about visiting mountains in certain seasons, because they offer something worth seeing at any time of year. Winters can be cold and brutal but these conditions may also drive hard-to-find wildlife onto lower slopes where they're easier to view. Springtime and early summer in the mountains is a sheer delight, with babbling brooks and fields of flowers. And autumn almost always brings stunning autumn colours. In temperate zones, mountains are also the last hideouts for rare large carnivores such as bears, wolves and big cats, although it takes patience and hard work to track them down.

MACHU PICCHU PERU

 ANDEAN CONDORS, APRIL (P73)
High in the Peruvian Andes, Machu Picchu is a marvel of the ancient world, an exquisitely built city of stone perched on a knife ridge between soaring peaks and sheer canyons. Machu Picchu and the nearby Inca Trail are probably the most dramatic places in the world to see huge Andean condors in their mountain home.

KAVKAZSKIY NATURE RESERVE RUSSIA

 WOLVES & WEST CAUCASIAN TURS, JULY (P114-15)
Perched on the doorstep of Europe, this magnificent wilderness in the Western Caucasus Mountains is extremely remote and has seen little human disturbance for centuries. This is the only place in the world where temperate deciduous forests have persisted for 40 million years, creating stupendous old-growth forests and a home for many rare animals.

BAIMA SNOW MOUNTAIN NATURE RESERVE CHINA

YUNNAN SNUB-NOSED MONKEYS, JULY (P125)
This nature reserve on the incredibly rugged boundary region between China and Tibet has 20 peaks over 5000m and is home to one of the world's most enigmatic and poorly known primates. Snub-nosed monkeys move fast through impenetrable bamboo thickets and rugged canyons, making them enormously difficult to find. On this adventure you'll see why they were lost to science for 70 years.

AKSU-DZHABAGLY NATURE RESERVE KAZAKHSTAN

SIBERIAN IBEXES & SNOW LEOPARDS, NOVEMBER (P181)
You may never have heard of this alpine paradise of rugged peaks and brilliant green pastures in the Tien Shan Mountains, but it was the first reserve in the world to receive status as a UNESCO biosphere reserve. This place is stunningly beautiful and it's one of the best places to see the rare ibex and snow leopard.

CHITRAL GOL NATIONAL PARK PAKISTAN

MARKHOR ANTELOPE & SNOW LEOPARDS, DECEMBER (P205)
This hidden gem in the Hindu Kush Mountains is surprisingly welcoming and safe, not to mention a place of dramatic soaring peaks. Unfortunately, wildlife has fared poorly in this tribal area although markhor populations are reportedly on the rise.

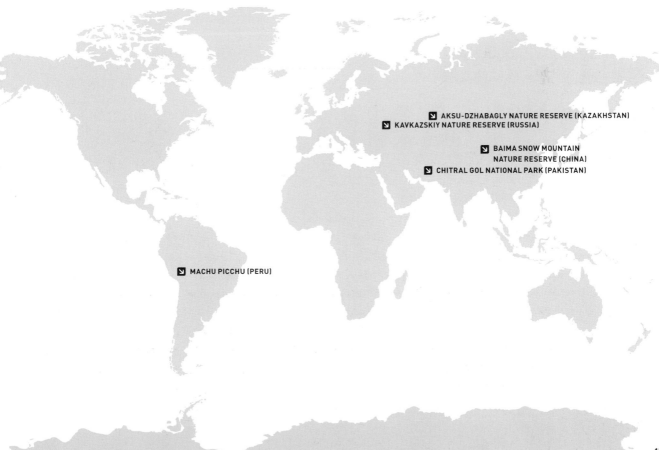

AKSU-DZHABAGLY NATURE RESERVE (KAZAKHSTAN)
KAVKAZSKIY NATURE RESERVE (RUSSIA)
BAIMA SNOW MOUNTAIN NATURE RESERVE (CHINA)
CHITRAL GOL NATIONAL PARK (PAKISTAN)
MACHU PICCHU (PERU)

↗ ISLANDS

ISLANDS ARE WORLDS UNTO THEMSELVES. Because they have been isolated from the continents for long periods of time, some strange things happen on them: populations can multiply in out-of-whack ways (such as the 120 million red crabs on Christmas Island); unusual creatures might evolve; or an island can become a beacon for huge numbers of animals living over the adjacent ocean. Sometimes animals evolved into pygmy forms or they developed into giants of their family. On islands with no predators, birds became flightless and animals lost their ability to protect themselves. Many of these unique island environments were lost forever when humans arrived and brought along predatory rats, cats and foxes or introduced other species. Only a lucky few islands escaped this fate or were large enough that the process is still ongoing, but these islands rank among the foremost sites in the world for wildlife-watching.

Strategies for protecting these islands vary widely. Some sites are off-limits, while others require that every visitor be checked for weed seeds or stowaway invaders. Some offer opportunities for volunteers to help restore native ecosystems and animals. Islands can be remote and hard to reach, while others may be close to mainlands or be popular destination resorts. Most of them are specialised destinations that you have to make an effort to reach, but after reading the following suggestions you'll be more than motivated to visit.

GALÁPAGOS ISLANDS ECUADOR

 MARINE IGUANAS & GIANT TORTOISES, JANUARY & MAY (P20, P86-7)

It goes without saying that the most famous islands in the world for wildlife-watching are the Galápagos Islands, but it's surprising how much there truly is to see here and how many options there are for seeing the 15 islands that are open to the public. Watch marine iguanas, snorkel with sea lions or walk among seabird colonies.

WRANGEL ISLAND RESERVE RUSSIA

 WALRUSES & POLAR BEARS, JULY (P118-19)

If you've ever wanted to explore a remote, rarely visited island, this frozen bit of wilderness north of Siberia might be your ticket. Only a few icebreakers in the world can make this journey, but your rewards are the massive gatherings of walruses, numerous polar bears and a strangely diverse flora that survived the Ice Ages.

MADAGASCAR INDIAN OCEAN

 CHAMELEONS & LEMURS, JANUARY & OCTOBER (P170-1)

Madagascar is home to the strangest and most unique animals in the world, but they are so highly threatened by habitat loss that this remarkable island is the most highly ranked conservation priority in the world. If you exclude bats and birds, 97% of the island's animals are found nowhere else on earth.

SOUTH GEORGIA ISLAND

 PENGUINS & ALBATROSS, NOVEMBER (P190-1)

South Georgia may be the best example of a remote island that attracts huge numbers of animals. Located some 2150km off the tip of South America at the edge of a phenomenally productive upwelling of nutrients, this island has over 30 million breeding seabirds and more than three million seals.

COCOS ISLAND NATIONAL PARK COSTA RICA

HAMMERHEAD SHARKS, DECEMBER (P197)

The famous oceanographer Jacques Cousteau called Cocos 'the most beautiful island in the world', and it is ranked as one of the top 10 dive sites in the world for the incredible number of sharks, manta rays, tuna and dolphins that gather around the island, including schools of 500 hammerheads at a time.

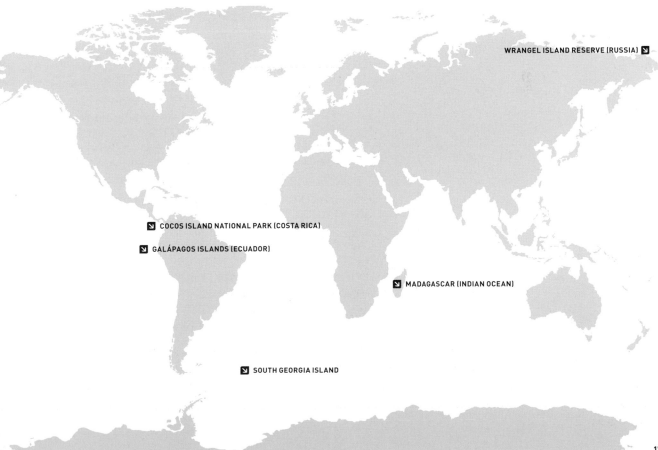

WRANGEL ISLAND RESERVE (RUSSIA)

COCOS ISLAND NATIONAL PARK (COSTA RICA)

GALÁPAGOS ISLANDS (ECUADOR)

MADAGASCAR (INDIAN OCEAN)

SOUTH GEORGIA ISLAND

↗ JANUARY
WEEK.01

WHAT YOU'LL SEE

- GREATER SPOTTED EAGLES
- SARUS CRANES
- DUCKS AND GEESE
- BLACKBUCKS
- FISHING CATS

KEOLADEO GHANA NATIONAL PARK INDIA

WHY NOW? Things get pretty exciting when wintering birds show up to join the residents

Once considered the premier duck-hunting destination in the British Empire, the wetlands at India's Bharatpur were elevated to national park status and renamed as Keoladeo Ghana National Park in 1982. Gone are the days when royal hunting parties would shoot 4000 ducks in a single day, and wildlife populations have soared in response, making this one of the finest birdwatching destinations in the world.

Even better, Bharatpur (as the park is still affectionately known) is ridiculously easy to visit. Just hop on a bike from town or one of the local lodges and toodle around the flat roads that weave among the park's clearly defined ponds and marshes. Wildlife is so densely packed into this relatively small (29 sq km) park that your foremost problem will be identifying everything you see among the crowds of birds and mammals.

How does one begin listing the virtues of these fabulous wetlands? From August to October the park's trees are chock-full of nesting herons, storks and egrets, with up to nine species per tree. From November to March bird diversity soars as countless migrants arrive from Asia and Europe, making it possible to see 180 species in a single day.

Everywhere around the marshes there is constant activity. Fifty species of fish (including freshwater sharks) ply the waters, while countless ducks, cranes and herons dabble, splash and stalk their prey as far as you can see. Mixed among the birds, handsome blackbucks, chital deer, sambar and nilgai wade in the shallows or wander nearby grasslands. You shouldn't have any problem spotting pythons, monkeys or one of the park's several species of cat.

And keep your eyes aloft to spot raptors; with 40 species of raptor and seven species of owl, Bharatpur is one of the best places on earth to see birds of prey. In fact, there is no better place in the world to catch the impressive greater spotted eagle.

Bharatpur is an easy add-on from Delhi, 180km to the north, or while visiting the Taj Mahal in Agra, 60km to the east. Local lodges and guides can help make sense of this overwhelming wildlife bonanza.
MORE INFO www.unep-wcmc.org/sites/wh/pdf /Keoladeo.pdf

MARINE IGUANAS GALÁPAGOS ISLANDS

LOCATION 1200km west of Guayaquil, Ecuador **WHY NOW?** The males are costumed in colour during breeding season **LEVEL OF DIFFICULTY** Low – what could be more fun than strolling along a beach in the Galápagos? **STATUS** Feral dogs and cats are killing many, but the iguanas are safe on some islands

Sure Darwin called them hideous and stupid, but you deserve to hop on a boat and see marine iguanas for yourself. No other sight is more iconic of the Galápagos shorelines than huddled masses of lava-black iguanas with salt-encrusted heads. Unlike your everyday modern dinosaur, these 1m-long lizards subsist on a diet of seaweed and they're willing to brave thrashing waves and bone-chilling waters to get it.

Actually it's the adult males – the strongest swimmers – that struggle through the whirlpool of offshore waves and dive up to 12m in search of underwater seaweed, while the females and juveniles feed in shallow reefs and intertidal areas at low tide. One meal a day is enough for these sluggish creatures, so the rest of the day is spent lying spread-eagled in the tropical sun and huddling in piles to keep warm at night. Salt water ingested during their feeding bouts is excreted by frequent sneezing, resulting in a salty crust of snot that accumulates on their faces.

Things get a little more interesting in January when males heat up to the task of mating. Flush with excitement, males assume a wonderful variety of red, orange and green splotches over their typically black background colour. These changes trigger head-butting and bobbing rituals between males that even flare up into full-blown fights, with dominant males accruing small harems for their efforts. Males on each island have slightly different behaviours and colour patterns, with those on Española Island being most famous for their spectacular colours.

MORE INFO www.galapagos.org

(LEFT) ↗
Marine iguanas on Isla Fernandina, Galápagos Islands, Ecuador.

(TOP RIGHT) ↗
Facing the destruction of its rainforest home, the harpy eagle has found refuge in Panama, where it is the national bird.

(BOTTOM RIGHT) ↗
Eight species of bat live inside the caves of Puerto Princesa Subterranean River National Park in the Philippines.

HARPY EAGLES PANANA

 LOCATION Punta Patiño Nature Reserve, 200km southeast of Panama City **WHY NOW?** You can see flowering trees and lush greenery in the dry season **LEVEL OF DIFFICULTY** Medium – some jungle scrambling required **STATUS** Harpy eagles are critically endangered but receive stringent protection in Panama

Though equipped with bone-crushing talons the size of grizzly-bear claws, the world's most powerful bird of prey is no match for the destruction of its rainforest home. As a result, harpy eagle populations have plummeted throughout Central and South America, though they have found a small refuge in Panama, where they were declared the national bird in 2002. At last count 41 active nests were known, many carefully monitored, and in some cases watched over by local Indian villages that benefit from guiding small parties of visitors to discreet observation sites.

Seeing a harpy eagle is at the top of the list for most birdwatchers, and for good reason. Decked out with a bonnet of ruffled feathers, this rare and fearsome predator specialises in swooping down and snatching monkeys and sloths from the tops of trees. When not hunting, harpy eagles spend much of the year looking after slow-growing chicks in their bulky stick nests. Panama's National Association for the Conservation of Nature (ANCON) manages the 263 sq km Punta Patiño Nature Reserve on the Gulf of San Miguel, where harpies can be observed at their nests almost any time of year. Local guides take you to where the action is.

MORE INFO www.ancon.org (in Spanish)

BATS & SWIFTLETS PHILIPPINES

 LOCATION Puerto Princesa Subterranean River National Park, 600km southwest of Manila **WHY NOW?** The beginning of the dry season is better for trail access **LEVEL OF DIFFICULTY** Low – being paddled around in a canoe isn't too hard **STATUS** The population is stable and well protected

Considered one of the greatest, if not *the* greatest, natural wonder of the Philippines, Puerto Princesa is touted as the longest navigable underground river in the world. When you canoe in from its mouth at the sea, this remarkable channel extends back more than 8km under the island of Palawan. Now protected as a national park, the subterranean river is the centerpiece of Palawan's commitment to preserving its natural heritage as its primary means of economic development.

Travellers may come simply for the river's fantastic limestone caverns and formations (some viewed as divinely shaped to mirror Catholic figures) but find themselves surprised by the wealth of wildlife both inside and outside the caverns. Eight species of bat as well as swiftlets are common, providing a lively and acrobatic accompaniment as boats glide in and out of the flickering shadows. Visitors are warned against putting their hands in the water due to snakes in the cave.

In addition to its underground features, the Puerto Princesa Subterranean River National Park was elevated to a World Heritage Site due to its fabulous cross-section of habitats, from ocean edge to mountain peak. Home to many highly endangered Palawan endemic species including rare birds, the park is a premier destination for birdwatchers.

MORE INFO www.puerto-undergroundriver.com

DID YOU KNOW?

Harpy eagles' feet clamp down with a force three times more powerful than the bite of a rottweiler, crushing bones and killing instantly.

Marine iguanas absorb sections of their spine and shorten their bodies when food is short, and regrow when food is abundant again.

↗ JANUARY
WEEK.02

YELLOWSTONE NATIONAL PARK
USA

WHAT YOU'LL SEE

WOLVES
BISON
ELK
PRONGHORN ANTELOPE
RAVENS

WHY NOW? Winter is a sublime time for wolf-watching

As soon as you pull into Yellowstone's Lamar Valley you begin to get a sense of why this place is often referred to as the Serengeti of North America. All along this sweeping river valley in the northeast corner of the world's oldest park there are clusters of elk, bison, moose and pronghorn antelope, as well as predators ranging from soaring bald eagles to swaggering grizzly bears. Year-round access and convenient viewing lookouts virtually guarantee crowds of noisy tourists in summer, but arrive in the depths of winter and you'll be greeted by an entirely different scene.

Perched on the mountainous slopes of North America's Continental Divide, Yellowstone National Park is a vast and complex landscape of geysers, hot springs, forests and remote wilderness. It's a rugged place and snow-bound winters can bite the end off a thermometer, so a drive into the Lamar Valley may feel suicidal on a January

morning before sunrise. You'll be shocked to discover, however, that roadside lay-bys are packed with cars full of wildlife groupies, all here for the same reason – wolves.

Since wolves were reintroduced to Yellowstone in 1995 and 1996, the Lamar Valley has become the top site in the world for watching wild wolves, and every single day of the year die-hard aficionados line up and wait for any glimpse they can get of the park's 12 wolf packs.

And these highly social predators seldom disappoint their fans. Whether you witness a pack bringing down a bison, chasing eagles away from a kill or frolicking with their bouncing pups, this is a wildlife adventure of the highest calibre. Chat with the gathered biologists

and eager onlookers (fondly nicknamed 'wolfies'), and you'll most likely hear the entire family history and life story of each individual wolf.

But winter in Yellowstone has many other equally stunning highlights. Seek out frost-covered bison around the park's steaming hot springs, or elk wandering among powdered mounds and ghosts of snow-covered trees. It's a landscape where every breath is etched in sharp little puffs of ice crystals, and when the morning sun rises golden over the horizon it *will* take your breath away.

MORE INFO www.nps.gov/yell

JELLYFISH LAKE PALAU

LOCATION Western Micronesia **WHY NOW?** January to March is considered the best time to dive in Palau's waters **LEVEL OF DIFFICULTY** Low – put on a snorkel and mask, hop in the water, and presto! **STATUS** An exotic anemone accidentally introduced to the lake threatens to alter the ecosystem

Is this heaven or a strange hallucination? You've come to Palau for its legendary reef diving and instead you're swimming in a lake full of jellyfish. And not just a few jellyfish but millions of them, many as large as cantaloupes, swirling in vast clouds and sliding past you as you snorkel along. But don't worry, they are a stingless variety and after the initial shock wears off you can try relaxing into the strangeness of this otherworldly experience.

Formed around 15,000 years ago, Palau's Jellyfish Lake is now completely enclosed by land, although salt water still seeps in through the porous limestone and supports the enormous population of jellyfish. According to some, there are an estimated 20 million jellyfish in the lake, and they spend their time swimming back and forth in pursuit of the sun's rays. By mid-afternoon the lake's entire population has congregated on the sunny west shore of the lake in numbers that stun the imagination.

Jellyfish don't do much more than pulsate with simple motion, but taken together the effect is like an eerie ballet or a slow-motion storm cloud. Jellyfish feed off sugars produced by algae that live inside their tissues, and algae need sunlight, so the jellyfish's primary goal is to stay in sunlight as much as possible. With tentacles trailing, they scull along slowly with mesmerising repetition and a serenity that matches the mood of this tropical paradise. For a while, you might even forget about the spectacular reefs that you'll be diving tomorrow.

MORE INFO www.visit-palau.com

[LEFT] ↗
Around 20 million stingless jellyfish populate Jellyfish Lake in Palau.

[TOP RIGHT] ↗
The breeding grounds of the James' flamingo were only discovered in 1957.

[BOTTOM RIGHT] ↗
Madagascar's many species of chameleon are threatened with extinction due to habitat loss and the demand for pets.

JAMES' FLAMINGOS BOLIVIA

 LOCATION Laguna Colorado, 600km south of La Paz **WHY NOW?** Flamingo numbers peak from November to January **LEVEL OF DIFFICULTY** Medium – travel easy, but expect intense sunlight and extreme elevation **STATUS** Flamingos were intensively hunted in Bolivia until 1986, but breeding colonies are now guarded

It is testament to the allure of flamingos that over 40,000 people a year now sojourn to the remote Laguna Colorado in southern Bolivia to see these magical birds. Here, at nearly 4300m, the sun is fierce and the air so thin that most people find it hard to sleep or breathe, but the chance to see this ethereal and haunting landscape of barren hills and shifting light is more than enough reason to visit.

Without a doubt, the stars of the show are the three species of flamingo that gather each November by the thousands to nest in this moody, red-stained lake. This is the most important breeding site in the world for the poorly known James' flamingo, a species whose breeding grounds were first discovered in 1957 and whose populations were counted for the first time in 1997. Volunteers organised by the Wildlife Conservation Society continue to survey and observe the flamingos in hopes of better understanding their status. Because nesting colonies are easily disturbed and the native ecosystems are so fragile, it is advisable to travel with guides from the local towns of Uyuni or San Juan and check in with the tourism office in Uyuni before entering the Eduardo Avaroa Faunal Reserve.

MORE INFO www.enjoybolivia.com/english/what-new/uyuni-eduardo-avaroa.shtml

CHAMELEONS MADAGASCAR

 LOCATION Off the east coast of Africa **WHY NOW?** The wet season is the time of chameleon courtship **LEVEL OF DIFFICULTY** Low to high – see them at local parks or on extreme expeditions **STATUS** Variable: some species are common while others are critically endangered

From pygmies you can barely see on the palm of your hand to 1m-long giants that eat small birds, the 75-odd species of chameleon in Madagascar are an ancient and remarkable clan of lizards. Most of the time these superb, slow-motion hunters move at a veritable snail's pace on vise-like feet, scanning leaves and branches with their turreted eyes then snagging prey in lightning-fast strikes with sticky tongues as long as their bodies.

This relatively placid picture changes during Madagascar's rainy season, when chameleons in habitats across the entire island emerge from seclusion and begin their flamboyant courtship and breeding rituals. Some species, especially those in which the males come equipped with horns, engage in rigorous head-butting manoeuvres that would put a goat to shame. Many species transform from camouflaged lumps of brown dirt to shimmering carpets of rainbow, with the startling capacity to change their colours within milliseconds. Both for their typically drab colouration and for their occasional bouts of ferocity, it is easy to see why they are named chameleon, which means 'earth lion'.

Sadly, widespread habitat loss and an insatiable demand for pet chameleons now threaten many species with impending extinction, although there are dozens of parks where you can still find them.

MORE INFO www.wildmadagascar.org

↗ JANUARY
WEEK.03

ASA WRIGHT NATURE CENTRE
TRINIDAD

WHAT YOU'LL SEE

10 SPECIES OF HUMMINGBIRD
GOLDEN-HEADED MANAKINS
PECCARIES
ARMADILLOS
OCELOTS

WHY NOW? The tail end of the rainy season is a particularly pleasant time to visit

Visitors to Trinidad benefit greatly from the island's enviable geographic location. Not only is it a classic Caribbean island, but it also sits a mere 12km off the Venezuelan coast (and was once connected to South America). So come to Trinidad for a bit of tropical paradise, and for its culture and easy access, while enjoying a remarkable mix of Caribbean and South American species.

Trinidad's relatively large size and its fairly enlightened conservation policies mean that significant examples of each vegetation type are well protected. This is especially true in the less-developed northern third of the island, where you can easily see excellent examples of Caribbean mangrove swamps, savannahs, woodlands and rainforests. For the nature lover there is no better base for exploring northern Trinidad

than the world-famous Asa Wright Nature Centre, where having tea and lunch on the veranda of the main lodge is like sitting in an aviary along with 200 species of wild bird. The centre welcomes both guests and day-trippers with equal enthusiasm.

It is not uncommon for visitors to see 10 species of hummingbird, or a total of 40 to 50 bird species, during a single morning session on the veranda. In fact, there'd be little reason to ever leave this ideal viewing platform except that the centre's wildlife sanctuary has five excellent trails and expert guides that can help you find peccaries, armadillos and maybe even an ocelot. You definitely want a guide along to help sort out the 600-plus species of butterfly you might see, or help you recognise poisonous snakes in the leaf litter. Even

better, don't miss golden-headed manakins doing their hilarious imitations of Michael Jackson's moonwalk while dancing on their leks.

Take time to see the many other parks and natural wonders that Trinidad has to offer, from its highest mountains to its glorious coastlines. If you visit in January you can also see as many as 12,000 scarlet ibises roosting at Caroni Swamp National Park. Local fishermen will offer to boat you out to the ibis roost, but you're more likely to find someone with a solid ecological background if you book a trip through a local tour company.

MORE INFO www.asawright.org

RED-CROWNED CRANES JAPAN

LOCATION Hokkaido, 250km east of Sapporo **WHY NOW?** Their courtship dances peak in mid-winter **LEVEL OF DIFFICULTY** Low – but prepare for bitter cold **STATUS** The crane population is stable and protected, both legally and in the national consciousness

Despite being mythological symbols of eternal life, the elegant red-crowned cranes were hunted into extinction in Japan by the late 1880s. Given their absence, it was regarded as a miracle when one reappeared in a Japanese field in 1910, and after a remnant band of cranes was discovered starving to death during the legendary winter of 1952, concerned farmers and schoolchildren began a tradition of feeding cranes that has continued ever since.

Today you can see several hundred cranes at once gathered on snow-covered fields outside Kushiro on the Japanese island of Hokkaido, where they are something of a national treasure. Among several observation points and feeding stations, one of the best known is the privately run Tancho no Sato reserve, adjacent to the Akan International Crane Center.

Of course it's interesting to watch majestic 1.5m-tall cranes striding back and forth across the fields, but that's not the reason visitors line up by the dozens and risk freezing their fingers and toes off. It's because red-crowned cranes have the most spectacular courtship dances of any of the world's cranes (all of which are renowned dancers).

The excitement is almost palpable among birds and humans alike as the flocks swoop in, their cries ringing off the hills with mounting ardour. Although pairs mate for life, it does little to dampen their enthusiasm for each other, and it doesn't take long before individuals, pairs and entire flocks are bowing, leaping, and prancing with the abandon of high schoolers at a be-bop. It has been said that human dance evolved from watching cranes, and if you catch yourself bobbing up and down you'll see why.

MORE INFO www.lake-akan.com/en

[LEFT] ↗
The courtship dance of the red-crowned crane draws many visitors to Hokkaido.

[TOP RIGHT] ↗
Mt Etna Caves National Park in Australia provides a maternity ward for the little bent-wing bat, although the young live under threat from the world's only bat-eating frog.

[BOTTOM RIGHT] ↗
The sociable coati looks like a mix between a raccoon and a monkey.

LITTLE BENT-WING BATS AUSTRALIA

LOCATION Mt Etna Caves National Park, 26km north of Rockhampton, Queensland **WHY NOW?** Watch clumsy babies making their first flights **LEVEL OF DIFFICULTY** Low – a park ranger-guided walk requires climbing steps up to the cave **STATUS** Stable

Bat Cleft Cave is one of many fascinating caves found on the limestone massif of Mt Etna, but it has gained worldwide fame for the unusual predators that hang out at the cave entrance to nab little bent-wing bats as they emerge from the cave each evening. Arrive on a guided park tour at 7pm and you'll see the first of 110,000 females ducking through the rocky obstacle course at the cave's entrance. This cave is the largest of five known maternity caves for the little bent-wing bat, and it is home for 80% of Australia's entire bent-wing bat population. Youngsters are born in December, and by mid-January they are making their first awkward attempts to join their mothers on their evening flights. Due to their inexperience, they stop frequently on the cave walls to rest and get their bearings.

January is the best time to see spotted and carpet pythons and brown tree snakes that cling to the walls and snatch bats out of mid-air. This sight alone is reason enough to visit Bat Cleft Cave, but even more bizarre are the 10cm-long green tree frogs on the cave floor snapping up exhausted babies that have fallen – the only known instance in the world of frogs that eat bats.
MORE INFO www.epa.qld.gov.au

COATIS USA

LOCATION Muleshoe Ranch, 80km east of Tucson, Arizona, USA **WHY NOW?** January and February are the best months to see coatis **LEVEL OF DIFFICULTY** Low – there's easy access to the ranch and hiking **STATUS** The population is stable and they are fairly common

First coveted by early ranchers for its permanent sources of water, the Muleshoe Ranch Cooperative Management Area is now a wildlife haven tucked away in the mountains and deserts of southeast Arizona. The site is easily reached by passenger vehicle, while backcountry portions of the management area can be further explored by 4WD, on horseback or on foot. You can even stay the night in a casita, or apply to volunteer for various management activities at the preserve.

Arizona's Sonoran Desert is a beautiful and lively landscape at any time of year, a place of buzzing hummingbirds, stealthy mountain lions and wildly grunting collared peccaries. Notable among this menagerie are troops of highly sociable coatis – looking like an odd cross between a raccoon and a monkey – that travel along streamside forests, nuzzling through leaf litter in search of grubs and small animals while making little chirruping and snorting noises. In the winter they descend out of hidden mountain canyons and fan out across desert lowlands where visitors have a better chance of encountering these fascinating creatures.

Coatis, also known as coatimundis or given various nicknames such as snookum bears, are endlessly entertaining to watch. Members of a troop ceaselessly interact both vocally and physically with each other as they climb trees, push their long noses into tangled vegetation and groom each other for ticks and other tasty morsels.
MORE INFO www.nature.org/wherewework/northamerica/states/arizona

WEEK.04

BANC D'ARGUIN NATIONAL PARK
MAURITANIA

WHAT YOU'LL SEE

BROAD-BILLED SANDPIPERS

DOLPHINS

SEA TURTLES

SAND CATS

JACKALS

WHY NOW? See the greatest concentration of wintering shorebirds in the world

Mauritania is a land of sand – few African countries are so completely dominated by the stuff – and Saharan sand dunes push further and further into Mauritania every year. This would be a bleak destination for a wildlife enthusiast if it weren't for the spectacular Banc D'Arguin National Park, which protects one of the world's richest marine areas.

Located on the coast just off the highway connecting the capital city of Nouakchott and the northern border town of Nouadhibou, Banc D'Arguin is a vast (11,750 sq km) World Heritage Site. Surprisingly, tourists rarely stop here, which is a shame because the park hosts phenomenal numbers of marine mammals and seabirds. Of course, you need an adventurous spirit because the 'roads' are little more than tracks in the sand and it's essential that you travel with a guide in a 4X4.

Fortunately, the shoreline is not far from the main highway and there you discover for the first time the true splendour of this park as you stumble upon flock after flock of waterbirds, rare monk seals, four species of sea turtle, five species of dolphin and porpoise, killer whales and much more, all drawn to the park's enormously productive coastal waters and super-abundant fish populations.

There are a lot of reasons to visit Banc D'Arguin, but without a doubt birds top the list. Fully a third of the waders that breed in Europe and Siberia come here to spend the winter, making this the foremost destination in the world for wintering shorebirds. Over two million broad-billed sandpipers alone have been counted here, plus vast numbers of plovers, godwits and dunlins,

congregating in dense flocks that you'll encounter every couple of kilometres as you travel along the coast. Or even better, try to catch the daily commute of shorebirds to and from their roosting sites on offshore islands, an especially impressive sight if you can visit the area on a sailboat.

Equally interesting are the few scattered villages of Imraguen tribesmen in the park who live by using traditional fishing techniques that they've handed down since the 15th century. Their livelihood and stewardship are an integral part of the park's long-term management.

MORE INFO www.mauritania-today.com

BOA CONSTRICTORS COSTA RICA

LOCATION Palo Verde National Park, 52km southwest of Liberia **WHY NOW?** The dry season is peak nesting time for water birds **LEVEL OF DIFFICULTY** Low– it's an easy and pleasant park to explore **STATUS** The population is stable in this well-protected park

Palo Verde National Park clearly holds its own against far more famous and heavily visited destinations in a country already full of wildlife superlatives. Fed by several major rivers in the driest province in Costa Rica, Palo Verde is an enormous natural sink that attracts the greatest congregations of waterfowl and water birds of any site in Central America.

This fact is immediately evident when you hop on a ranger-led boat tour down the Río Tempisque along the park's western boundary. Everywhere you look there are startling numbers of ducks, herons, egrets, spoonbills, ibises and cormorants, many of which take advantage of the abundant prey available during the dry season to form noisy gregarious nesting colonies. The colonies are particular dense on Isla Pájaros (Bird Island), where there are so many nesting birds that predators such as boa constrictors gather to feast on the countless eggs and chicks.

You'd be hard pressed to find a boa constrictor on a normal day anywhere else in Costa Rica, but here (from the safety of your boat) you're likely to see as many fat and happy boa constrictors as you could wish for. Boa constrictors are surprisingly attractive snakes and it's a rare treat to observe their behaviour up close, but don't be shocked if you see them eating eggs and chicks that have fallen out of their nests. Access to the park is on a road open year-round, 28km from the town of Bagaces (located on the InterAmerican Hwy), where you can find accommodation if you don't want to camp in the park.

MORE INFO http://costa-rica-guide.com

(LEFT) ↗
Eggs and chicks that have fallen from nests are easy prey for the attractive boa constrictors in Costa Rica's Palo Verde National Park.

(TOP RIGHT) ↗
A roving gang of kea, the intelligent but destructive New Zealand parrot, may leave the rubber on your car in tatters.

(BOTTOM RIGHT) ↗
Extreme weather and a fragile landscape make seeing the Bactrian camel a challenge.

KEA NEW ZEALAND

LOCATION Arthur's Pass National Park, 100km northwest of Christchurch **WHY NOW?** There are large flocks of kea in January **LEVEL OF DIFFICULTY** Low – they are common around mountain towns and parking lots **STATUS** The population is low and their habitats may be threatened

As soon as you encounter kea on New Zealand's South Island, you'll see why these remarkable alpine parrots are described as playful, highly inquisitive, tame and extremely bold. You may even witness them at their favourite pastimes of rolling playfully in the snow or tumbling gleefully through the air like Chinese acrobats. However, when you turn around you may just as easily learn one of their other commonly ascribed attributes – incredibly destructive – when you discover that behind your back a gang of kea has stripped the wiper blades and windshield seals from your car.

Unfortunately, it's not a stretch to call them a gang. Most of the birds that hang around parking lots and popular tourist sites are young shiftless males, like a bunch of street punks in search of a thrill. In part, these 1kg parrots are merely using their famed intelligence and curiosity to test out their world. It is extremely difficult to find food in their alpine environments so these parrots have evolved to constantly taste and try new food sources, whether it's a tourist's knapsack or a pile of interesting garbage. Until 1986, thousands of these birds were killed because it was thought they were eating sheep on a regular basis. It remains uncertain whether their populations will recover.
MORE INFO www.apinfo.co.nz

BACTRIAN CAMELS CHINA

LOCATION Lop Nur Wild Camel Nature Reserve, northeastern Xinjiang Uighur Autonomous Region **WHY NOW?** It's the camel mating season **LEVEL OF DIFFICULTY** High – few places in the world present such extreme bureaucratic and logistical challenges for travellers **STATUS** The camels are critically endangered and are facing imminent extinction unless there is prompt intervention

Think 'camel' and you probably envision caravans of pack animals on the Silk Road, but few people realise that the wild ancestors of all domesticated camels still survive in the incredibly remote corners of the Gobi Desert of western China and Mongolia. Although a few tourists commute into Mongolia's Great Gobi Biosphere Reserve, where about 400 people reside on 53,000 sq km, hardly any travellers venture into the adjacent Lop Nur Reserve of China, which is home to many of the world's 950 remaining Bactrian camels.

Though this is the mating season for wild camels, winter is not an easy time to visit the Gobi. If you do go and find yourself wondering about the sanity of battling -40° C temperatures, realise that the alternative is withering to a husk under the sizzling sun in a region that sees 100mm of rain every two to three years. People who have mounted expeditions into this vexing region have come back with dazzling tales of camel herds, wild asses, gazelles, wolves, bears and snow leopards, but remember that the camels are already facing incredible threats and disturbance in this increasingly fragile landscape, and your very presence could keep them from reaching a vital watering hole if you're not careful.
MORE INFO www.wildcamels.com

↗ **FEBRUARY**

WEEK.01

GUNUNG LEUSER NATIONAL PARK INDONESIA

WHAT YOU'LL SEE

HORNBILLS
BARBETS
ORANG-UTANS
GIBBONS
BEARDED PIGS

WHY NOW? Escape the dreary winter of the northern hemisphere

Although tropical rainforests are rightly thought of as immensely complex habitats, there is one common and easily overlooked pillar around which the entire ecosystem seems to be built – the ubiquitous fig. In some rainforests up to 70% of the resident animals' diets consist of figs, revealing the enormous importance of these common plants.

Figs range from inconspicuous vines to gigantic 50m strangler trees, with each species producing copious crops of succulent fruit at different times. On any given day there will be, somewhere in the vicinity, one or more species of fig producing fruit, and if the rainforest could be said to have a rush-hour traffic jam of wildlife it would occur at a fruiting fig.

While you can look for fruiting figs at virtually any tropical forest site in the world, why not make your first encounter at Gunung Leuser National Park, just west of the

Sumatran capital Medan. This pristine park is the only site in the world where you can encounter the big four Southeast Asian animals – orang-utans, tigers, elephants and rhinos – in one location. Because fig-watching involves hiding quietly next to a fruiting fig, you will not only get to see a veritable circus of birds and primates, but you stand a reasonably good chance of having one of the big four wander by. You will certainly see some of Gunung Leuser's 5000 orang-utans because the giant red apes absolutely love these yummy fruits.

Equally exciting are prehistoric-looking hornbills that fly far and wide in search of fig crops. Up to 50 at a time (sometimes three or four species at once) may descend on a single fruiting fig. Of Sumatra's nine species, the most impressive are the helmeted hornbills, which are nearly 2m long including their tails, and the 1m-long rhinoceros hornbills with a flamboyantly curled 'horn' on their bills. When troops of these cautious giants swoop in with their raucous cries ringing through the forest it will send chills up your spine.

Visitors may want to avoid the touristy town of Bukit Lawang and head straight to Gurah in the centre of the park (accessible by bus from Medan), where there are trails and guides available.

MORE INFO www.wcsip.org

CHEETAHS TANZANIA

LOCATION Serengeti National Park, 250km northwest of Arusha **WHY NOW?** Avoid the crowds that come to see the famous wildebeest migration **LEVEL OF DIFFICULTY** Low – trips are guided and meticulously arranged **STATUS** Numbers are stable but they are highly inbred, creating a risk that disease could devastate the wild population

While you're almost guaranteed to see a big cat on an African safari, the only one you're likely to see bringing down a kill is the cheetah. This is because the cheetah is a diurnal hunter with a taste for speed, making them easy to spot on the open plains of the Serengeti. Targeting only the fastest sprinters among the antelope – impalas and gazelles – a cheetah springs from cover, reaching speeds of 110km/h and making 7m-long bounds in a headlong attempt to snag its prey before the cat runs out of steam. This chase is one of the most thrilling events you'll encounter in Africa.

Keep an eye out for hunting cheetahs during the cooler hours of early morning or late afternoon, when you might run across a cheetah perched atop a termite mound (or on the bonnet of your safari vehicle), scanning the horizon for prey. During the heat of the day, cheetahs wisely stick to shade or take it easy, like the other animals. Ironically, the exquisite adaptations that make the cheetah the fastest runner in the animal world also render it relatively helpless when protecting its food or cubs from predators. Adults scarf down their food in minutes, before other predators can be drawn to the excitement, and about half of all cheetah cubs are killed by other carnivores by the age of three months.

Although widespread on the plains of Africa, cheetahs are thought to reach their greatest density near the Wandamu River in Serengeti National Park.

MORE INFO www.serengeti.org

(LEFT) ↗
Cheetahs use termite mounds for elevation to scan the horizon for prey.

(TOP RIGHT) ↗
Hunting to meet the demand for shark fins has left many species endangered.

(BOTTOM RIGHT) ↗
Up to 1000 eagles may hang around a red-billed quelea colony, waiting for a baby quelea to eat.

REEF SHARKS MARSHALL ISLANDS

LOCATION Bikini Atoll, 750km northwest of Majuro **WHY NOW?** There's less rain and lower temperatures at this time of year **LEVEL OF DIFFICULTY** Medium – the flight schedules are casual and arrangements require some flexibility **STATUS** Shark populations, even in this protected zone, are being seriously depleted for their fins

With shark populations hunted into near-extinction all over the globe, you have to travel further to find these magnificent creatures. Fortunately, a brief flight from Majuro, the capital of the Marshall Islands, gives you access to what is still considered the world's foremost concentration of sharks. Here at Bikini Atoll, divers report seeing hundreds and perhaps thousands of sharks around a break in the circular coral reef that forms the atoll. This is where sharks gather to feed on a steady flow of fish flushed back and forth in the rush of currents through the break.

The majority of these sharks are grey reef sharks, an active social species found throughout the South Pacific and coastal regions of Australia and Southeast Asia. At least 10 other species of shark have been reported so far, but the list will surely grow higher as more divers visit this newly opened region that already consistently ranks among the top 10 dive sites in the world. These sharks are considered relatively harmless, but should be treated with great respect because they may bite if harassed or if food is present. Fortunately, they generally stick to 'Shark Pass', leaving the rest of the atoll to the divers.

MORE INFO www.bikiniatoll.com

DID YOU KNOW?

 Though not fully understood, shark brains are comparable in size and complexity to the brains of birds and mammals.

Th flocks of red-billed queleas are so huge in Africa that at a distance they look like the smoke of a fast-moving wildfire.

RED-BILLED QUELEAS SOUTH AFRICA

LOCATION Kruger National Park, 350km east of Johannesburg **WHY NOW?** The peak nesting season attracts many predators **LEVEL OF DIFFICULTY** Low – you may need to hire a jeep and guide within the park **STATUS** There's an abundant population

Many animals in this book could be called 'the most' or 'the greatest' but none trump Africa's humble red-billed quelea, the world's most abundant bird. So numerous are queleas (there are an estimated 1.5 million in Africa) that a flock of these finches may take five hours to pass an observer, and the weight of roosting birds has been known to break thick tree branches. In much of the continent this species is considered a serious pest because they consume every grain and can demolish entire fields in minutes.

These superlatives carry over to the nesting season, when vast colonies with up to 500 nests per tree extend many kilometres in length. And when you have that many nesting birds you end up with a lot of baby birds and a lot of food for predators. A single giant colony in Kruger National Park may attract over 1000 eagles that hang around to eat baby queleas. Other hungry eaters include vultures, storks, hornbills, hyenas, civets, baboons and leopards. Some predators simply wait for baby birds to fall out of their nests, while others actively tear nests apart.

These colonies can be found in the thorny thickets that dot the savannahs or line the valley bottoms on Kruger's central plains. They aren't hard to find – just look for a traffic jam of eagles.

MORE INFO www.sanparks.org

↗ FEBRUARY
WEEK.02

EVERGLADES NATIONAL PARK
USA

WHAT YOU'LL SEE

- ROSEATE SPOONBILLS
- PURPLE GALLINULES
- ANHINGAS
- ALLIGATORS AND CROCODILES
- RIVER OTTERS

WHY NOW? The dry season means that wildlife is concentrated around water holes
Although at first glance Florida's Everglades may look like a big soggy lawn, it won't take long before you realise why this is one of North America's foremost wildlife destinations. All you have to do is wander along one of the park's many trails or boardwalks to encounter a profusion of birds and alligators; or even better, hop in a canoe and get eye-to-eye with wildlife on one of the park's countless waterways.

During the summer this vast, seasonally flooded sawgrass prairie functions like a slow-moving river, teeming with aquatic organisms and the countless animals that prey on them. But in the winter dry season these waters retreat to small pockets and the wildlife becomes even more concentrated and dramatic, making this the best time of year for a visit.

Unfortunately, this renowned 'river of grass' suffered immensely after upstream waters at Lake Okeechobee were diverted and dammed in the early 1900s. In recent years the Everglades have become the target of the largest ecosystem restoration project ever undertaken, and there is new hope on the horizon for the park and its 14 threatened and endangered species.

Because the Everglades National Park is vast in size and largely inaccessible, your best introduction would be the popular Anhinga Trail near the park entrance, 70km southwest of Miami. Here you are virtually guaranteed sightings of the bizarre anhinga, nicknamed the snake bird for the way it swims partially submerged with only its snake-like head and neck projecting above the water. In February this is probably the best place in the US to see tropical wading birds such as roseate spoonbills, not to mention alligators, turtles and snakes. Other popular water holes for wildlife and tourists alike are Paurotis Pond, Nine-Mile Pond and Mrazek Pond.

For an incredible experience, venture onto the water for a canoe trip on the 166km Wilderness Waterway, a legendary boating route on the park's western boundary, and get lost in an endless maze of channels while exploring the largest mangrove ecosystem in the western hemisphere. Trips range from a few hours to multiday excursions. Don't forget the insect repellent; part of the Everglades wilderness experience includes encountering its 40 species of mosquito.
MORE INFO www.nps.gov/ever

↗ **FEBRUARY**
WEEK.02

ADÉLIE PENGUINS ANTARCTICA

LOCATION Cape Adere, 750km north of McMurdo Station **WHY NOW?** Chicks must make a solo dash through a gauntlet of predators to reach the sea **LEVEL OF DIFFICULTY** Medium – it's incredibly remote but visited by some cruise ships **STATUS** The population rises and falls with ocean conditions, but is not currently threatened

It must be fun to be a penguin. First of all you get to wear a snappy handsome suit and look pretty cute. Then you get to hang out in big noisy groups with all your buddies. And, if you're an Adélie penguin, you've had your image replicated as a character in movies, books and advertisements all over the world. It's no wonder that these comical penguins have been one of the premier attractions for generations of Antarctic travellers.

As the most common and widespread penguin in the world, the Adélie is readily observed by visitors throughout the Antarctic region, especially from December to March when these 70cm-tall birds gather to nest on the ice-free slopes of rocky coastlines. In the Ross Sea region alone, there are an estimated five to seven million Adélie penguins, including the largest known colony – 250,000 pairs – on Ridley Beach at Cape Adere. There is no feeling like standing among a chaotic sea of squabbling penguins sitting on their little pebble nests or tending their fuzz-ball chicks.

One of the most interesting penguin behaviours occurs in the first half of February when all the Adélie chicks line up in preparation for making a mad dash to the ocean to join their departing parents. It is a terribly anxious and raucous time because their number one predator, the leopard seal, waits for them at the surf's edge hoping to snag a meal.

MORE INFO www.antarctica.ac.uk

[LEFT] ↗
A quarter of a million pairs of Adélie penguins nest at Cape Adare in Antarctica, creating the largest known colony in the world.

[TOP RIGHT] ↗
Gelada baboons have opposable thumbs and rival humans for dexterity.

[BOTTOM RIGHT] ↗
Platypuses use their highly sensitive ducklike 'bills' to dig in the mud for prey.

GELADA BABOONS ETHIOPIA

LOCATION Simien Mountains National Park, 470km north of Addis Ababa
WHY NOW? You've got the best chance of seeing baby baboons **LEVEL OF DIFFICULTY** Medium – the tourist infrastructure is improving but is still rudimentary **STATUS** Exploding human pressure is putting a huge strain on this fragile ecosystem but the gelada are stable for now

The soaring mountains around Ethiopia's highest peak, Ras Dashen Terara (4620m), are considered among the most beautiful landscapes in the world by the few tourists who've visited this mystical place. Fantastically eroded, the Simien massif is a place of deep gorges, knife-edged ridges, sheer cliffs and some of Africa's most critically endangered wildlife. While you won't encounter all these animals in one visit, you will certainly see the gelada, baboon-like monkeys that congregate in large troops along the cliff edges.

Gelada are among the world's most unusual primates, making them of great interest to biologists. Unlike other primates, they graze almost exclusively on grass and have opposable thumbs that rival humans in dexterity. Their social displays involve flashing their shiny teeth and naked red chests at each other like sunburned lifeguards, and at night entire troops scamper down the sheer cliffs to sleep. Gelada society is extraordinarily complex, being built around harems of females that cooperate to make decisions, and it's not rare to see 300 to 600 gelada grazing peacefully together. Access to the remarkable Simien Mountains is best made from the northern city of Debark, where it's possible, though tricky, to hire dependable guides and supplies for a journey into the highlands.
MORE INFO www.selamta.net

PLATYPUSES AUSTRALIA

LOCATION Eungella National Park, 80km west of Mackay, Queensland
WHY NOW? It's your best chance of seeing babies making their first forays into the world **LEVEL OF DIFFICULTY** Low – viewing platforms make for easy sighting opportunities **STATUS** The platypus population is stable and generally well protected

Australia has a lot of odd creatures, but none are as hard to fathom as the platypus. So strange in appearance that early biologists thought they were a hoax, platypuses seem part duck, part otter and part beaver. It didn't help doubters when it was discovered that this semi-aquatic anomaly also laid reptilian eggs and possessed poison-bearing spurs on its hind legs. Fortunately, it is fairly easy to see this remarkable animal for yourself from the viewing platforms on the Broken River in eastern Queensland's Eungella National Park. Between December and February you may even catch a glimpse of baby platypuses (sometimes affectionately called puggles) appearing from their burrow for the first time and swimming along behind their mother.

Most platypus sightings are made in the early morning or late afternoon, when platypuses emerge from their streamside burrows and repeatedly dive in search of bottom-dwelling prey along placid stretches of river. Their ducklike 'bills' are covered in ultra-sensitive nerves that detect prey buried in the mud by touch and by the faint electric currents emitted by living organisms. Platypuses must eat for about 12 hours a day in order to survive, and they use their beaver-like tails as a place to store excess fat.
MORE INFO www.epa.qld.gov.au/parks_and_forests

DID YOU KNOW?

 Adélie penguins stopped eating fish 200 years ago and switched to a diet of krill, possibly because humans hunted out whales and seals.

 The poison in a male platypus' spurs won't kill a human, but leaves the victim incapacitated; the excruciating pain can last for months.

⬈ FEBRUARY
WEEK.03

KGALAGADI TRANSFRONTIER PARK AFRICA

WHAT YOU'LL SEE

KALAHARI LIONS
CHEETAHS
GEMSBOKS
SPRINGBOKS
BAT-EARED FOXES

WHY NOW? There's a lot of excitement when the rains arrive in February. Kgalagadi, or 'land of thirst', is the indigenous San word for the parched Kalahari Desert for good reason – it rains a mere 200mm a year and the two river courses in this 52,000 sq km park flow with water only once every 10 years or so. It's a harsh place, but surprisingly rich in wildlife. In recognition of the region's extraordinary values, this vast corner of northwestern South Africa and western Botswana was declared Africa's first peace park in 2000.

Widely thought of as a desert, complete with immense solitude and fields of orange-red sand dunes stretching to the horizon, these ecosystems are technically semi-arid savannahs. This fact becomes abundantly clear when the rainy season arrives in February and unexpectedly transforms the landscape with a flush of brilliant green grasses. In particular, check out the river courses where gemsboks, springboks and

wildebeests come from far and wide in search of the tallest and sweetest vegetation.

It would be hard to overstate the excitement of this time of year in the Kalahari. Dominant male antelope stake out territories and try to round up newly arriving females while fighting each other for access to these harems. Predators, including famous black-maned Kalahari lions as well as surprisingly abundant cheetahs, lurk on the perimeter, and a rich assortment of raptors perch on streamside trees.

Visitors to the park typically journey along two 2WD roads in the South African portion of the park. These roads follow the fossil riverbeds of the Auob and Nossob Rivers, where major rivers flowed thousands of years ago. Despite an absence of surface water, deep-rooted trees can still access subterranean water and the river courses are well marked by meandering bands of acacia trees. All along these routes, and scattered elsewhere in the park, wind-powered pumps create small water holes where some of your best wildlife watching will occur. Roads in the remote Botswana section of the park are 4WD and require that you travel in a convoy of vehicles for safety.

Although Kgagaladi can be accessed from Namibia, Botswana or South Africa, travel is easiest from the South Africa side, especially from Upington, which is 400km south of the park and accessed from other airports in the country.

MORE INFO www.sanparks.org

MONARCH BUTTERFLIES MEXICO

LOCATION El Rosario Butterfly Sanctuary, 210km west of Mexico City **WHY NOW?** Monarchs become increasingly active on sunny days **LEVEL OF DIFFICULTY** Low – the uphill climb to the sanctuary is somewhat strenuous **STATUS** Despite international attention, continued deforestation greatly imperils the entire population of wintering monarchs

Local Mexican villagers call them *las palomas* – 'souls of the lost children' – because as long as they can remember, monarch butterflies have arrived in time for the Mexican holiday of the Day of the Dead. Ironically, the villagers didn't know that they held the answer to one of the great wildlife mysteries of the 20th century: where do the 120 million monarchs of North America go each winter? It wasn't until 1975 that the truly incredible story of Mexico's wintering monarchs reached the scientific community and the world.

The experience of seeing 120 million sleeping butterflies is almost impossible to comprehend without seeing it for yourself at El Rosario or one of the other butterfly sanctuaries now open to the public in the mountains of Mexico's Michoacán state. Here, in the cool depths of the Oyamel fir forests, the monarchs completely cover every single tree like a cloak of orange leaves. For four to five months the butterflies remain nearly motionless, but on the first warming days in February they begin to stir in the beckoning sun. Soon, their short flights turn the air into a flurry that resembles a snowstorm of orange flakes as they drift to the ground in search of water and nectar to replenish their dwindling fat reserves.

There are daily buses from Mexico City to the gateway community of Angangueo, where it's possible to access at least two of the main sanctuaries at El Rosario and Sierra Chincua by vehicle or on foot.
MORE INFO www.mbsf.org

[LEFT] ↗
Monarch butterflies stay virtually motionless for four or five months of the year.

[TOP RIGHT] ↗
Female grey whales migrate to Baja California to give birth to their 600kg calves; the males migrate there to mate with the females.

[BOTTOM RIGHT] ↗
The dhole family pack stays in touch by emitting an odd collection of noises.

GREY WHALES BAJA CALIFORNIA

LOCATION San Ignacio Lagoon, 400km northwest of La Paz **WHY NOW?** It's the best time to see mothers and calves up close **LEVEL OF DIFFICULTY** Low – see the whales from small local boats **STATUS** They were virtually extinct in 1850s but the population is now stable

Grey whales are the happy story of an animal that nearly became extinct then made a remarkable recovery back to its historic levels of around 20,000. Today it is once again possible to witness them return each December to their legendary calving grounds on the coasts of Baja California. This fantastic experience is made all the more compelling because the whales have recently begun responding positively to human presence, with countless tales of mother whales bringing their calves over to boatloads of visitors so the babies can be petted and scratched. And it seems that San Ignacio Lagoon, on the Pacific Ocean side of the peninsula, has the friendliest whales of all, making it Baja's foremost must-see destination for wildlife enthusiasts of every age.

Grey whales make the most extraordinary migration of any known mammal, travelling 10,000km from the Bering Sea to Baja California for the sole purpose of finding a warm safe place for their 600kg calves to be born. Males tag along to mate with the many gathered females, and February is the all-around best time to see the whales.

San Ignacio Lagoon is a reasonable 860km drive south from the US border, although many tour groups fly into Loreto for a much shorter drive. **MORE INFO** www.netconnection.com/bajawhales.html

DHOLES INDIA

LOCATION Kanha National Park, 175km southeast of Jabalpur, Madhya Pradesh **WHY NOW?** There's a good chance of seeing pups **LEVEL OF DIFFICULTY** Low – many visitors to the park see dholes during their stay **STATUS** Dholes are highly threatened across Asia and are probably extirpated from most areas

Dholes were at one time the definitive wild dogs of Asia, but in recent decades they have virtually disappeared across vast swathes of their range and little is known about their current status. Only in central and northern India do you have a reasonable chance of encountering these unique dogs. Reddish in colour and about the size of a border collie, dholes cannot be neatly classified with foxes or wolves so they are placed in their own genus. They are one of the few dogs that regularly hunt in social, cooperative packs, a behaviour that requires high levels of intelligence, coordination and courage. Packs of five to 12 dholes specialise in singling out and taking down medium-sized antelope, but in a pinch they will not hesitate to tackle massive guar, buffalo, young rhinos or tigers, even though some members of a pack may be killed in the process. Packs are based on extended family units that stay in touch with a peculiar repertoire of whistles, screams, mews and clucks that no other dog in the world seems to share. Kanha National Park preserves India's last great sal forests, a habitat favoured by herds of antelope that dholes prey on. Access Kanha from Jabalpur via rail or bus.
MORE INFO www.cuon.net/dholes

↗ FEBRUARY
WEEK.04

RAJA AMPAT ISLANDS
INDONESIA

WHAT YOU'LL SEE

- REEF FISH
- CORALS
- SEA TURTLES
- LIMESTONE PINNACLES
- PALM TREES AND SANDY BEACHES

WHY NOW? Every time is a good time on the equator

If you spend much time flipping through magazines and websites researching the 'Top 10' dive sites in the world, you'll see a lot of the same names and superlatives popping up over and over again. After a while you can be excused if the different destinations begin to swirl together in your mind, but don't let this stop you from discovering one truly outstanding destination that doesn't make it onto many lists – the Raja Ampat Islands.

This sprawling archipelago of 1500 small islands off the northwest tip of West Papua (formerly known as Irian Jaya) is remote, expensive to visit and lacks any significant infrastructure for mass tourism. So why bother visiting? Sure there are mazes of eerie limestone pinnacles and palm-lined beaches as far as you can see, but the answer is revealed as soon as you dive underwater: the display of corals and reef fish will blow

[LEFT] ↖
More than 1000 species of fish have been identified in the Raja Ampat reefs.

your mind. This is, without a doubt, the most pristine and diverse underwater ecosystem anywhere on the planet.

A 2002 survey of the Raja Ampat reefs found over 1000 species of fish and more than 500 species of coral living in an unbelievably complex matrix of colours and forms. During the survey one biologist recorded 284 species of fish on a single dive (a world record), while more than 50% of the sites surveyed had over 200 species of fish per dive, far surpassing the numbers found at any other location in the world.

At a time when tropical reefs are being decimated by overfishing, insensitive tourism and the impacts of global warming, it is incredible that this site has survived. And because the Raja Ampat Islands are located in the channel where waters flow between the Indian and Pacific oceans, biologists believe that these phenomenally diverse coral reefs disperse prodigious amounts of larvae into the passing currents and play a major role in replenishing coral reefs of the neighbouring oceans.

About the only way to access the Raja Ampat Islands is to fly to the West Papuan port city of Sorong from Jakarta or Manado (North Sulawesi) and join a 'liveaboard' charter boat for a week or more of intensive cruising and diving.
MORE INFO http://rajaampat.org

STELLER'S SEA EAGLES JAPAN

↘ **LOCATION** Hokkaido, 320km east of Sapporo **WHY NOW?** You can see large numbers of sea eagles gathering on the sea ice **LEVEL OF DIFFICULTY** Low – it's logistically easy but be prepared for cold temperatures **STATUS** There are about 5000 left in the world but the population is probably stable due to the remoteness of their breeding range

A trip to the port city of Rausu on the northeastern tip of Hokkaido in the middle of winter is a trip to the wild edge of the Arctic. By February the sea reaches its coldest temperatures and has either locked the fishing harbour in a sheet of sea ice or filled the nearby Numuro Strait with floating blocks of snow-covered icebergs. Unless you do well in bitter cold it's not an inviting time of year to visit, but it's also the peak time to see the world's heaviest (at 9kg) and most beautiful eagle, the majestic Steller's sea eagle. They are here because freezing water pushes them out of their breeding range on the remote and largely inaccessible Kamchatka Peninsula and forces them south towards northern Japan in search of open water and abundant fish.

With huge orange bills and bold white patches on their dark brown bodies, these eagles cut a dashing figure at any time, but in February when they gather around Rausu by the hundreds they are even more impressive. Conditions permitting, you can charter a boat that will take you out into the strait for some eye-popping views of eagles perched on the floating ice in the first rays of sunrise.

You may also witness the excitement of early courtship activity or see some of the region's other winter birds, including white-tailed sea eagles, whooping swans and the highly sought-after Blakiston's fish-owl, which fearlessly wades into icy water to catch fish.

MORE INFO www.fadr.msu.ru/o-washinet/spsynop.html

[LEFT] ↗
Weighing in at approximately 9kg, the world's heaviest eagle is the Steller's sea eagle.

[TOP RIGHT] ↗
Pink dolphins make up the world's largest population of river dolphins, as other species are extinct or close to extinction.

[BOTTOM RIGHT] ↗
Up to 50 Tasmanian devils are born in a single litter; they must compete for access to one of their mother's four teats for survival.

PINK RIVER DOLPHINS PERU

LOCATION Yarapa River, 150km upstream from Iquitos **WHY NOW?** It's possible to see calves **LEVEL OF DIFFICULTY** Low – the logistics are straightforward on a guided tour, but more difficult if you arrange your own transport **STATUS** The dolphins are vulnerable and increasingly threatened by fishing nets

No you haven't been drinking too much cachaça; those really are pink dolphins! And what odd-looking creatures, with long beaks, tiny eyes and strangely flexible necks. No wonder local peoples have until recently treated the Amazon's river dolphins with a degree of respect and superstition. In return, these intelligent animals (with a brain capacity 40% larger than humans) show a high degree of curiosity and readily interact with humans in areas where they aren't hunted.

Finding them in any numbers is another story altogether. Although pink dolphins congregate at river confluences to cooperate in chasing fish into shallow waters, they also disperse individually into flooded forests during the rainy season. Sure you can spot them swimming away in the distance, but why not have a more intimate encounter with these unique creatures? One possibility is to find them at traditionally dependable sites such as the confluence of the Yarapa and Amazon Rivers, where you have the added benefit of staying at a lodge and watching mothers and calves gather to play (www.isptr-pard.org). Another option is to volunteer with a research team engaged in long-term studies of hundreds of marked individuals at the confluence of the Japura and Solimoes Rivers just west of Manaus, Brazil. **MORE INFO** www.projetoboto.com

TASMANIAN DEVILS AUSTRALIA

LOCATION Cradle Mountain–Lake St Clair National Park, 120km northwest of Hobart, Tasmania **WHY NOW?** Now is your best chance of spotting a devil because inexperienced youngsters are on their own for the first time **LEVEL OF DIFFICULTY** Low – as long as you don't mind driving around at night **STATUS** They are seriously threatened by a mysterious facial cancer that is decimating the wild population

Along with its sensational name, Australia's largest marsupial carnivore has a notoriety that is largely undeserved. True, there are the threatening growls, gnashing teeth and blood-chilling screams that can be heard several kilometres away as a horde of devils devour a carcass. And even more unnerving is the sight of a dead wombat bulging and heaving as a devil emerges from inside the body covered in gore – they commonly eat large corpses from the inside out. However, in general they are shy and solitary creatures rather than the devils of lore.

Life is a struggle from birth for Tasmanian devils. As many as 50 offspring are born at the same time, each about the size of a rice grain, and they must scramble 8cm from the birth canal to their mother's pouch where they battle for access to their mother's four teats. There are only four winners and it seems that evolution favours devils that are particularly fierce and strong. The best way to see these nocturnal carnivores is to drive along forest roads an hour or two after sunset. Newly independent young that are too inexperienced to avoid detection can be spotted in January and February, especially around Cradle Mountain Lodge.
MORE INFO www.parks.tas.gov.au

DID YOU KNOW?

The pink river dolphin's vertebrae are unfused, giving them flexibility for hunting fish in the tangled vegetation of a flooded forest.

Relative to their size, Tasmanian devils have the strongest bite of any mammal, enabling them to devour every part of a carcass.

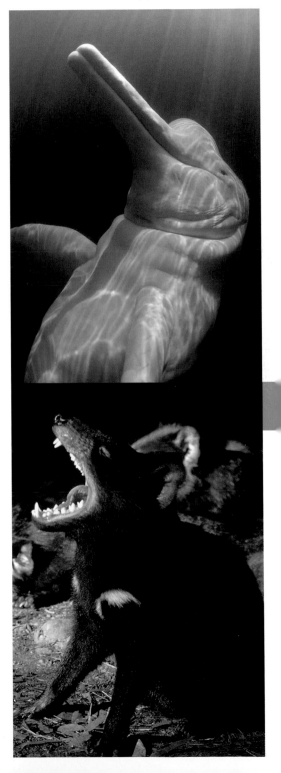

↗ MARCH
WEEK.01

CIÉNAGA DE ZAPATA NATIONAL PARK CUBA

WHAT YOU'LL SEE

WHY NOW? It's the best time for cooler, drier weather

If your image of Cuba is simply of a culture of cigars and political isolation, you are missing Cuba's true wealth. Go with the eyes of a wildlife traveller and prepare to be amazed. Few people realise it, but Cuba is the crown jewel of the world's fourth most important biodiversity hot spot, and on a scale of endemic species per unit area it may surpass every other location in the world. And even better, Cuba's endemic species are not your ordinary local varieties; they are truly bizarre. Consider the newly discovered frog that is 1cm long and lays only one egg a year. Or the dwarf scorpions that are also only 1cm long. Or the butterfly bats that have 12cm wingspans. Then there are orchids with flowers that are 2mm wide. But best of all is the bee hummingbird, the world's smallest bird – only 5.5cm long and weighing little more than a standard paper clip. The size of a large bee, this tiny hummingbird has the wonderful local name

zunzuncito for the sound it makes when it flies.

In some ways Cuba is still a relatively pristine island, with ample opportunities to explore its native species or to discover some new species on your own. For a wide range of habitats, check out Ciénaga de Zapata, a vast area of marshes, mangroves and coral reefs comparable to the Florida Everglades. Zapata Swamp is famous among birdwatchers because it is home to 18 of Cuba's 22 endemic bird species, including the highly localised Zapata wren, Zapata rail and Zapata sparrow, not to mention the bee hummingbird. The swamp has also been the last refuge for the Cuban crocodile and a sanctuary for West Indian manatees.

Once you've whetted your appetite for Cuban wildlife at Zapata, you could arrange an expedition to check out the colony of 70,000 nesting flamingos within the rugged Humedal Río Máximo-Cagüey region. Or take it easy at the Alejandro de Humboldt National Park, a World Heritage Site that is considered the most biologically diverse tropical island habitat in the world.

This is a challenging destination to the extent that there are few national park guidelines, maps or tourism policies in Cuba, but for the adventurous traveller that's part of the charm.

MORE INFO www.havana-guide.com

HARP SEALS CANADA

LOCATION Magdalen Islands, 700km east of Quebec City, Quebec **WHY NOW?** There's a narrow window of time to see white seal pups **LEVEL OF DIFFICULTY** Low – it's cold and a little slippery on the sea ice **STATUS** The seals are hunted for fur and oil but the population is relatively stable

As you fly over the sea ice in Quebec's Gulf of St Lawrence, it looks as if the snow is speckled with dark spots across the entire vista. You are seeing some of the 1.3 million harp seals that have hauled themselves out of the water to give birth to their pups in what is one of the world's greatest marine mammal events.

Unlike their dark-complexioned mothers, the pups are born with soft woolly white fur that they keep for the first two to four weeks of their life. They grow about 2.5kg a day on a diet of rich mother's milk, getting so fat that they grow into little blimps with flippers. Mother seals are eager to wean their pups as soon as possible because the ice begins to break up before the pups are hardly ready to swim, and the pups need to be as fat and large as possible to withstand the icy waters. Mother seals have another agenda too: soon after giving birth they become reproductively fertile and large numbers of males are anxiously circling at the ice's edge waiting for opportunities to mate.

All of this would be an idyllic life except for the annual hunt of seal pups for fur and oil by fishermen. Despite intense international condemnation and boycotts, over 200,000 harp seal pups continue to be harvested in Canada each year.

MORE INFO www.pinnipeds.org/species/harp.htm

(LEFT) ↗
Baby harp seals gain up to 2.5kg a day to insulate them against the icy temperatures of the Gulf of St Lawrence.

(TOP RIGHT) ↗
The iridescent resplendent quetzal is Montverde's flagship bird.

(BOTTOM RIGHT) ↗
The Gulf of Corcovado in Chile functions as a maternity ward for the incredible blue whale.

RESPLENDENT QUETZALS COSTA RICA

LOCATION Monteverde Cloud Forest Preserve, 180km northwest of San José **WHY NOW?** Quetzals come lower in trees to nest during the breeding season **LEVEL OF DIFFICULTY** Low – some jungle scrambling is required **STATUS** Quetzals are widely threatened due to habitat destruction but are stable in Costa Rica preserves

Among conservationists and tourists, Monteverde is shorthand for one of the most famous and accessible rainforest reserves in the world. Thousands of visitors a year descend on Monteverde and few leave disappointed. Most visitors come for a glimpse of Monteverde's flagship bird, the resplendent quetzal, generally considered one of the world's most beautiful birds because of its iridescent green plumage, crimson belly and elegant streaming tail. But what's amazing is how much diverse wildlife this preserve, and a handful of neighbouring preserves, have to offer.

Once you survive the long bumpy bus or rental-car ride up to the preserve area, you'll want to settle in for a long stay at one of the many ecolodges or hotels to take advantage of the excellent local guides, trail systems and numerous volunteer opportunities. You could see up to three species of monkey, tapir, ocelot, coati, agouti, kinkajou and more. Birdwatchers covet this area for its 400 species of bird, including an astounding 26 species of hummingbird that gather each day at the Hummingbird Gallery feeders. One of the things that makes this area so fun to visit is that there are so many interesting biologists, wildlife enthusiasts and conservationists to meet here.
MORE INFO www.cct.or.cr/english

BLUE WHALES CHILE

LOCATION Gulf of Corcovado, 250km south of Puerto Montt **WHY NOW?** It's the calving season **LEVEL OF DIFFICULTY** Low – there are some logistics involved in getting to viewing points around the gulf **STATUS** The future is uncertain due to low population numbers and the growing impact of salmon farms

By the time the hunting of blue whales was outlawed in 1966, an estimated half a million had been killed, leaving so few that it was widely believed this gigantic 180,000kg mammal would soon become extinct. In 1997 a team of scientists surveyed 4000km of Chilean coastline in the hope of learning how many blue whales remained in this once productive area. Sadly, they only found a total of 40 by the end of the project, but a miracle occurred when team members hopped a ride back home on a cruise ship crossing the Gulf of Corcovado – they found 60 blue whales in four hours and discovered what may turn out to be the world's most important nursery ground for the species.

The pristine waters of the gulf appear to be an ideal haven for nursing whales, whose calves grow an astonishing 90kg a day and require prodigious quantities of tiny shrimplike krill. Little is known about blue whales in the Gulf of Corcovado but a Blue Whale Center (Centro Ballena Azul) has been set up in the island town of Melinka as a base camp for scientists conducting research and conservationists working to educate local communities and the Chilean government about this incredible mammal.
MORE INFO www.ballenazul.org

DID YOU KNOW?

 Resplendent quetzals eat avocado-like fruits that they swallow whole, coughing up the pits later.

 The blue whale's scientific name means 'little mouse' and it's thought that someone came up with this name as a joke.

DANUM VALLEY CONSERVATION
AREA MALAYSIAN BORNEO

WHAT YOU'LL SEE

ORANG-UTANS
GIANT FLYING SQUIRRELS
MOUSE DEER
GREAT ARGUS PHEASANTS
BARBETS

WHY NOW? It's the tail end of the rainy season and before Sabah's busy festival season

Even before it officially opened in 1986, tropical biologists were buzzing about the fabulous wildlife and untouched rainforests being found in Sabah's Danum Valley. Historically there had been no villages in the area so the habitats were completely undisturbed, and were home to everything from the last remnant bands of Sumatran rhinos left in Borneo to herds of elephants and numerous orang-utans. As biologists dug deeper the discoveries kept unfolding, and today Danum Valley is widely considered one of the foremost conservation sites in Borneo and all of Southeast Asia.

Courtesy of the new Borneo Rainforest Lodge it is now possible (though expensive) for tourists to explore this famous destination, along with scientists who are still uncovering the riches of Danum Valley. Not only are there substantial canopy walkways and platforms

for viewing treetop wildlife, but visitors will also enjoy ready access to 50km of trails.

There may be no other place where you can observe all of northern Borneo's primates (except one) in a single location, or see so many orang-utans. Visitors have equally good chances of running across four species of cat and two species of mouse deer (they look like deer but are the size of a rabbit), plus bearded pigs and elephants. Or if you wait on the swinging bridge at dusk you may spot a giant flying squirrel gliding across the river.

Danum Valley may also be one of the last significant locations for finding lowland rainforest birds in Borneo. You could come for any of the 275 known species here, but why not search for the seven species of pitta,

the glowing jewels of the forest floor; or the great argus pheasant performing its grand courtship ritual; or the enigmatic and poorly known Borneon bristlehead lurking in the canopy.

Fortunately, it is fairly easy to access this destination. There are daily flights from Kuala Lumpur to Tawau, Sabah. From there you can take a 120km bus or taxi ride to the gateway village of Lahad Datu, where there are regular shuttles into the Conservation Area. It is said that even a year at Danum Valley isn't enough time, so make sure you arrange to stay as long as possible.

MORE INFO www.sabahtourism.com

SANDHILL CRANES USA

↘ **LOCATION** Platte River, 24km east of Kearney, Nebraska, USA **WHY NOW?** You can see absolutely incredible numbers of cranes **LEVEL OF DIFFICULTY** Low – bundle up if you want to see the morning fly-out **STATUS** Cranes are increasingly crowded on a river that's being dammed and diverted into near-oblivion

It's an hour before sunrise and you're sitting on a cold wooden bench freezing your butt off in an unheated wildlife blind, but you have to admit that between bouts of shivering your heart is racing with excitement. Out there in the darkness you're hearing the resounding cries of one of the world's loudest birds, and not just a single bird, but 30,000 at once. Then, as the sun suddenly peeks over the horizon, their cries reach an outrageous crescendo as flock upon flock of sandhill cranes takes flight at once. Welcome to the spectacle of crane-watching on the Platte River!

Maybe it's because sandhill cranes are among the oldest living birds, but their cries rank up there with wolf howls as one of the most primeval and bone-chilling natural sounds you will ever hear. And there's nothing like being on the stretch of the Platte River between Kearney and Grand Island, Nebraska, in mid-March when 500,000 of them stop to fatten up for their final flight to their Canadian breeding grounds. If you wander along local country roads during the day you'll find thousands of cranes gathering in agricultural fields to eat leftover grains, but it's the late-afternoon and early-morning flights to and from their riverside sleeping areas that are truly breathtaking. The National Audubon Society manages a popular viewing area along one 8km stretch of river at the Lillian Annette Rowe Sanctuary. Book ahead to save a seat at the viewing blinds and show up before sunrise.

MORE INFO www.rowesanctuary.org

(LEFT) ↗
Around half a million sandhill cranes stop on Platte River in Nebraska in mid-March to fatten up before heading onwards to Canada.

(TOP RIGHT) ↗
The 110km of protected coastline in Quirimbas National Park is home to at least 375 species of tropical fish.

(BOTTOM RIGHT) ↗
Leatherback turtles on Matura Beach are protected during egg-laying by volunteers from local villages.

REEF FISH & DANCING SCALLOPS
MOZAMBIQUE

LOCATION Quirimbas National Park, north of Pemba **WHY NOW?** You can see resident wildlife plus migrant birds **LEVEL OF DIFFICULTY** Medium – it's expensive, logistically challenging and information is difficult to find **STATUS** In this scarcely known region, the greatest threat is developers snapping up land for high-end resorts

Imagine an unspoiled paradise of clear blue water and powder-white sand beaches and you'll come close to imagining Mozambique's unexploited and little-known north coast. Overlooked due to a near absence of infrastructure, this region of traditional villages, coastal wilderness and abundant natural resources has survived largely intact into the 21st century. With much fanfare, local villages and communities asked for and received national park status in 2002, making it perhaps the first national park in the world established at the request of the area's inhabitants. If you're not staying at one of the new expensive resorts that predictably sprouted up, expect to have a hell of a journey accessing this region on a variety of boats or trucks leaving Pemba.

But the rewards are worth it. Over 375 species of tropical fish have been found in relatively pristine reef settings along 110km of protected coast, along with three species of dolphin, hammerhead shark and sea turtle. The area reportedly has exceptionally large parrotfish, angelfish and moray eels, and on a slow dive through the seagrass beds you might see swimming scallops that come up and dance in midwater. With a little research, budget travellers can find inexpensive local homestays.

MORE INFO www.mozguide.com

- -

LEATHERBACK TURTLES TRINIDAD

LOCATION Matura Beach, 50km east of Port-of-Spain **WHY NOW?** It's the beginning of the nesting season **LEVEL OF DIFFICULTY** Low – walk the beach at night with local guides to see the turtles **STATUS** The turtles are globally threatened by fishing nets, pollution and loss of nesting grounds

In the sad, sad story of sea turtle conservation, the village of Matura, Trinidad, is a very bright light indeed. Globally, the populations of the world's seven sea turtle species have plummeted from hundreds of thousands, perhaps millions, to mere handfuls. In response to this environmental crisis, the government of Trinidad acted to protect the world's largest leatherback turtle nesting colony at Matura Beach in 1990. However, when government patrols shut off the area, local villagers protested the loss of their favourite beach and source of income so they formed a group called Nature Seekers and took charge of monitoring and safeguarding the turtles themselves. These proud villagers, many of whom are women with families, donate their nights to help patrol the beaches and in honour of their efforts they have won numerous international awards and earned recognition from the United Nations.

Each night during the egg-laying season, these majestic 900kg turtles lumber out of the ocean to lay their eggs in the sand. On peak nights up to 150 turtles can be found on Matura Beach and the Nature Seekers will be out too, measuring, monitoring and guarding against egg-poachers. Volunteer for this amazing organisation through Earthwatch Institute (earthwatch.org) or contact the Nature Seekers directly.

MORE INFO www.natureseekers.org

DID YOU KNOW?

 The reefs of the Quirimbas Archipelago are virtually unexplored but may turn out to have the richest coral diversity in the Indian Ocean.

- -

 When diving to 1200m, leatherback turtles don't crack because their shells are formed of flexible cartilage and miniature bones.

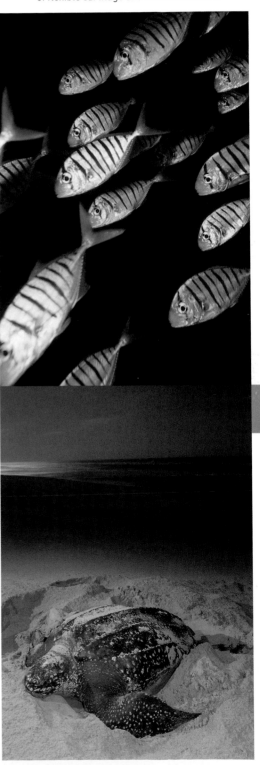

↗ MARCH
WEEK.03

ANAVILHANAS ARCHIPELAGO
BRAZIL

WHAT YOU'LL SEE

- HOATZINS
- ZIGZAG HERONS
- PARROTS
- CAPYBARAS
- DOLPHINS

↘ **WHY NOW?** The excellent weather coincides with high water levels

The ultimate Amazon fantasy trip would be to rent a boat in Manaus and set sail on an extended expedition up the world's mightiest river. Dozens of such boats – complete with captain and crew, living quarters, kitchen and showers – are available for multiweek journeys tailored to your every whim. Loaded up with as much food and supplies as you want, these boats serve as moving base-camps and observation platforms that putter along backchannels or set anchor for in-depth explorations at any point.

Manaus sits at an important crossroads in the Amazon and offers access to several major rivers and minor tributaries, but there is no better option than to motor 60km up the Rio Negro and weave into the 80km-long web of hundreds of channels, lakes and islands that make up the Anavilhanas Archipelago Ecological Station. From November

to April river levels are at their highest, flooding vast stretches of *igapo* forest and putting your boat eye-to-eye with treetop-level parrots, toucans and monkeys. Lie in a hammock on the deck and soak up the scenery, or hop in a canoe and explore mysterious sidechannels to your heart's content.

Other than a bit of poaching, massive annual floods prevent these forests from human encroachment, making the archipelago a haven for wildlife. You're likely to see both species of Amazon dolphin and plenty of monkeys, or as your boat slides quietly along you might spot a jaguar, tapir or capybara.

Birds are prolific here, especially water birds and parrots. If you can pull your eyes away from all the egrets and herons, look for primitive-looking hoatzins as well as the specialised and highly sought-after sungrebes and sunbitterns. Parrots are everywhere too, and at sunrise they put on a fun show when great noisy flocks fly out from their nightly roosts and swoop off to feed in nearby forests.

With a small group of people splitting the costs, these river trips are surprisingly inexpensive and boats are booked many months in advance during the peak season. Alternatively, you could rent a large canoe and sleep on shore in hammocks each night, but nothing compares to the luxury of sharing your own private floating hotel with some friends.

MORE INFO www.v-brazil.com/tourism/amazonas/manaus.html

KILLER WHALES ARGENTINA

LOCATION Valdés Peninsula, 1400km south of Buenos Aires **WHY NOW?** The killer whales arrive to eat seal pups **LEVEL OF DIFFICULTY** Low – it's remote but on a well-established tourist circuit **STATUS** The South Atlantic is the world's fastest-growing fishery, depriving both seals and killer whales of their food

Killer whales (orcas) surely rank as one of the world's most spectacular animals, and of all their incredible behaviours nothing beats the show they put on at Argentina's Valdés Peninsula. This enormous World Heritage Site is a desolate, sparsely inhabited thumb of land jutting into the Southern Atlantic Ocean, long famous for attracting large numbers of breeding right whales, sea lions, elephant seals and magellanic penguins. In 1975 an orca project (www.fundorca.org.ar) began to identify, name and monitor the killer whales that occurred in the area, and team members discovered a remarkable behaviour that they brought to international attention in 1985.

From December to March, 7000 sea lions gather to mate and give birth on beaches protected by the peninsula's sheer cliffs. Towards the end of March, there is a narrow window of time when all the seal pups line up on the beach and make their first tentative forays into the ocean. With exquisite timing, killer whales show up at the same time. These ferocious 10m-long predators catch seal pups by ramming forward with such speed that the whales actually launch themselves out of the water in an explosion of foam, land on the beach, grab a pup, and slide back into the ocean. A recent survey by BBC's *Wildlife* magazine rated this as number three of the top 10 wildlife spectacles in the world – you don't want to miss it.

Reach the nearest city, Puerto Madryn, by bus from Buenos Aires or after a domestic flight to Trelew. **MORE INFO** www.patagonia-argentina.com

(LEFT) ↗
Killer whales have learned to show up on the Valdés Peninsula during the sea lion breeding season as they are likely to catch a feed of seal pups.

(TOP RIGHT) ↗
Male kob perform on leks for hours at a time in the hopes of attracting a female.

(BOTTOM RIGHT) ↗
Standing up to 1m high and weighing 22kg, a great bustard in full display could be mistaken for a sheep.

UGANDA KOB UGANDA

⬊ **LOCATION** Queen Elizabeth National Park, 480km west of Kampala **WHY NOW?** The end of the dry season triggers peak mating activity **LEVEL OF DIFFICULTY** Low – it involves the typical safari logistics **STATUS** The population is fast-growing and recovering after Uganda's civil war

These elegant, high-strutting antelope of Africa's equatorial savannahs might be scarcely noticed if it weren't for the extraordinary mating rituals of the males as they gather on 'dance floors' (leks) to attract females. Courtship activity reaches an apex towards the end of the dry season when kob bunch up on the green grassy fringes of drying waterways and the presence of so many females sends the hormonal males into overdrive.

Leks are located in the middle of prime grazing pastures or along main travelling routes so females can watch the males' strange antics and determine which ones are the strongest and most dominant. Male behaviour is highly ritualised, with erect walking and head shaking, and often leads to savage fights. Constant activity wears away all the grass on these distinctive 'kob fields'; after several hours or a day of intense activity, males stagger away to drink, eat and rest up for their next round of showing off.

Although most visitors come to Queen Elizabeth National Park for fabulous hippo-viewing along the Kazinga Channel or for the park's stunning 606 species of bird, it's worth driving the Kasenyi Track to observe the park's 31,000 kob. You can reach the park on public transport from Kampala, but to really see the park you need a private vehicle.
MORE INFO www.uwa.or.ug/queen.html

DID YOU KNOW?

↗ Killer whales often play with seal pups, tossing them in the air like volleyballs then releasing them unharmed.

↗ Kobs convert poor-quality grass into meat faster than other bovids, making them a valuable food source for predators.

GREAT BUSTARDS SPAIN

⬊ **LOCATION** Extremadura, 250km southwest of Madrid **WHY NOW?** It's the beginning of the courtship season **LEVEL OF DIFFICULTY** Low – you can see them from the idyllic pastoral roads **STATUS** The population is declining and is not well protected

To see the world's largest flying bird, try driving the rolling pastoral roads of Extremadura on a March or April morning. There are few farmsteads in this sparsely inhabited region and you're likely to have the narrow country roads, the big vault of sky and countless singing birds all to yourself. Scan open grasslands for groups of 22kg birds that tower 1m high. It shouldn't be a problem spotting these birds except that when they are all fluffed out and displaying their white feathers they look more like sheep standing in the distance and are surprisingly easy to overlook.

Bustards are famous for their elaborate courtship displays that involve the male inflating big air sacs in his throat, throwing back his head, cocking his tail forward and almost turning his wings inside out in order to nearly cover himself in a shower of vibrating snowy-white feathers.

With a population (in 2006) of 6900 great bustards, Extremadura is the last great place for observing these magnificent – although rapidly declining in numbers – birds. It is also a fantastic location for other grassland birds such as the more common little bustard, which has an equally interesting courtship display, or the scarce pin-tailed sandgrouse. Not far away, Monfragüe National Park, 60km north of Truijillo, is a great place to look for 16 species of breeding raptor.
MORE INFO www.iberianature.com

↗ MARCH
WEEK.04

NINGALOO MARINE PARK
AUSTRALIA

WHAT YOU'LL SEE

WHALE SHARKS
SEA TURTLES
DUGONGS
CORALS
REEF FISH

WHY NOW? There's a good chance of seeing spawning coral

You're likely to come to Western Australia's Ningaloo Reef to see its biggest animal, but count yourself lucky if you see the smallest. Each year, on a single night a few days after the full moons in March and April, the entire reef gives 'birth'. This mass coral spawning happens suddenly, and without warning, and for just a few hours the ocean turns into a surreal pinkish haze as trillions of packets of coral sperm and eggs flood the waters. It is one of the most astounding events that a diver will ever see and its fame has grown over time because it's notoriously hard to predict.

Not only is the synchronised release itself beautiful to watch, but it also attracts swarms of zooplankton and bait fish for a massive feeding frenzy. This in turn draws in large numbers of whale sharks, jellyfish and manta rays that appear offshore. The 12m-long whale sharks hang around in good numbers until June, making this the best time

of year to see this stupendous, slow-moving freight train of a fish.

Does anyone really need a good reason to visit Ningaloo? This is, after all, Australia's largest fringing coral reef, a reef you can easily swim to from shore (as opposed to a barrier reef that you'd have to take a boat to see); and everywhere you look there are profusions of corals and reef fish that rival the legendary Great Barrier Reef.

Spanning 260km of coastline, Ningaloo Reef has many different facets. At Coral Bay on calm days the seas are crystal clear and you can swim out to the coral gardens to explore beds of lavender coral and forests of blue staghorn with endless schools of iridescent reef fish. Look for flame-coloured false clown anemonefish lurking among sea anemones, or reef octopuses and golden seasnakes weaving over the sea floor. Further north around the Oyster Stacks you'll encounter massive domed or petal-like corals jewelled with sea urchins and nudibranchs.

Located 1200km north of Perth, Ningaloo Reef runs along the west shore of Cape Range National Park, where you can take a break to wander rock gorges and tracks in search of rock wallabies and wedge-tailed eagles. Camp in the park or shack up in nearby Exmouth.

MORE INFO www.environment.gov.au/coasts/mpa /ningaloo/index.html

MEERKATS SOUTH AFRICA

LOCATION Addo Elephant National Park, 72km northeast of Port Elizabeth **WHY NOW?** There's a good chance of seeing youngsters **LEVEL OF DIFFICULTY** Low – they are easily viewed and readily adapt to human presence **STATUS** Meerkats are common and widespread in South Africa

Not many animals have enough charisma to pull off a wildly popular television series watched in 164 countries, but it's all in a day's work for South Africa's goofy meerkats. Based on the life and drama of several neighbouring meerkat clans, the popular TV show *Meerkat Manor* highlights the unique behaviour and cooperative social structure of these mongoose cousins, but why not appreciate meerkat antics yourself in one of South Africa's parks? Some ecolodges even have dedicated meerkat wardens who track meerkat activities for guests who want to see these television stars first-hand.

Meerkat life is built around a social pack of 10 to 30 meerkats, and all members benefit if the group stays large and healthy. A meerkat's day starts with a session of sunbathing and grooming before the pack bounds off on its daily foraging expedition. A sentry is always posted to cry out if a hawk flies over, but if a ground predator appears the pack jumps up and down together to give the illusion that they're charging. Otherwise their day is spent tousling, rolling around like kids and playing 'follow the leader'. Everyone pays attention to the pups that emerge from their burrows sometime after January, and the pack takes turns at nursery duty to give the mothers time to find some food for themselves.

From their constant human-like murmuring to their upright stances, there is something comforting about meerkats. And almost everything they do will generate a laugh. Very tame groups can be observed along the Woodlands-Harpoor Loop in Addo Elephant National Park, but also at many other locales.

MORE INFO www.sanparks.org/parks/addo

(LEFT) ↗
Meerkats start their day with a sunbathing session.

(TOP RIGHT) ↗
Mature male gharials emit a loud flatulent sound from their snouts to woo the females and deter challengers.

(BOTTOM RIGHT) ↗
The resident black flying fox roost at Tooan Tooan Creek in Queensland is also seasonally populated with grey-headed and little red flying foxes.

GHARIALS NEPAL

LOCATION Royal Chitwan National Park, 120km southwest of Kathmandu **WHY NOW?** It's the beginning of spring **LEVEL OF DIFFICULTY** Low – the park's logistics and infrastructure are well organised **STATUS** Gharials are critically endangered despite intensive management efforts

Most visitors to Royal Chitwan, Nepal's oldest and most popular park, come to ride around on elephants in search of rhinos and tigers, but totally overlook the bizarre gharial, a highly endangered crocodilian with a set of long, unbelievably skinny jaws that it uses like chopsticks to capture fish. Strictly limited to rivers and living on a diet of fish, the gharial once roamed thousands of kilometres of rivers from Pakistan to Myanmar, but its population today is found on less than 200 kilometres and is dwindling rapidly.

Mature male gharials develop a wart-like appendage which presses down on their nostrils at the tips of their snout, so that when they breathe out forcefully they produce a big flatulent sound, a 'buzz-snort' that attracts females and warns off challengers. Rival males engage in fierce territorial combat, clashing their snouts like swords in mid-air and thrashing the water with their tails. Females likewise fight for access to the best nesting spots on sandy beaches, where they lay a clutch of 50 large eggs then retreat to stand guard from the nearby water.

Unfortunately, there are only eight gharial remaining in Royal Chitwan, their last stronghold in Nepal. Around 200 can be found in India's National Chambal Sanctuary but the sanctuary is understaffed and threatened by local mafia gangs that profit from killing wildlife.

MORE INFO www.gharialconservation.org

DID YOU KNOW?

Although gharials lack the strength of a crocodile's blunt heavy jaws, their lightweight skulls and slender snouts allow them to catch fast-moving fish with quick grabs.

Black flying foxes will travel up to 50km a night in search of food.

FLYING FOXES AUSTRALIA

LOCATION Tooan Tooan Creek, 250km north of Brisbane, Queensland **WHY NOW?** The roosting colony is at peak numbers **LEVEL OF DIFFICULTY** Low – there's easy access and viewing **STATUS** The flying foxes are stable and well protected

If you have never seen a flying fox, prepare to have your definition of 'bat' revised dramatically, because these giant bats with 1m wingspans are closer to a pterodactyl than one of those small flitty things you normally see. In fact, bats of this size are a little frightening and even more so when they roost in massive colonies like the one at Tooan Tooan Creek in Hervey Bay, Queensland.

This particular roost site is especially intriguing because the resident colony of several thousand black flying foxes is seasonally augmented by the arrival of hundreds of thousands of nomadic grey-headed flying foxes and little red flying foxes. These wanderers apparently follow the flowering cycles of tea trees and move on to find new flower crops after a few weeks at Tooan Tooan. The migratory patterns are still poorly understood so the Queensland National Parks and Wildlife Service is monitoring flying fox roosts all over Queensland in an attempt to track the movements and behaviour of these nomadic species.

Meanwhile, the resident black flying foxes are content to hang around and spend their days sleeping on the same tree branches. See them winging off at dusk in search of flowering eucalyptus trees. Fortunately, the Hervey Bay community seems to recognise the ecological and economic value of their odd neighbours.

MORE INFO www.herveybay.qld.gov.au/community/environment/wildlife.shtml

SINHARAJA NATIONAL PARK
SRI LANKA

WHAT YOU'LL SEE

- LEOPARDS
- INDIAN ELEPHANTS
- PURPLE-FACED LEAF MONKEYS
- SRI LANKAN PIGEONS
- WHITE-FACED STARLINGS

↘ **WHY NOW?** The beginning of the rainy season in April brings everything back to life

You could say that Sri Lanka's Sinharaja National Park is a real conservation success story. First set aside in the 3rd century BC as a *thahanakelle* (protected forest) by tribal law, it held sway in local legend as the home of Sinharaja, 'the Lion King', a mythological lion who ruled the region until vanquished. In recognition of the forest's stellar biodiversity, Dutch colonists declared the area a reserve in 1875, and it was further protected by the new Sri Lankan government in 1977 after national outcry over logging activity.

Even though tiny Sinharaja National Park constitutes a mere 0.7% of Sri Lanka's land area, it is home to half of the island's endemic species. Sadly, 98.5% of the island's lowland rainforests have already been logged, with most of the wood turned into cheap

plywood, but half of the remaining 1.5% has been protected in Sinharaja, making this the last great place to see Sri Lanka's native trees and wildlife.

Birdwatchers are probably the park's primary visitors, drawn to the vibrant mix of endemic birds with unusual names. See if you can find a red-faced malkoha or the white-faced starling, or look for the Ceylon hanging-parrot or Ceylon frogmouth. This is also virtually the only place in Sri Lanka you can see the endemic green-billed coucal.

Sri Lanka's lowland forest trees consist mostly of spectacular members of the *dipterocarp* family, with 55 of the island's 56 species found nowhere else in the world. These dense forests, with their towering 45m-high canopies, are crisscrossed by countless clear streams and are home to many interesting animals such as the slender loris, the purple-faced leaf monkey, whistling lizards, wrinkled frogs and torrent toads. It would be a stroke of good fortune to see a leopard, but you can console yourself with seeing the world's largest butterflies.

Go at the very beginning of the rainy season to experience the resurgence of life, but don't wait too long or else prepare for the worst – rainfall can reach 6m a year and the trails will be a bit of a slog. Tourist infrastructure is well established in Sri Lanka, although Sinharaja is still three hours by rough road south of Ratnapura.

MORE INFO www.slwcs.org

SEA OTTERS USA

↘ **LOCATION** Monterey Bay, 140km southeast of San Francisco, California, USA **WHY NOW?** You can enjoy beautiful weather and observe the otter pups **LEVEL OF DIFFICULTY** Low – kick back on a park bench with binoculars and a picnic basket **STATUS** The otters are threatened and the population has recently declined

The dramatic beauty of California's rugged coastline is greatly enhanced by the presence of the smallest, and what must be the cutest, marine mammal of all. Sea otters are a sheer delight to watch, whether they are rolling around in play, banging on a crab with a rock or scrubbing their faces with deft hands. They are all soft fur, adorable faces and goofy personalities, and it's a stroke of good fortune that they're still around because it was thought that they'd been hunted into extinction by the early 1900s. However, a tiny remnant population of 50 was discovered on California's remote Big Sur coast in 1911 and today, with constant monitoring and stringent protection, their population hovers at around 2000.

Sea otters continue to be found in small pockets along the Big Sur coast, but there is no better place for observing them than from the charming village of Pacific Grove, at Monterey Bay. Grab a seat on one of the many shoreline park benches to watch sea otters bob in gently undulating kelp beds. Stay on the lookout for adults surfacing with clams, crabs or sea urchins. They specialise in cracking open these hard-shelled foods by using their stomachs as a table while they pound away at their prey with a rock. Mothers do double-duty by carrying their pup at the same time, and there are few natural sights as heart-warming as a baby sea otter squawking for food. For even closer views, it's worth visiting the otter exhibit at the world-class Monterey Bay Aquarium.

MORE INFO www.monterey.com

(LEFT) ↗
Back from the brink of extinction, sea otters now number around 2000 and gather in small pods along the Big Sur coast in California.

(TOP RIGHT) ↗
The hard-to-find horned guan resides in the El Triunfo Biosphere Reserve alongside tapira, five species of cat and over 400 species of tropical bird..

(BOTTOM RIGHT) ↗
Sulawesi's 12cm-long spectral tarsier can jump up to 1.5m from branch to branch.

HORNED GUANS MEXICO

LOCATION El Triunfo Biosphere Reserve, 250km east of Tuxtla, Chiapas **WHY NOW?** Go in the dry season, especially during March or April, because the trails are impassable in the wet season **LEVEL OF DIFFICULTY** Medium – hiking, camping and jungle scrambling are all required **STATUS** The horned guan is highly endangered and its forest home is under serious threat

Nearly always enveloped in a mantle of fog, the mystical cloud forests of El Triunfo are like a lost world preserved against all odds. Remote and pristine, this biosphere reserve near the Guatemalan border is considered one of the most important natural areas in Mexico, both for its forests and its wildlife. It is here, among cloud-drenched trees densely covered with orchids and bromeliads, that the rare and little-known horned guan makes its last stand. This boldly patterned, turkey-like bird with a red, unicorn-like horn is the reserve's star attraction among a host of other exciting animals ranging from furtive tapirs and five species of cat to over 400 species of tropical bird.

Coming across a horned guan is another story altogether, and numerous birding groups make the long, tiring trek to the El Triunfo base camp, where they camp for days and explore the excellent trail system with local naturalists and park rangers. The reserve is located on the continental divide of the Sierra Madre de Chiapas, and countless generations of farmers and villagers have crossed the mountains here. When not looking for horned guans you may have a chance to experience some of the local customs.

MORE INFO http://parksinperil.org/wherewework/mexico/protectedarea/eltriunfo.html

SPECTRAL TARSIERS INDONESIA

LOCATION Bogani Nani Wartabone National Park, 100km southwest of Manado, Sulawesi **WHY NOW?** The beginning of the rainy season (April to May) is when the babies are born **LEVEL OF DIFFICULTY** Medium – tourism and park infrastructures are limited to nonexistent **STATUS** Both the tarsiers and the national park are highly threatened

Sulawesi's remarkable wildlife story started 40 million years ago when part of Australia began drifting north and collided with Asia. In the process a lot of very different plants and animals got mixed together and then evolved in unexpected directions on an isolated island for millions of years. As a result, Sulawesi has one of the highest rates of endemism of any location in the world, and sadly it also has one of the highest rates of lowland forest loss of any site in the world. Despite national park status and being ranked as the most important conservation site in Sulawesi, Bogani Nani Wartabone is little more than a park on paper; it is threatened by uncontrolled logging, poaching and gold mining.

Imperilled with eventual extinction are truly bizarre creatures such as the babirusa ('pig-deer') with two spiral tusks, and a goat-sized buffalo called the anoa. Also at risk is the world's smallest primate, the spectral tarsier, an adorable nocturnal gnome with massive eyes. This tiny mite has a body that's only 12cm long but it makes prodigious 1.5m leaps from branch to branch. Because it can't move its huge eyes in their sockets, the tarsier swivels its head 180 degrees back and forth to look around.

MORE INFO www.north-sulawesi.com

DID YOU KNOW?

 Sea otters lack blubber so they stay warm with a coat of super-dense silky hairs, with about 61,500 hairs per sq cm.

 A female spectral tarsier carries its infant in its mouth while leaping through the forest.

↗ APRIL
WEEK.02

WHAT YOU'LL SEE

JAGUARS

MANATEES

CROCODILES

BARRIER REEFS

PRISTINE RAINFOREST

BELIZE

WHY NOW? The end of the dry season enables easy access to many sites

Belize is a diminutive and easily overlooked wildlife gem tucked into the upper northeast corner of Central America under the protective hook of Yucatan's arm. In this location it's almost lost between its larger and more famous neighbours Mexico and Guatemala, but Belize more than makes up the difference by being an entirely accessible and friendly country easily explored on a reasonably short trip.

The first-time visitor can be excused for thinking it would be a toss-up whether to journey to Belize for its splendid rainforest preserves (nearly 50% of the country's area receives some sort of protection) or for its barrier reefs – the second longest in the world after Australia's Great Barrier Reef – but you'll soon learn you don't have to make these kinds of decisions in a country this small.

And why not dream big? Maybe you'll cross paths with a jaguar. Belize is home to so many that it has the world's only preserve solely devoted to their protection, the Cockscomb Basin Wildlife Sanctuary. You're not likely to see a jaguar in such a vast protected area but don't give up hope; check out the roads in the Río Bravo Conservation and Management Area, or at the luxurious Chan Chich Lodge, where they have an astonishing 60 to 70 jaguar sightings a year.

Meanwhile, you can't help but notice Belize's dramatic mix of migratory and resident birds. The many different species, from jacamars and manakins, to ornate hawk-eagles and jabiru storks, fill your days with vibrant sounds and colours. It's easy to see why this is such a popular destination for birdwatching tours.

Water enthusiasts also find a lot to love in this delightful tropical paradise, with everything from coastal waterways awash with crocodiles, birds and monkeys to world-famous offshore reefs and cays that are home to manatees, sea turtles and a fabulous assortment of marine fish. It's a short flight or boat trip out to one of several laid-back island towns, where you can easily arrange an endless succession of dive trips or visits to hundreds of uninhabited islands. No matter what you do, you'll soon get the hang of the country's unofficial motto, 'Go slow, mon!'

MORE INFO www.destinationsbelize.com

CHIMPANZEES UGANDA

LOCATION Kibale Forest National Park, 320km west of Kampala **WHY NOW?** The wet season means fewer tourists and premier wildlife-viewing **LEVEL OF DIFFICULTY** Low – a strong infrastructure and community support make your visit easy **STATUS** The chimpanzee population is stable and watched over by local communities who benefit from the tourism

Kibale is both a patch of highly diverse, unspoiled rainforest and the site of a successful ecotourism project involving local communities and hiring about 90 people. Without doubt the park's main attraction is its numerous primates – 13 species in all, including a large population of chimpanzees – but birdlife is also prolific and a birdwatching trail has been developed at Bigodi Wetland. Because the park lies at the intersection of several vegetation zones, some 250 tree species occur here, most festooned with dense mats of moss and orchids, while fruiting figs attract birds, chimps, monkeys and other primates.

Chimp-watching is a delightful experience and an estimated 600 chimpanzees divided up into several groups live in Kibale. The population at Kanyanchu has been habituated to visitors and Primate Walks (basically an exercise in tracking chimps) are led daily by local naturalists, while organised Night Walks from Kanyanchu search out nocturnal primates such as galagos. Although chimps can be silent and difficult to locate, they are by far the noisiest African primates. From the time they leave their nests in the early morning – which they announce by drumming on tree trunks – until settling down at night, the forest echoes with their hoots and screams. Tracking these 'drama queens' is largely a matter of following their sounds, but your first sighting may be nothing more than a tantalising glimpse of a backside retreating into the foliage. It is a rare privilege if your tracking rewards you with prolonged views, and it's likely to be worth every minute of your effort. **MORE INFO**www.uwa.or.ug/kibale.html

[LEFT] ↗
Chimpanzees are the noisiest African primates, from drumming on tree trunks to hooting and screaming through the forest.

[TOP RIGHT] ↗
With a 3m wingspan, condors can travel more than 200km a day.

[BOTTOM RIGHT] ↗
The threatened red squirrel has a sizable population in Scotland's Abernethy Forest Reserve.

ANDEAN CONDORS PERU

 LOCATION Machu Picchu, 80km northwest of Cusco **WHY NOW?** You should visit in April for good weather and to avoid tourist season **LEVEL OF DIFFICULTY** Low – it's Peru's most visited site **STATUS** The condors are threatened by habitat loss and secondary poisoning

Although the most dependable place in the world to see Andean condors is at La Cruz del Condor in Colca Canyon (160km northwest of Arequipa), it pales in comparison with the experience of seeing one of these ponderous birds soaring around the ancient Inca city of Machu Picchu. Here among towering cliffs and picturesque ruins, the sight of a condor wheeling in majestic circles on its 310cm wingspan will take your breath away, but count yourself lucky if you see one. These specialists of the High Andes were once widespread from Colombia to Tierra del Fuego, but today occur in low numbers and with a fragmented population, despite being the most symbolically important bird in South America.

By April, parents may be observed making regular forays in search of food for their one or two newly hatched chicks that wait patiently at nests on remote sheer cliffs. Most of the year, condors inhabit large territories and travel more than 200km a day, but it's likely that they'll stay closer to their nests during the breeding season. Condors spend their time soaring over paramo grasslands and rocky mountain areas, and they are often observed along the popular Inca Trail above Machu Picchu. They eat dead animals and can die from eating poisoned carcasses or lead bullets.
MORE INFO www.incatrail-peru.com

RED SQUIRRELS SCOTLAND

 LOCATION Abernethy Forest, 1km southwest of Nethy Bridge **WHY NOW?** It's springtime and the chance of seeing baby squirrels makes this an ideal time to visit **LEVEL OF DIFFICULTY** Low – just a walk in the woods, so to speak **STATUS** The population is markedly declining

If the sheer number of devoted websites and working groups is any measure, the red squirrel would rank as one of Great Britain's most beloved creatures. These pointy-eared squirrels are charismatic and energetic, but their population is suffering from a bourgeoning influx of eastern grey squirrels from North America. The latest count was red squirrels, 140,000 and dropping; grey squirrels 2.5 million and growing – an imbalance that apparently brings out the best in Britain's animal lovers.

Red squirrels were one of the original denizens of the great pine woods extensively felled more than 1000 years ago. By the 1800s, red squirrels were absent over significant portions of their former range, and the introduction of the dominant grey squirrel was simply the last straw.

About 85% of Great Britain's current red squirrel population survives in small fragmented habitats across Scotland, with a sizable number surviving in the extensive Scots pine woods at the Abernethy Forest Reserve. Here you can watch these delightful squirrels as they scamper and scold and chase and introduce their babies to the world. If you miss them in person you can watch them on a webcam (www.rspb.org.uk/webcams/feeders). Check with the Forestry Commission of Great Britain for other viewing locations.
MORE INFO www.forestry.gov.uk/forestry/Redsquirrel

DID YOU KNOW?

One of the 'charms' of the Andean condors is that it defecates liquid waste onto its legs so that it will evaporate and help cool it down.

Red squirrels have long claws and double-jointed ankles that are highly adapted to their arboreal lifestyle.

↗ APRIL
WEEK.03

WHAT YOU'LL SEE

EUROPEAN BISON
LYNXES
RACCOON-DOGS
MOOSE
EURASIAN OTTERS

BIALOWIEZA NATIONAL PARK
POLAND

↘ **WHY NOW?** Go before the summer rains and mosquitoes take over in mid-May

The vast and ancient Bialowieza Forest, straddling the border of Poland and Belarus, is often overlooked even though it is the European equivalent of Africa's Serengeti or North America's Yellowstone. The primary difference at Bialowieza is that you'll have to bushwhack through a lot of big, and in some cases really big, trees in order to see your wildlife.

But what a place! This is Europe at its primeval best, a snapshot of a time when howling wolves and mythological creatures roamed dark and gloomy forests surrounding tiny isolated villages. Nearly all of this original wilderness and its inhabitants have been lost, but here among the giant pines, firs, oaks and birches of Bialowieza Forest, it is still possible to find healthy populations of moose, grey wolves,

elk, lynxes, beavers, otters and over 200 species of bird.

This forest was originally the favourite hunting grounds for Polish and Russian royalty, providing a level of protection that also made it the last stronghold for the 1000kg European bison, a mighty animal that once roamed from the Atlantic coast to the South and East China Seas. Even though killing a bison if you weren't a member of the royal family was punishable by death, the bison was eliminated in the wild by 1927. It's a major conservation triumph that 12 carefully managed individuals from zoos and private collections were eventually bred into a current population of 3000 bison.

Today most people visit Bialowieza Forest to find the park's iconic bison in their native habitat, without even realising how many other animals they're likely to see. Core wildlife-rich areas of the park are completely wild and can only be accessed with permits and guides, but around these core areas there are hundreds of kilometres of surrounding forest available for unlimited hiking and riding. Snows melt off by mid-March and mosquitoes arrive in furious numbers in mid-May so make sure you arrive in that magic window of time when the forest is a true pleasure to explore.

The Polish section (Puszcza Bialowieska) and the Belarus section (Belovezhskaya Pushcha) are each easily accessed from their respective capitals. Head to the Polish town of Bialowieza or the Belarusian town of Brest to find visitor facilities and detailed information.
MORE INFO http://whc.unesco.org

SUPERB LYREBIRDS AUSTRALIA

↘ **LOCATION** Royal National Park, 30km south of Sydney **WHY NOW?** You can see the 'superb' courtship display **LEVEL OF DIFFICULTY** Low – it's easy to observe lyrebirds on a morning drive **STATUS** The lyrebird is common

Sweeping south from the tidal mudflats of Port Hacking, the second oldest park in the world has beaches, heathlands, pockets of rainforest and 300m-high coastal cliffs, not to mention a surprising abundance of wildlife given that Australia's largest city sits on the north side of the park. Lady Carrington Drive is one of the best places in New South Wales to see the superb lyrebird. These normally wary birds often cross the track and forage in the open here, and you could see up to a dozen on a morning visit. During winter they sometimes display close to the track, affording good views if they are approached quietly.

Male lyrebirds may be drably coloured but they perform stunning courtship displays and vocalisations that are remarkable to witness. The male conducts his songs of love from atop a mound of leaf litter that he scratches together. In display, the male's long tail, which usually trails behind, is thrown over his head so that the broad, curved outer feathers form the arms of a 'lyre' around a fan of quivering white filamentous feathers. Simultaneously, he mimics the sounds of other common birds and mixes them with his own rich buzzing and clicking calls into a symphony that lasts up to 20 minutes. During the peak courting season, the forested valleys of the park may ring with the calls of multiple birds at once.

Afterwards, stop at the Audley picnic area on your way back to Sydney to see other birds of these moist forests; look for Lewin's honeyeaters, satin bowerbirds, green catbirds and azure kingfishers to top off the morning.

MORE INFO www.environment.nsw.gov.au/nationalparks

[LEFT] ↗
The superb lyrebird incorporates the calls of other common birds into its courtship song through mimicry.

[TOP RIGHT] ↗
Giant pandas lead solitary lives, staying in one place as they gorge on up to 50kg of bamboo a day.

[BOTTOM RIGHT] ↗
Instead of webbed feet, the coqui has small sticky pads on the ends of its toes, allowing it to climb trees easily.

GIANT PANDAS CHINA

LOCATION Wolong Nature Reserve, 140km northwest of Chengdu, Sichuan **WHY NOW?** It's your best chance of hearing the love songs of mating pandas **LEVEL OF DIFFICULTY** Medium – this trip requires research and planning to figure out how to explore the huge reserve **STATUS** The panda is highly endangered but intensively protected and managed

Everyone knows the iconic giant panda, perhaps one of the world's most famous endangered animals, but how many people have ever seen a panda in the wild? According to a 2006 study, there may now be 3000 free-roaming pandas in the mountains of central China, a significant improvement after decades of intensive and expensive conservation efforts by the Chinese government and international organisations.

About 100 pandas live in the rugged mountain forests of the 2000 sq km Wolong Nature Reserve, the best known of China's 50 panda reserves. Unfortunately for naturalists, pandas are thinly dispersed and lead solitary lives amid dense bamboo thickets, so it takes a supreme effort or stroke of good fortune to spot one under these conditions. Because pandas eat up to half their 100kg weight in bamboo each day, they seldom leave their feeding places. April, however, is the season when females are reproductively fertile for a couple of days and dim-sighted males must seek them out by scent and by making soft calls. Even if you don't cross paths with a panda, this is a fantastic time to visit because entire hillsides of rhododendrons are likely to be in full bloom. Arrange tours and accommodation from Chengdu.
MORE INFO www.chinagiantpanda.com/site/wolong.htm

DID YOU KNOW?

 Newborn pandas are small relative to their mother's weight, the equivalent of a human baby having a mother who weighs 2700kg.

 Coqui populations grow till they eat all the insects in an area and start cannibalising, which reduces the population and restarts the cycle.

COQUIS PUERTO RICO

LOCATION Luquillo Biosphere Reserve, 50km southeast of San Juan **WHY NOW?** The beginning of the rainy season is a beautiful time to visit **LEVEL OF DIFFICULTY** Low – paved trails make for easy walking **STATUS** The coqui is abundant

It is said that the heart and soul of Puerto Rico lies in the tiny *coquí*. Never more than 80mm long, this diminutive tree frog lives in every nook and cranny of the island, and at night its characteristic *ko-kee* songs can be heard and felt everywhere, as if the land itself was singing. It is estimated that there are 20,000 coquis per hectare at Luquillo (formerly known as El Yunque or Caribbean National Forest), but densities of up to 20 per sq metre have been reported elsewhere and their songs can be deafening at full volume (up to 100 decibels).

These tree frogs don't have webbed feet but use small sticky disks at the end of each toe to climb. Most of their lives are spent in trees, even to the extent that females lay their eggs on leaves or in abandoned bird nests. Males guard the eggs and keep them moist until they hatch into little froglets.

The Luquillo Biosphere Reserve is small but extremely diverse. The area was first set aside by the Spanish Crown in 1876 in order to protect an ancient forest unchanged since Christopher Columbus visited the island 500 years previously. Wander the 60km of paved trails among 1000-year-old trees draped with deep mats of ferns, epiphytes and orchids.
MORE INFO www.fs.fed.us/r8/caribbean

↗ **APRIL**

WEEK.04

HIGH ISLAND USA

WHAT YOU'LL SEE

WOOD WARBLERS
SCARLET TANAGERS
ROSE-BREASTED GROSBEAKS
SHOREBIRDS
ROSEATE SPOONBILLS

WHY NOW? It's your best chance of seeing a legendary fallout event

Wander into the woods on High Island on a spring afternoon and you'll feel like you've stepped into a candy store of birds. This little patch of trees on the otherwise flat and barren Texas Gulf Coast attracts more than its fair share of birds; in fact, High Island easily rates as one of the top 10 birding sites in North America. But what makes High Island so fascinating is not that it's a great birding location, but that it's the site of one of North America's most amazing bird phenomena. Come in the summer and you'll be distinctly underwhelmed, but arrive during spring fallout and you'll have one of the top birding experiences of your life.

Each spring, uncounted millions of songbirds pile up on the northern tip of the Yucatan Peninsula waiting for ideal conditions for their 960km journey across the Gulf of Mexico to North America. When conditions are just right they depart after dusk and arrive on the Gulf Coast around midday, with some stopping at High Island but most continuing onward.

However, one or two times each spring, strong cold fronts form over Texas and move south into the gulf by late morning, creating a headwind that exhausts migrating birds. A day like this is called a 'fallout' and it can linger in birdwatching legends for decades because the birds literally fall from the sky in vast numbers. It's not uncommon to see 30 colourful species of warbler, not to mention countless tanagers, grosbeaks, thrushes and other birds, sometimes all in the same small patch of trees. You might see as many birds in a single view as you'd encounter over thousands of square kilometres of prime breeding habitat, and the birds are so exhausted that they pay no attention to watching humans.

Most visitors come to High Island, about 100km east of Houston, planning to stay a week or more because fallouts are unpredictable. Fortunately, it's easy to fill your days with other natural attractions while waiting for the migration to pick up. This is also a fantastic time to birdwatch at the nearby Anahuac National Wildlife Refuge because the adjacent rice fields are flooded in April and birds swarm all over them.
MORE INFO www.houstonaudubon.org

PACIFIC HERRING SPAWN USA

LOCATION Sitka Sound, 150km southwest of Juneau, Alaska, USA **WHY NOW?** It's the peak of the spawning season **LEVEL OF DIFFICULTY** Low – watch the spawning from the city streets or ride out in a boat **STATUS** They occur in unbelievable numbers but it's likely they are overfished

When herring spawn by the millions the ocean turns milk-white with sperm and eggs, the silvery bodies of adults boil the water with movement and there is sheer pandemonium among predators. This exciting, and overlooked, wildlife event happens every spring along the West Coast of North America. Sure you can catch it in San Francisco Bay in December or January, but why not see it in Alaska in April instead, with hundreds of humpback whales, sea lions, bald eagles and thousands of gulls joining the party?

The 30cm-long Pacific herring is a phenomenally productive species whose vast numbers once supported entire food chains of predators. To avoid these predators, the herrings first congregate in tremendous schools in deep, offshore channels then rush up into the intertidal zone and spawn all together in a boiling mass of bodies. Over the course of a few hours, billions of herrings lay an entire year's worth of eggs, leaving behind up to six million eggs per sq metre. And for those same few hours, whales and sea lions scoop up mouthfuls of fish as fast as they can, while eagles snatch herring from the surf and gulls pluck eggs off rocks.

Natives and old-timers tell of herring spawns that stretched 160km along the shores of Alaska's Sitka Sound, but biologists recorded only 60km of spawning in 2007 and many people are arguing that the herring are being fished out by boats that can catch 500 tonnes in a single net run. Herring fisheries have already collapsed at several sites but tourism dollars may be a sustainable alternative to fishing.
MORE INFO www.sitka.com

[LEFT] ↗
A herring spawn results in up to six million eggs per sq metre.

[TOP RIGHT] ↗
One gluttonous meal allows a gila monster to survive for 12 months, which is necessary as they sleep in burrows for up to 95% of the year.

[BOTTOM RIGHT] ↗
Bird Island, in the Seychelles, becomes home to 1.5 million sooty terns during the nesting season.

GILA MONSTERS USA

LOCATION Organ Pipe Cactus National Monument, 20km south of Ajo, Arizona, USA **WHY NOW?** It's the beginning of the active courtship season **LEVEL OF DIFFICULTY** Medium – finding one may require some extended desert exploration **STATUS** They are little-known but the population is declining outside of protected areas

You don't have much reason to fear a gila monster unless you plan to stick your hand in its mouth and dare it to bite down on you. Still, running across one of these boldly patterned venomous lizards will make you jump back in your tracks because it's a pretty sinister looking creature and it'll probably hiss fiercely at you. About as thick as your forearm, heavily beaded, with stumpy legs and a sausage-like tail, the gila monster doesn't look like any other lizard you've ever seen and scientists say they're more closely related to snakes than to lizards.

Gila monsters spend over 95% of their year sleeping in burrows, but in the spring males awaken and wander widely in search of females and food. If two males run into each other they may engage in extremely physical wrestling matches that last for hours or even an entire day. Food comes in the form of baby rabbits, squirrels or birds, with a gila monster eating 50% of its body weight in a single meal and laying down enough fat from one gluttonous feast to survive for an entire year of sleep. Their active season begins in April and often peaks in May, when their own babies emerge from the soil.
MORE INFO www.nps.gov/orpi

DID YOU KNOW?

 The herring's silvery colour is created by guanine crystals embedded in their scales, creating a camouflaging illusion of light.

 Gila monster venom causes excruciating pain but also contains a peptide that shows great promise for treating type-2 diabetes.

SOOTY TERNS SEYCHELLES

LOCATION Bird Island, 100km north of Victoria **WHY NOW?** Tern numbers here grow almost daily in preparation for nesting **LEVEL OF DIFFICULTY** Low – it would be impossible to miss this many terns **STATUS** The population is stable and seemingly well protected

By the end of April, sooty terns are beginning to gather by the hundreds of thousands on a tiny speck of land on the northern fringe of the Seychelles Archipelago called Bird Island. Within weeks, about 1.5 million sooty terns will arrive for the nesting season. Until they settle down and begin nesting, this immense colony of birds spends the day feeding, but each evening they return en masse to the colony like a giant cloud of bats in the sunset – an incredible sight.

These ground-nesting terns make a lot of raucous noise during their brief nesting season, flying back and forth continuously while adults take turns incubating their eggs in June and feeding their chicks in July. The owners of this private island and their small ecotourism lodge have worked hard to return the island to its native condition and rebuild the tern colony from a low of 18,000 pairs in the 1960s. Because of the limited area sooty terns nest in, this gathering of 1.5 million terns now forms one of the densest bird populations in the world. Scientists and visitors come today to study all 20 species of bird on the island, including dainty white fairy terns, tropicbirds and frigatebirds.
MORE INFO www.birdislandseychelles.com

↗ **MAY**
WEEK.01

WHAT YOU'LL SEE

TAKINS
BHARALS
SNOW LEOPARDS
SATYR TRAGOPANS
BLOOD PHEASANTS

BHUTAN

WHY NOW? There's great weather and absolutely stunning displays of flowers. If you travel to Bhutan for its exceptionally pristine habitats and wildlife populations, expect to also come away deeply affected by this tiny nation's remarkable people and culture. Ruled in accordance with Buddhist values, the people of Bhutan practise a kind of voluntary simplicity and respect for life that leaves you wishing all countries could be like this. Television was unknown in Bhutan until 1999, and the country strictly limits the number of foreign visitors (21,000 in 2007) to preserve the character of its culture.

Bhutan has also banned hunting and logging, and vowed to maintain at least 60% of its land under forest cover for all time, in accordance with the belief that a healthy environment is essential for both material and spiritual happiness. The lucky few who travel to Bhutan come back with stories of unspoiled landscapes as far as you can see, and of otherwise rare animals that in Bhutan verge on common and tame. For instance,

the three-week Tashitang trek into the high mountains
of northwestern Bhutan is probably the best place
on earth to see a snow leopard, as well as a bharal,
Himalayan tahr, red panda and the bizarre takin (likened
to an oxen with a goat's head). From March to May, the
country's 50 species of rhododendron are in full bloom
and birds will be singing almost everywhere you travel.

Encompassing a full range of habitats, from the
Indian plain to 7000m peaks, Bhutan is home to an
incredible cross-section of eastern Himalayan wildlife,
a fact that is abundantly revealed on the Limithang
Road where, starting from the small town of Jakar,
you descend 3000m in 100km, with pristine habitats
at every turn in the road. In the lowlands, visit the vast
and remote Royal Manas National Park (adjacent to

India's Manas National Park) in search of elephants,
rhinoceros, leopards, tigers and pygmy hogs.

All visitors must come either on an organised
tour or be guests of the government, and you can
expect to pay a hefty daily tariff for the honour of
visiting Bhutan. You are generally not allowed to travel
freely on your own but the fee you pay covers your
accommmodation, meals, guides and transport while
you're in the country.
MORE INFO www.kingdomofbhutan.com

RED-SIDED GARTER SNAKES CANADA

 LOCATION Narcisse Snake Dens, 130km north of Winnipeg, Manitoba **WHY NOW?** It's the largest concentration of snakes in the world **LEVEL OF DIFFICULTY** Low – the dens are well marked and easily visited **STATUS** It's the most widespread and common snake in North America

If snakes make you nervous, you will want to approach the Narcisse Snake Dens with caution because the ground will be covered with hundreds, perhaps thousands, and maybe even more, snakes. Awakened from hibernation by the warming air, males emerge all together from deep cracks in the bedrock, where they have been sleeping in wriggling masses safely hidden from Canada's frosty winter fingers. Once peak numbers are on the surface in early May, females emerge one by one over the course of several weeks, triggering frantic 'mating balls' where 100 males at a time furiously weave around any receptive female they find.

Relatively unknown a few decades ago, this incredible phenomenon is now a popular event in Manitoba, where there are about 70 hibernacula (hibernation dens), some with more than 10,000 snakes. Scientists have begun to study this phenomenon as well, and one of the strangest things they've discovered is that some males ('she-males') also release female mating pheromones and get swarmed by eager males. Because 'she-males' remain interested in mating with females, they sometimes get confused and chase, and try to mate with, their own tails to the point of exhaustion.

The red-sided garter snake ranges further north than any other North American snake but they can only survive at northern latitudes by hibernating for six to seven months of the year. The short summer season requires that they get a fast start on the breeding season by coordinating their mating behaviour. Later in the summer, when females have fattened up and are in peak health, they give birth to a litter of 10 to 40 finger-length little snakelets.
MORE INFO www.gov.mb.ca/conservation/wildlife/managing/snakes.html

[LEFT] ↗
During the mating season, writhing masses of red-sided garter snakes weave around any receptive female.

[TOP RIGHT] ↗
Giraffes have 45cm-long tongues, giving them access to food that few other herbivores can reach.

[BOTTOM RIGHT] ↗
Over half of Fiji's native birds, including the orange fruit dove (pictured) and the silktail, live on the island of Taveuni.

GIRAFFES ZAMBIA

LOCATION South Luangwa National Park, 700km northeast of Lusaka **WHY NOW?** The giraffes are concentrated here at the end of the wet season **LEVEL OF DIFFICULTY** Medium – they are best seen on walking safaris, which require some planning **STATUS** The population is low in numbers but fairly well protected

Spanning an area 700km long and 100km wide, the Luangwa Valley is part of the Great Rift Valley and is an isolated haven for a unique race of giraffe called Thornicroft's giraffe. Here the Luangwa River carves a tortuous and ever-changing course south to the Zambezi River through a mosaic of mopane, miombo woodlands and grasslands that flood during the wet season (November to April). When the park floods, the sandy soils around Mfuwe remain above water, which is a bonus for both the park's visitors and for the park's 700 giraffes who gather here while waiting for other areas to dry out.

Thornicroft's giraffes are recognised by their dark brown neck spots and the lack of blotches below the knees, but they share with all giraffes the long necks and 45cm-long tongues that give them access to foods few other herbivores can reach. Look for mothers with calves, a fairly rare sight because up to 75% of the calves are killed by predators in their first year. Also watch for males engaged in 'necking' battles that involve pushing and swinging their heads at each other; it may look languid but necks and jaws can be broken. May is also the month when the rarely visited North Luangwa National Park becomes accessible.

MORE INFO www.zambiatourism.com/travel/nationalparks/sluangwa.htm

DID YOU KNOW?

Bhutan's economy operates on guidelines designed to maintain a high 'Gross National Happiness', Bhutan's alternative to GDP.

A giraffe's size means it needs to dissipate prodigious amounts of heat; its markings help channel heat out through the skin.

ORANGE FRUIT DOVES FIJI

LOCATION Taveuni, 250km northeast of Nadi **WHY NOW?** It's the beginning of the dry season **LEVEL OF DIFFICULTY** Low – there may be no more idyllic spot in the world to watch birds **STATUS** The population is stable and well protected

If travelling in comfort among superbly friendly people on a tropical island is your ideal adventure, then here's a great excuse for a trip to Fiji – tell everyone back at the office you'll be out of touch for a while because you have to go and see some orange fruit doves. You'll surely want to see this electric orange bird, but who's going to fault you if you sneak in some snorkelling on Fiji's fabulous coral reefs or kick back with your new friends and some rounds of fermented *yaqona*.

Of Fiji's 300-plus islands, none offers the wildlife enthusiast such riches as Taveuni, 'the Garden Island of Fiji', where 60% of the original forests remain intact and much of the island is protected by the internationally recognised Bouma National Heritage Park. Over half of Fiji's endemic birds occur in this slice of paradise, from orange fruit doves to the even more surreal many-coloured fruit doves or enigmatic silktails (a bird that has no certain affinities to other birds).

If you can pull yourself away from the enchantingly clear waters and palm-lined beaches, arrange a journey into the cool, misty montane rainforests on Des Voeux Peak, a lofty realm of giant tree ferns and the highest diversity of birds found anywhere on the islands.

MORE INFO www.fiji-island.com

WHAT YOU'LL SEE

- GALÁPAGOS SEA LIONS
- GALÁPAGOS PENGUINS
- BLUE-FOOTED BOOBIES
- GIANT TORTOISES
- MARINE IGUANAS

GALÁPAGOS ISLANDS
ECUADOR

↘ **WHY NOW?** The water is at its warmest and clearest

Where does one start in the Galápagos? This may be the most famous wildlife-watching destination in the world, and there are so many options. Fifteen islands are open to visitors and you can put together countless combinations of stops and routes to explore this cradle of evolution. There is no wrong time to visit the Galápagos, but prices are low and crowds greatly diminished in May, which is coincidentally one of the very best times to see these equatorial islands. The transition period between the rainy days of April and the dry days of June is renowned for its dramatic skies, calm seas and clear waters that make for superb snorkelling conditions.

Seabirds reach their peak nesting activity in June, but May is a good time to see courtship and territorial behaviour. Check out the world's entire population of 12,000 waved albatross or observe elegantly attired red-billed tropicbirds on Española Island.

Hike to the rim of the volcano on Genovesa, the youngest island in the archipelago, and wander among 140,000 pairs of nesting red-footed boobies. Even better, witness the comical courtship of the blue-footed boobies on Isabela as they alternately lift their stunning blue feet and waggle them in the air at each other.

Isabela is also a great place to watch marine iguanas, and to see the world's only tropical penguins and groups of golden rays. There are sea lions at Isabela but San Cristóbal and Santa Fé are considered the top islands for snorkelling, with calm water and playful sea lions. You'll be utterly charmed by the curious and fearless manner of Galápagos' animals.

The only way to see the islands is on an extended boat tour that makes different stops each day or lingers for a few days at individual islands. Many boats depart from Puerto Ayora on Santa Cruz, the tourist hub of the islands, where a visit to the Charles Darwin Research Station is an ideal introduction to the Galápagos. Discover how scientists think so many plants and animals made it to islands that are 1000km off the coast of South America, or check ahead to learn about opportunities to volunteer with wildlife surveys, habitat restoration work and other projects in the Galápagos. **MORE INFO** www.darwinfoundation.org/en

EURASIAN OTTERS ENGLAND

LOCATION North Devon, 250km west of London **WHY NOW?** In some areas this is a good time to look for cubs **LEVEL OF DIFFICULTY** Medium – access and viewing are easy but the low numbers mean that it may take some effort to find them **STATUS** They are clawing back very slowly after local extinctions

After Henry Williamson published his classic novel *Tarka the Otter* in 1927, the delightful and charismatic otter gained superstar status as England's favourite animal. Sadly, decades of pesticide poisoning almost completely extirpated otters from Great Britain between 1950 and 1990, and their populations are only now very slowly recovering. It takes a lot of effort, or a healthy dose of luck, but once again there is a reasonably good chance of finding them in northwest Scotland, Cumbria, Devon and Cornwall. They actually verge on common along the south coast of Shetland, but there's something special about looking for them on the same, little-changed byways of North Devon where Williamson chronicled Tarka's adventures.

Otters rarely stray far from unpolluted waters and they are equally at home on rivers, lakes and coastlines, although those living in salt water need frequent dips in freshwater to wash the salt off. At all times, otters are irrepressible bundles of energy and goofy antics. They swim or bound along the ground with the same vigour, stopping often to look around, and occasionally chattering with excitement. In the water they swim with a rolling motion that easily turns into playful somersaults, especially when there are several otters together, as when mothers and youngsters set out on foraging expeditions.

While in North Devon, pay homage to Williamson's legacy and visit the simple hut he lived in (www .henrywilliamson.co.uk), or venture out in search of otters on the 48km Tarka Trail through pastoral countryside that has remained largely unspoiled for 80 years.
MORE INFO www.devon.gov.uk/tarkatrail

(LEFT) ↗
Otters that live in saltwater need to dip into freshwater frequently to get rid of the salt on their coats.

(TOP RIGHT) ↗
Oilbirds are similar to bats in that they use echolocation in addition to eyesight and smell for navigation.

(BOTTOM RIGHT) ↗
The 'Great American Desert' was once home to 30 million bison.

OILBIRDS VENEZUELA

LOCATION Cueva de los Guacharos National Park, 12km west of Caripe **WHY NOW?** You'll be blown away by hordes of screaming nocturnal birds **LEVEL OF DIFFICULTY** Low – join a guided walk to the cave entrance **STATUS** They're little known but are not a current conservation concern

Chalk this one up to the list of 'world's strangest birds', because here you are staring into the mouth of a cave that sounds like a portal into the underworld. From deep within there rises a cacophony of clicks, squawks and shrieks that builds inexorably into a deafening roar of loud screaming and snarling calls, then suddenly thousands of birds with 1m wingspans erupt like a river of dark demons passing in the dusk. You have just witnessed the nightly exodus of *guacharos* ('those who wail/lament'), the world's only nocturnal, fruit-eating birds. By day, the 15,000 oilbirds sleep and nest on high ledges down in their namesake cave, and at sunset they fly into the night to eat and engage in behaviours that remain unknown to scientists.

Even stranger, oilbirds echolocate by emitting clicks in the manner of bats. In conjunction with their excellent eyesight and keen sense of smell, these audible sounds allow them to navigate through the rainforest at night. Although they migrate seasonally to follow fruiting crops, they predictably occur at Cueva de Los Guacharos in peak numbers from April to June because this is their nesting season. Chicks take four months to grow and become so fat that they can be rendered for their excellent oil.
MORE INFO www.caucanet.net.co/nf/nf/guacharos/pnnguacharos.htm

AMERICAN BISON USA

LOCATION Tallgrass Prairie Preserve, 70km northwest of Tulsa, Oklahoma, USA **WHY NOW?** You'll see the prairie in its full splendour **LEVEL OF DIFFICULTY** Low – access is via a nature trail and scenic vehicle loop **STATUS** They're in low numbers but are well managed

You may come to the Tallgrass Prairie Preserve to see its 2500 bison and not even realise that these 1000kg giants are merely the most prominent animals in a fabulously rich web of life that once stretched across 14 states. Don't worry, you're not alone; the first European explorers who tried to cross the Great Plains called this the 'Great American Desert'. Yet this so-called desert was home to 30 million bison and staggering numbers of pronghorn antelope, elk, bears, wolves and wildcats. Native tallgrass prairie, named for its undulating sea of grasses that tower 2m to 3m tall, now exists in scattered fragments, with the largest fully functioning example of this ecosystem found here in Oklahoma.

What is most surprising as you drive around in May looking for newborn bison calves is how vibrant the prairie feels. Everywhere there are profusions of wildflowers, birdsong and the steady hum of insects. You may hear the booming courtship calls of greater prairie chickens in the distance, or encounter bobcats, coyotes, armadillos and badgers. Free-roaming bison herds wander widely over the 160 sq km preserve so count yourself lucky if you run across any; if you do find them you'll be seeing this great American icon in its native habitat, which is an even rarer event.
MORE INFO www.nature.org/wherewework/northamerica/states/oklahoma

DID YOU KNOW?

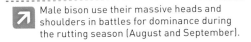

Scientists don't know how oilbirds produce the clicks they use to echolocate at night – with their bills, their tongues or their syrinx.

Male bison use their massive heads and shoulders in battles for dominance during the rutting season (August and September).

WHAT YOU'LL SEE

KORGALZHYN STATE NATURE RESERVE KAZAKHSTAN

WHY NOW? See the steppe when it's a carpet of iridescent flowers and singing birds

While much of the vast Central Asian steppe has been converted into farms, there remains an area of staggering and pristine beauty in northern Kazakhstan, protected in the 2589 sq km Korgalzhyn State Nature Preserve. Scarcely known, even within Kazakhstan, this astounding preserve is dominated by immense lakes, wetlands and gorgeous grasslands of delicate feather grass. And when you're not exploring this paradise, you'll find that the local people are warm and inviting, and you are likely to be welcomed to a feast of traditional *beshparmak* washed down with *kumys*, the 'Kazakh champagne' made from fermented mare's milk.

Located at the crossroads of two major migration routes, Korgalzhyn is one of the most important bird areas in Asia. Over 15 million birds stop here to feed, with five

species showing up in the hundreds of thousands and 19 species numbering in the tens of thousands. Nowhere else in the world can you see black-throated divers and greater flamingos breeding in the same place, along with over 300 other species.

In May the steppes are utterly transformed by tulips and wildflowers as far as you can see. Wander in search of wolves, marmots, gyrfalcons and demoiselle cranes. This is a great area to explore on foot, bike or horseback.

Keep your eyes open for the critically endangered saiga antelope, one of the strangest mammals you'll ever see, and restricted to only a couple of remote sites in the world. While physically they look like antelope, they have a peculiar trunk-like nose that is halfway between cute and scary in appearance. Unfortunately,

saiga have been hunted to near extinction with stunning speed, going from a population of more than one million in the late 1980s to around 35,000 today, after conservation groups suggested that their horns might be a suitable replacement for rhino horns.

This area is seldom visited by tourists and you're likely to have the entire place to yourself. The preserve is 160km northwest of Astana, where the official headquarters and museum are located; stop here for a permit and to give advance notice that you'll be visiting the site. Travel to the preserve is easily done on local buses, while homestays in local guesthouses are readily arranged.

MORE INFO www.kazakhstan.orexca.com/korgalzhyn _reserve_kazakhstan.shtml

KOMODO DRAGONS INDONESIA

↘ **LOCATION** Komodo National Park, 450km east of Bali **WHY NOW?** You can see giant lizards fighting and mating, and encounter newly hatched babies **LEVEL OF DIFFICULTY** Low – access is off the beaten path, but is not a problem **STATUS** There are about 3000 in the world, but only 350 breeding females remain

It's hard to deny the allure of a prehistoric lizard that weighs upwards of 166kg and has the power to take down and kill a full-grown water buffalo. Not surprisingly, the Komodo dragon looms large in the imagination of local people, who revere it as a mythical ancestor. Reaching lengths of 3m, the dragon is the top predator on the few islands where it lives, and every living animal is its potential prey, including humans. Fortunately, Komodo dragons have a preference for dead animals and use their uncanny sense of smell to find carrion up to 10km away.

Komodo dragons are today a popular attraction and centrepiece of the 1800 sq km Komodo National Park, which has been recently expanded to protect both terrestrial ecosystems and a fabulously unspoiled coral reef system. Visitors to the islands will almost certainly see dragons stalking ponderously with their huge heads swinging from side to side as they sniff the air for food. During the courting season, you may spot big males standing on their hind legs and struggling fiercely to pin each other to the ground in a show of dominance. Dragon courtship can be equally interesting because females fight back so ferociously that an amorous male must fully restrain the female in order to avoid being seriously hurt by her claws and teeth while they're mating. Courtship is also the time when babies hatch from their eggs and scamper up into trees to avoid being eaten by adults.

MORE INFO www.komodonationalpark.org

(LEFT) ↗
Komodo dragons can smell out a carcass from up to 10km away.

(TOP RIGHT) ↗
California condors are as popular as the Grand Canyon itself, with at least 65 free-flying birds soaring overhead on the winds rising from the canyon.

(BOTTOM RIGHT) ↗
The 2m- to 3m-long grouper uses its mottled colouring to sneak up on its prey.

CALIFORNIA CONDORS USA

LOCATION Grand Canyon National Park, 95km north of Flagstaff, Arizona, USA **WHY NOW?** You'll avoid summer crowds and high temperatures **LEVEL OF DIFFICULTY** Low – it's accessible for anyone **STATUS** The condors are highly threatened

There is no better way to see North America's largest land birds than to stand at the South Rim of the Grand Canyon and watch the show unfold. After a 100-year absence, these massive vultures with 3m wingspans were reintroduced to Arizona in 1996 and they now rank with the canyon's stellar scenery as one of the most popular attractions in the park. In fact, the huge crowds of people who gather daily on the South Rim seem to be a powerful attractant for a scavenger that likes to hang around large mammals waiting for one of them to die. It is nothing short of exhilarating to watch these majestic birds circle back and forth on winds rising out of the canyon, especially because condors seem to take a perverse delight in swooping up the cliff face and rocketing across the stone parapet right over people's heads. You can almost imagine that they're trying to frighten someone into falling off the cliff, like they would if they were scaring deer or other animals they could eat.

Climbing back from a low point in 1987, when only 22 captive birds remained in the world, there are now upwards of 65 free-flying condors soaring over the wild landscapes of the Grand Canyon. Each bird is numbered and monitored by biologists who are on hand to help answer questions.

MORE INFO www.nps.gov/grca

QUEENSLAND GROUPERS AUSTRALIA

LOCATION Great Barrier Reef Marine Park, stretching 2300km along the coast of Queensland **WHY NOW?** This is the tail end of Australia's busy summer season **LEVEL OF DIFFICULTY** Medium – deeper dives require training and experience **STATUS** Groupers are vulnerable due to large adults being hunted in most of the world

Queensland groupers, also known as giant groupers, are widespread from the coast of South Africa eastward to Hawaii, but you'd have a hard time finding one of the famously huge adults because they have been mostly hunted out. A good bet for seeing these legendary 2m- to 3m-long fish might be in the protected waters of the Great Barrier Reef, where groupers weighing upwards of 400kg still haunt dark shelters and slowly patrol reefs for prey items. Built like a tank with a huge mouth, the grouper relies on its mottled colouration to sneak up on other fish or sea turtles and make lightning-fast lunges to catch its food.

It's a little frightening to swim with these monster fish, but divers consider groupers to be intelligent and inquisitive and enjoy running across them. One place where giant groupers are known to hang out is around the renowned wreck dive at the SS *Yongala,* 22km from Alva Beach, but divers can expect them at many other sites along the entire barrier reef. Another option is to see one of their close relatives, a wonderfully patterned grouper popularly known as the potato cod, that can be readily observed at Cod Hole on Ribbon Reef number 10.

MORE INFO www.cairnsvisitorcentre.com

DID YOU KNOW?

 If a Komodo dragon's 2.5cm-long serrated, biting teeth don't kill, the toxic microbes in their saliva will cause death from infection.

Groupers are born female but turn male when they reach 1m long. Huge males are often seen surrounded by harems of smaller females.

↗ **MAY**

WEEK.04

WHAT YOU'LL SEE

BARNACLE GEESE

BEAN GEESE

DIVERS

WADERS

OWLS

BIRDWATCHING
FINLAND

↘ **WHY NOW?** You can witness a massive migration of birds while avoiding massive attacks by biting insects

With unspoiled countryside and superlative numbers of birds, Finland is quickly gaining popularity among birdwatchers who are willing to travel to this sparsely populated country on the far northeast fringes of Europe. Twice the size of England but with only five million residents, Finland is dominated by forests (69% of the country) and lakes (180,000) rather than humans. Birdwatchers frequently come to Finland to see its 10 species of owl, but a visit in the second half of May gives you front-row seats to one of Europe's most impressive bird migrations as millions of birds cross the Gulf of Finland.

Single-day counts on the south coast of Finland readily reach 70,000 barnacle geese, 150,000 brent geese, 50,000 bean geese and 10,000 divers. These numbers can't possibly convey, however, the sheer excitement of birds rolling overhead in almost

continuous processions. And not only are there geese and divers but also countless flocks of various ducks (hundreds of thousands of long-tailed ducks a day are possible) and waders, along with songbirds and raptors, all eagerly migrating north.

To see this event, it's helpful to contact one of Finland's many bird clubs or bird leaders who can direct you to favourable locations along the coast. Another option is to start at the Hanko Bird Observatory situated at the tip of the Hanko Peninsula, Finland's southwesternmost point of land, where biologists conduct counts of birds and you can learn more about the dynamics of the migration.

A well-rounded birdwatching trip to Finland has to include a visit to the country's interior forests, lakes and marshes to see numerous species that are difficult to find elsewhere in Europe, such as Blyth's reed warbler or red-flanked bluetail. Check out the thousands of lekking ruff (a kind of wader with outrageous courtship displays) in fields around Liminka Bay. Or search for capercaille, black grouse, hazel and willow grouse, along with eagle owls and other owls on a night drive. No matter where you travel in Finland, this is a fantastic time to catch the peak migration of Arctic birds that are heading north to breed and to hear the songs of birds that stick around to nest in Finland's many rich habitats. **MORE INFO** www.fatbirder.com/links_geo/europe/finland.html

HORSESHOE CRABS USA

LOCATION Delaware Bay, 160km east of Washington DC, Delaware & New Jersey, USA **WHY NOW?** You can walk beaches covered in crabs and shorebirds **LEVEL OF DIFFICULTY** Low – there's easy access and viewing **STATUS** Their future is uncertain; numbers are dramatically down in the face of heavy harvesting

Despite their name, horseshoe crabs are actually close relatives of spiders, ticks and scorpions. In fact, they seem to be descendants of ancient trilobites and haven't changed much in 445 million years, a fact that only adds to their eerie prehistoric mystique. Walking among hundreds of thousands of horseshoe crabs at Delaware Bay is an even stranger experience. Millions formerly crawled onto these beaches to spawn with high tides on full moon or new moon evenings. Numbers are currently down to around 200,000 and it is not known whether this is due to cyclic population levels or overharvesting of spawning crabs, but it's leading to some concern. The state of New Jersey banned crab harvests in 2008, and countless volunteers walk the beaches each day turning over crabs that have been flipped on their backs by waves or by their frenzied mating activities.

Reaching lengths of 60cm, with turtle-like carapaces and long spiked tails, these odd marine animals gather in huge numbers to mate and lay their eggs in 20cm-deep holes they dig on the beach. Much smaller males cling to the backs of females and drop sperm into the holes along with the 4000 eggs the female lays. She may lay four to five clutches during each venture onto the beach, and return with subsequent tides to lay a total of 15,000 to 64,000 eggs. In turn, eggs exposed by waves provide the primary food source for up to one million shorebirds that gather on these beaches to fatten up on their flights from South America to their Arctic breeding grounds. **MORE INFO** www.horseshoecrab.org

[LEFT] ↗
Up to a million seabirds gather on the beaches of Delaware Bay to feed on the 200,000 breeding horseshoe crabs.

[TOP RIGHT] ↗
Black howler monkeys in the Bermudian Landing area of Belize now number up to 250 per hectare.

[BOTTOM RIGHT] ↗
Charles Darwin lobbied to have the Aldabra tortoise protected, making it one of the first protected species in the world.

BLACK HOWLER MONKEYS BELIZE

LOCATION Community Baboon Sanctuary, 42km west of Belize City **WHY NOW?** You'll catch the end of the dry season **LEVEL OF DIFFICULTY** Low – local guides will help you find the monkeys **STATUS** The monkeys are common and widespread

In Belize, black howler monkeys are known as baboons (though they're not related) and this sanctuary is the only area established entirely for their conservation. It's a wholly community-based initiative founded in 1985 at the village of Bermudian Landing. Landowners voluntarily pledge to manage their land in a monkey-friendly fashion by maintaining forested strips along the Belize River and along property boundaries to create corridors for howlers, while not cutting important food trees such as figs and hogplums. The scheme has spread to surrounding villages and now includes over 100 landowners, resulting in the densest populations of howlers found anywhere – up to 250 individuals per hectare.

This density of monkeys makes for outstanding viewing but places a premium on space, creating one of the most aggressive and vocal populations of howlers on the planet. When you hear their deafening, roaring calls resonating through the forest, you'll quickly understand how they got their name. Howlers are often visible from the main road, but a maze of trails provides the best views. The routes traverse private property so stop by the visitor centre at Bermudian Landing to hire a local guide who can find the most habituated troops, some of which can be approached to within a metre – a privilege unique to the sanctuary.

MORE INFO www.howlermonkeys.org

ALDABRA TORTOISES SEYCHELLES

LOCATION Aldabra Atoll, 150km southwest of Mahé **WHY NOW?** It's the beginning of the dry season **LEVEL OF DIFFICULTY** Medium – the atoll is extremely remote and all visits must adhere to strict guidelines **STATUS** They have a limited range but are well protected

Lying closer to Africa and Madagascar than the capital of the Seychelles, the Aldabra coral atoll is one of the most unspoiled and remote ecosystems in the world. Visitors are few and far between, consisting primarily of a few charter boats from Mahé. The atoll is so strictly protected that every visitor activity is tightly monitored and guided, down to checking your shoes and clothing for any seeds and alien species hitching a ride before you're allowed to step foot onto land. The reward for your visit is witnessing a tropical paradise that remains virtually untouched by humans, including the world's largest population of giant tortoises and phenomenally pristine coral reefs.

The tortoises of Aldabra are the atoll's most famous inhabitants, even catching the attention of Charles Darwin who lobbied to have them become one of the world's first protected species. Unfortunately, in some areas the atoll's 150,000 giant tortoises have seriously outgrown the space available to them. In these areas, 40 to 50 tortoises vie for the shade of each scarce tree, piling up two to three tortoises deep to avoid the searing sun. Other creatures include endemic birds such as the flightless rail and the Aldabra sacred ibis, in addition to 7000 pairs of frigatebirds and hundreds of nesting hawksbill and green sea turtles.

MORE INFO www.seychellesislandsfoundation.org

DID YOU KNOW?

Howler monkeys rely on a diet of leaves that, although abundant, are full of hard-to-digest toxins and don't offer much energy.

A 320kg Aldabra tortoise fulfills the same ecological role as an elephant, knocking down trees and creating trails through vegetation.

↗ JUNE
WEEK.01

ARCTIC NATIONAL WILDLIFE REFUGE USA

WHAT YOU'LL SEE

- BUFF-BREASTED SANDPIPERS
- SNOWY OWLS
- MUSK OXEN
- POLAR BEARS
- BOWHEAD WHALES

WHY NOW? You can enjoy the peak breeding season before the onslaught of mosquitoes begins

If you had to pick one place in the world to see wildlife in June it would have to be the Arctic National Wildlife Refuge on the north slope of Alaska. Not only is this 81,000 sq km refuge one of the largest and northernmost conservation areas in the world, it is also home to so much wildlife and adventure you'll have a hard time deciding where to start. Will you raft down one of the refuge's 18 major rivers for an exhilarating cross-section of habitats? Do you kayak the edge of the Arctic Ocean with bowhead whales, belugas and polar bears? Or will you set up base camp on the coastal plain to observe caribou, musk oxen, wolves and grizzly bears? And those are just the most popular options in a wilderness so vast that you could have entire mountain ranges to yourself or hike for months without seeing anyone else.

One of the best reasons to visit is to witness the unbelievable explosion of life on the refuge's north coastal plain. Here, around an endless lacework of braided rivers and lagoons, the air practically buzzes with the energy of courting, singing and nesting birds. The soft spongy ground is utterly carpeted with wildflowers, and predators wander casually among an endless feast of prey animals and newborn babies. Because the growing season is so short and because most birds must begin their southbound migration as soon as possible, all this activity is hyperconcentrated into mere weeks. Male buff-breasted sandpipers, for instance, gather on leks to attract females with flashy wing-lifting ceremonies that are stunning to watch, then a week or two later the males leave.

The refuge is a particularly impressive place for predators such as black, grizzly and polar bears, scarce wolverines and common arctic foxes. And for good reason: everywhere you look you'll see abundant food animals ranging from ringed seals along the coast to moose among the willow thickets and Dall sheep on rocky slopes.

Charter planes from local villages such as Fort Yukon, Deadhorse or Katovik can take you into this very remote refuge, but there are no roads, trails or lodges so you must be self-sufficient for this adventure.
MORE INFO http://arctic.fws.gov

HIPPOPOTAMUSES GABON

LOCATION Loango National Park, 250km south of Libreville **WHY NOW?** It's the beginning of the dry season **LEVEL OF DIFFICULTY** Medium – coastal portions of the park are easily reached but the infrastructure is still in its infancy **STATUS** The area is likely to be logged unless tourism starts to generate revenue and publicity for the park

Alternately called 'Africa's Last Eden' or the jewel of Africa's west coast, Loango National Park was brought to international attention by American ecologist Michael Fay in 1997, then set aside as one of Gabon's first national parks in 2002. Spanning 1550 sq km, this park was initially nicknamed 'the land of surfing hippos' for the stunning discovery that hippopotamuses come out of the forest to swim in the ocean surf along the Loango coast. And nowhere else in the world can you watch hippos, elephants, leopards and forest buffalo walking on a white sand beach next to the ocean.

Only recently did scientists realise that the 100km of uninhabited coastline is also home to the second greatest concentration and diversity of whales and dolphins in the world. Among the 14 species found here are 1500 to 3000 humpback whales that arrive in June to calve and spend the winter.

Away from the shorelines and coastal lagoons, Loango protects rainforests and papyrus swamps full of exotic animals such as sitatungas, red river hogs, dwarf crocodiles and lowland gorillas. You're more likely to encounter hippos here as well, giving you ample opportunity to watch their behaviour as 3200kg males defend groups of females and calves. Look for males challenging each other with loud hoots and 'yawning' displays to show off 50cm tusks that can chop a crocodile in half. At all costs they try to avoid fighting, so you might even see two males back up and shower each other with urine and faeces as a sign of respect. **MORE INFO** www.africas-eden.com

[LEFT] ↗
Hippopotamuses, despite their placid appearance, are considered one of the most aggressive animals on earth.

[TOP RIGHT] ↗
Sharing many characterisitcs with the larger giant panda, including opposable thumbs, the red panda is only about the size of a housecat.

[BOTTOM RIGHT] ↗
Long-tailed layflies must complete their entire breeding cycle before their minuscule fat reserves run out.

RED PANDAS CHINA

LOCATION Bingzhongluo National Park, 550km northwest of Kunming, Yunnan **WHY NOW?** The climate is agreeable **LEVEL OF DIFFICULTY** Medium – the infrastructure is in its infancy and there are very few Western tourists **STATUS** There are fewer than 2500 left in the world and that number is declining due to habitat fragmentation

This is a park you've never heard of because it might not even exist. Prompted by the efforts of international conservation organisations such as the Nature Conservancy, this brand-new park in the fabulous Gaoligong Mountains of western Yunnan has a new headquarters and hotel but may be rendered obsolete by the construction of 13 dams on the Nu River (Salween). A temporary halt in plans to build dams has raised hopes that increased tourism can stop these projects from destroying one of the least known and most important biodiversity hot spots in the world.

Among the region's many interesting mammals are raccoon-like red pandas, no larger than housecats but 120cm long and coloured flaming red with dark masks. Sharing many features with giant pandas, including living on a diet of bamboo leaves, these smaller cousins live in mountain forests between 1800m and 4800m, and are most active at dawn and dusk. Like giant pandas, they have a 'thumb' bone that gives them the dexterity to hold bamboo shoots. Red pandas give birth in June but many details of their lives in the wild remain unknown.

Bingzhongluo is home to Tibetan and Nu peoples, and just like Tibet the region has many temples and snow-capped peaks. Nearby is the 320km-long Nu River Gorge, called the 'Grand Canyon of the East'.

MORE INFO http://chinarivers.com/nujiang.html

LONG-TAILED MAYFLIES HUNGARY

LOCATION Tisza River, 100km east of Budapest **WHY NOW?** Mating swarms happen over the course of a few hours **LEVEL OF DIFFICULTY** Low – they're easy to see but it's hard to get word of when the hatch is happening **STATUS** Once widespread in European rivers, the mayflies are now restricted to the Tisza River and are vulnerable to water pollution

Locals call it Tiszavirágzás (the blooming of the Tisza River) in celebration of the annual hatch of long-tailed mayflies, an event that no longer occurs anywhere else in Europe due to widespread river pollution. It all begins on an early June afternoon when the placid, sun-dappled water of the Tisza River is broken by the forms of mayflies as they climb out of their larval skins and rise into soft-winged flight. What starts as one or two mayflies quickly builds into a crescendo of millions of mayflies. The first to emerge are 12cm-long males, the largest mayflies in Europe, but females arise moments later.

After two to three years spent living as worm-like larvae in the river's muddy bottom, this hours-long mating flight is the final act in the mayfly's life. Adults that emerge from the water have no mouths or stomachs and they must complete their entire breeding cycle before their minuscule fat reserves run out. The countless males are particularly desperate to find females, and each emerging female is mobbed by a dozen males. Backlit by the setting sun, the exquisite ballet of millions of gossamer long-tailed mayflies may be the most exquisite blossoming you've ever seen.

MORE INFO www.icpdr.org/icpdr-pages/dw0802_p_10.htm

↗ JUNE
WEEK.02

SARDINE RUN
SOUTH AFRICA

WHAT YOU'LL SEE

- COMMON DOLPHINS
- BRONZE WHALER SHARKS
- CAPE FUR SEALS
- HUMPBACK WHALES
- CAPE GANNETS

WHY NOW? You'll see 'the Greatest Shoal on Earth'

In June and July South Africa's east coast experiences the biggest marine show on the planet, the annual 'sardine run', an event that easily rivals the wildebeest migrations in terms of sheer biomass. No one knows how many sardines (Southern African pilchards) actually make this 'run' up the east coast, but there may be hundreds of shoals of fish along the 1000km of coastline, with each shoal as large as 15km long, 4km wide and 40m deep. Unless you're a scuba diver you're not likely to see the fish themselves, but everyone can see the swirling crowds of predators that follow the food, including 20,000 common dolphins, thousands of sharks, Cape fur seals and tens of thousands of gannets.

It is remarkable how little is known about this phenomenon, although scientists believe that the fish are spillovers from the immense breeding grounds south of Cape

Town. An estimated 2% of the Cape's population is eventually pushed up the east coast by northward-flowing cold waters during winter, creating the only site in the world where sardine runs are found near a coastline.

'Sardine fever' is a highly anticipated event in South Africa, with spotter planes searching for feeding frenzies and local dive boats dashing out to catch the show. The action starts when herds of common dolphins scare a group of sardines into a dense 'baitball' by blowing bubbles all around the fish. Attracted by the excitement of hundreds of dolphins, predators converge so rapidly that the water literally boils with action as thousands of sharks, cormorants and seals dive, chase and thrash in the water. Tens of thousands of gannets soon converge overhead and begin raining into the water like laser-guided missiles. And as a backdrop to the whole show you'll spot the spectacular breaches of gigantic humpback whales that gather here to mate and raise their calves during this time of superabundant food.

Divers and underwater photographers relish the thrill of watching the storm of predators around a baitball, but even non-divers will see plenty of action from the boatside, while snorkellers get to watch the feeding close-up with the added thrill of having gannets plunging into the water all around them. South African dive companies now offer specialised trips to see 'the Greatest Shoal'.

MORE INFO www.sardinerun.net

BARREN GROUND CARIBOU CANADA

LOCATION There are multiple sites in northern Canada and northeast Alaska, USA **WHY NOW?** You can see the last great herds in North America on their calving grounds **LEVEL OF DIFFICULTY** Medium – it's logistically challenging and expensive due to the remote locations **STATUS** The population is stable and protected by the inaccessibility of its range

If you can find a way to travel to the vast open stretches of northern Canada, go in June to see the last great herds of wildlife left in North America. Here, in over 100 herds (each named for their distinct calving grounds), millions of barren ground caribou follow timeless routes and deeply rutted paths on their annual 3000km to 5000km migration. Eight of these caribou herds number over 100,000 – including the George River Herd in eastern Nunavut, which numbers between 400,000 and 800,000 – and when they're on the move they form a seamless river of caribou that carpets the landscape.

Like the wildebeests of East Africa, barren ground caribou (the same species as the European reindeer) spend much of their life on the move and you can pick almost any month to see some aspect of their migratory life cycle. In April and May the caribou stream northward from Canada's boreal forests to their far northern calving grounds. Females lead the way, so eager to reach their destination that calves born en route may be abandoned. Most calves are born in mid-June and, after a week or two, thousands of caribou mass up as tightly as possible and proceed north again to escape clouds of mosquitoes that are so dense you can hardly breathe unless you keep walking.

For sheer numbers the George River Herd would be a good bet (www.nunavutparks.com), but most famous of all is the Porcupine Herd of the Arctic National Wildlife Refuge and adjacent Ivvavik National Park. **MORE INFO** www.pc.gc.ca/pn-np/yt/ivvavik/index_E.asp

(LEFT) ↗
Barren ground caribou are heavily migratory animals, travelling 3000 to 5000km a year.

(TOP RIGHT) ↗
The Caucasus black grouse population is low but remains protected by the rugged mountainous habitat.

(BOTTOM RIGHT) ↗
The orchestrated lightshows of fireflies allow the males and females to find each other.

CAUCASUS BLACK GROUSE TURKEY

LOCATION Kaçkar Mountains, 90km east of Trabzon **WHY NOW?**
The mountains are still snow-bound but you'll see grouse courtship
LEVEL OF DIFFICULTY Medium – this involves hiking into high mountains
before sunrise **STATUS** They are highly susceptible to disturbance but are
protected by their rugged habitat

The 4000m-high Kaçkar Mountains of eastern Turkey are a spectacular
landscape of history, ancient village traditions, wildlife and stellar hiking trails.
This alpine mountain range, also known as the Pontic Alps or the Lesser
Caucasus, was set aside as a national park in 1994, partly to protect its famous
black grouse leks.

Fewer than 1500 of these magnificent gamebirds survive in remote
mountain meadows of northeast Turkey, and in the first half of June they
perform their legendary flutter-jump courtship displays (popular enough that
there is an annual festival to celebrate the bird). Unfortunately, they only
perform in high meadows above the treeline and in order to catch their sunrise
displays you have to leave the warmth of your hotel at 3am and follow a
trusted guide on a strenuous hike into the mountains. Even in June you are
likely to face deep snows and frigid temperatures, but it will all be worth it
when you get to witness the stunning black males show off by leaping into
quick fluttering flight, flipping 180 degrees in mid-air to flash hidden white
wings, then landing. The village of Sivrikaya hosts the best-known grouse lek,
but check out the new ecotourism project at Ayder for a less publicised site.
MORE INFO www.kackarlar.org

FIREFLIES USA

LOCATION Great Smoky Mountains National Park, 10km southwest of
Gatlinburg, Tennessee, USA **WHY NOW?** The firefly display lasts for two
to three weeks **LEVEL OF DIFFICULTY** Low – you should plan ahead to get
a space on the bus, then kick back with a lawn chair and enjoy **STATUS** The
firefly population is stable and well protected

First described in 1577 by Sir Francis Drake, the fireflies of Southeast Asia are
celebrated for their synchronised flashing. In the mid-1990s someone reported
finding the only known synchronous firefly displays in the western hemisphere –
in a clearing on the edge of Great Smoky Mountains National Park, where fireflies
gather every year for two weeks of breathtakingly beautiful displays. Each night
from early to late June, hundreds of people ride park buses from the Sugarlands
Visitor Center to the Elkmont Trailhead and wait, their eager conversations fading
into awed murmurs as the show begins between 9pm and 10pm.

What draws everyone is not the sheer numbers of fireflies, but the
remarkable way that dozens, then hundreds, then thousands of fireflies begin
flashing in perfect synchrony as if orchestrated. As soon as a few fireflies
tentatively flash, the entire forest of fireflies flashes in a spontaneous chain
reaction, over and over again, three seconds of flashing followed by six second
pauses. Because adult fireflies live for only two weeks, these brilliant light
shows are the only way that males and females find each other and they
seem to pour their heart and soul into the event. Reserve a space at Elkmont
Campground and you can stay behind when the buses leave.
MORE INFO www.nps.gov/grsm

DID YOU KNOW?

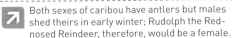

Both sexes of caribou have antlers but males
shed theirs in early winter; Rudolph the Red-
nosed Reindeer, therefore, would be a female.

As soon as females of some firefly species
mate they begin deceptive flashing to lure in
males of other species that they then eat.

↗ JUNE
WEEK.03

NORTH ATLANTIC SEABIRDS
GREAT BRITAIN

WHAT YOU'LL SEE

ATLANTIC PUFFINS
NORTHERN GANNETS
GREAT SKUAS
GUILLEMOTS
KITTIWAKES

WHY NOW? Catch the seabirds in peak breeding activity and numbers

In a way, the vast seabird colonies of Great Britain are the quintessential wildlife image of the North Atlantic region – lovely green pastures ending in sheer cliffs that plunge into the pounding waves of the North Atlantic with thousands of birds floating in stiff winds in front of sculpted rock faces utterly covered in nesting birds. Not only are these places of breathtaking beauty, but they are also among the most important seabird colonies in the northern hemisphere. Many such sites exist around the perimeter of Great Britain, with varying numbers of seabirds and varying degrees of accessibility ranging from treacherous boat rides to pleasant pastoral ambles.

Seabirds gather in vast numbers on these cliffs so they can safely nest out of reach of predators but with ready access to the immense food riches of the Atlantic Ocean.

Because June is the period of peak food supplies, seabirds time the nesting season so that their chicks hatch this month. Cliff faces are difficult places to nest, so every single nook and cranny is crammed with squawking seabirds, creating a visual tapestry of birds shimmering with constant activity. When they're not jostling for space on tiny perches, birds launch into open space and float like pieces of kinetic art in the endless winds. If this doesn't make you want to fly then nothing will!

St Kilda, 64km west of the Outer Hebrides, is the top seabird site in Europe, with 500,000 pairs of nesting seabirds, including significant portions of the total population of bird species such as the northern gannet, Leach's storm-petrels and Atlantic puffins. The 400m cliffs of St Kilda are a splendid sight, but access is limited and difficult unless you join an organised group (www.kilda.org.uk). Much easier to access and equally magnificent are the cliffs of Foula, off the coast of Shetland, where 18 species of seabird nest in massive, uncounted colonies.

Part of the fun of chasing seabirds is sniffing around and researching the numerous viewpoints, reserves and boat trips that offer views of nesting colonies all over the different islands. Everyone has their favourite sites so contact bird clubs, check out guidebooks, grab a pair of binoculars and prepare to have some memorable bird sightings.

MORE INFO www.rspb.org.uk

NIGHT DRIVES SOUTH AFRICA

LOCATION Kruger National Park, 460km east of Pretoria **WHY NOW?** The beginning of the dry season means there is less vegetation to block viewing, and more animals gathering at watering holes **LEVEL OF DIFFICULTY** Low – the park has an efficient system for joining night drives **STATUS** The animals are well protected in the park and local private reserves

If you think all the African safari action occurs in the daytime, then it's time to sign up for a guided night drive at Kruger National Park to see what happens when the sun goes down. Rousing from their drowsy daytime sleep, this is the magic hour for hungry predators. While a mostly unseen chess game of predator-and-prey plays out in the brush all around you, the tension and thrill grows with each cracking branch and flickering shadow. Glowing eyes dart between trees, yelps and roars rise up in the night, and you may stumble across a fresh kill with lions, hyenas and jackals squaring off over the feast.

The immense Kruger National Park is a perfect place for this drama to play out. Home to large numbers of the Big Five and countless smaller animals, this sprawling 20,000 sq km park is laced with thousands of kilometres of roads and numerous camps offering night drives that take you deep into the bush. Gates are closed at night to protect the camps and private vehicles are forbidden, but you won't miss out on the action from your seat on one of the official safari trucks.

Happily, not all night-time events involve high drama and killing, because this is also the best time to see smaller creatures such as bush babies, genets, civets, owls and nightjars, plus many lesser known nocturnal critters. Bathed in the gleam of your vehicle's spotlights, expect to see all the action up close and personal. **MORE INFO** www.sanparks.org/parks/kruger

(LEFT) ↗
The predators in Kruger National Park are at their most active overnight; when the sun rises again, they rest after their night of hunting.

(TOP RIGHT) ↗
In June and early July, mountain goats emerge in search of the sulphur minerals needed to grow shaggy new coats.

(BOTTOM RIGHT) ↗
Magpie-geese are well protected in Australia's Kakadu National Park.

MOUNTAIN GOATS CANADA

LOCATION Jasper National Park, 38km south of Jasper, Alberta **WHY NOW?** It's the time when mountain goats come down for mineral licks **LEVEL OF DIFFICULTY** Low – the goats can be observed at close range from roadside viewpoints **STATUS** The population is stable and well protected

The mountain goats of the Canadian Rockies are best known as white dots barely discernable on distant cliffs, the kind of thing you find tourists staring at through binoculars and arguing over whether they've found sleeping goats or if they're seeing clumps of snow. Closely related to the mountain antelope of Asia (like serows or gorals), these snow-white animals rarely leave the alpine cliffs where they are astonishingly adept and safe from predators. It's nearly impossible to see them at close range except in June and early July, when they moult their heavy white coats and descend out of the mountains in search of sulphur minerals that are essential for regrowing shaggy new coats.

Fortunately for human visitors, sulphur occurs naturally in glacial silt deposits at low elevations and for a brief window of time the normally wary goats and their newborn kids are so desperate for minerals that they pay little attention to the people watching them at close range. Check out the Goats and Glaciers Viewpoint along the Icefields Parkway 38km south of Jasper, and the Disaster Point lick 29km east of Jasper on Highway 16. The Disaster Point lick is also an excellent place to observe the equally skittish bighorn sheep in good numbers.
MORE INFO www.pc.gc.ca/pn-np/ab/jasper

MAGPIE-GEESE AUSTRALIA

LOCATION Kakadu National Park, 170km east of Darwin, Northern Territory **WHY NOW?** The dry season concentrates birds in smaller areas **LEVEL OF DIFFICULTY** Low – they're best seen on a boat cruise **STATUS** Magpie-geese are numerous and well protected

As the largest national park in Australia, Kakadu offers so much that you'll have a hard time deciding where to start. Diverse wildlife can be found throughout the park's four primary habitats – sandstone cliffs on the 500km-long Arnheim escarpment, floodplains along the Alligator Rivers, vast areas of tropical savannah, or scattered patches of rainforest. June to July is the 'cold weather' season (what the Aboriginal peoples of the area call Wurrgeng), when creeks and floodplains dry out and the park's many water birds are forced into much smaller wet areas. This is a perfect time to see the 1.6 million magpie-geese that live at Kakadu, when they are fat and healthy after weeks of abundant food.

These striking black-and-white birds of uncertain ancestry congregate by the hundreds of thousands in wet grasslands, milling about in search of roots and bulbs and making a tremendous honking racket. One fantastic way to appreciate magpie-geese and other floodplain wildlife is to sign up for an early departure on the daily boat cruises up the Yellow Water billabong, a source of vitally important permanent water at the height of the dry season. Keep your eyes open for unique comb-crested jacanas, green pygmy geese, storks, cranes and, of course, the massive saltwater crocodiles that are abundant here.
MORE INFO www.environment.gov.au/parks/kakadu

DID YOU KNOW?

 Mountain goats typically live for 12 to 15 years but the gradual wearing down of their teeth limits their lifespan.

Magpie-geese usually nest in trios: each male has two females that lay their eggs in a single nest.

↗ JUNE
WEEK.04

WILDEBEEST MIGRATION
TANZANIA & KENYA

WHAT YOU'LL SEE

WILDEBEESTS
GAZELLES
ZEBRAS
LIONS
CROCODILES

WHY NOW? Things get pretty exciting when over a million wildebeests cross crocodile-infested rivers

Although Africa's wildebeests are sometimes called 'clowns of the plains', they are deadly serious when they set out on their annual trek from the calving grounds in Tanzania's Serengeti National Park to fresh grazing areas in Kenya's Masai Mara National Reserve. Despite the perils of migration, males have sex on their minds, which drives them to bouts of frantic jumping, snorting and slobbering, while females struggle to keep newborn calves in tow and navigate through a gauntlet of predators and lusty males.

The result is the most famous mammal migration on earth, and perhaps the best known of all wildlife events, as over a million wildebeests are joined by 500,000 gazelles and 200,000 zebras on a sweeping 800km journey in search of food. Predators are

in close attendance all along the path, with none as impressive as the giant 6m-long Nile crocodiles that lie in wait at each river crossing.

These river crossings – first the Grumeti River in Tanzania, then the Talek and Mara River crossings in Kenya – are terrifying episodes for the wildebeests, who line up on the riverbank, pushing each other towards steep slippery banks and the river below. Many perish here, the victims of broken bones, exhaustion or crocodile attack, and numerous bawling calves and mothers are forever separated in the turmoil.

What few people realise is that the wildebeest migration is an ongoing, year-round event because wildebeests are constantly on the move, making one complete 800km to 1600km circumnavigation of the Serengeti Plains each year. The timing of their movements and the routes they take vary each year, so the best thing to do is call ahead, or ask for updates when you arrive, and plan accordingly.

In late June the wildebeests turn north and head towards Masai Mara, so this is a good time to catch them as they cross northern Serengeti National Park. While searching for the wildebeests and their travelling companions, you will see many elephants, rhinos, cheetahs, lions, giraffes, vultures and eagles – part of the park's 95 species of mammal and 500 species of bird. Serengeti National Park is located 325km northwest of Arusha, Tanzania, and has excellent infrastructure and guides to help you find the action.
MORE INFO www.serengeti.org

PACIFIC WALRUSES USA

LOCATION Walrus Islands State Game Sanctuary, 700km southwest of Anchorage, Alaska, USA **WHY NOW?** You'll see thousands of male walruses **LEVEL OF DIFFICULTY** Medium – camping on the island is a true wilderness experience **STATUS** The population is successfully rebounding from early-20th-century hunting

When female and immature walruses head north each summer to follow the receding ice pack through the Bering Strait, the males stay behind and whoop it up with 'the guys'. Actually they spend their time sleeping and sunbathing on beaches around Alaska's Bristol Bay, with occasionally forays to catch some crabs and shrimp for dinner. That isn't to say walruses are boring to watch; in fact, they do quite a bit of jostling and mock fighting as they pack together on wave-swept beaches and argue over prime sleeping spots. And the action gets pretty exciting on Round Island, where anywhere from 2000 to 14,000 males jostle for space on a single small beach.

Part of the State Game Sanctuary just west of Dillingham, Round Island is one of four major 'haul-outs' in Alaska, and probably the best known. Two other sites – Cape Peirce and Newenham – can be found on the adjacent Togiak National Wildlife Refuge, and a third is located at Seniavin near Port Moller. Round Island is a brooding steep-sided cone of rock in Bristol Bay, with cliffs plunging into rocky beaches covered in walruses. Steller's sea lions haul out nearby, while 250,000 seabirds nest on the rock faces above and 16 species of marine mammal ply the offshore waters.

Visitors can charter a boat from one of three licensed operators in Dillingham and visit Round Island on a day trip or be dropped off for a wild and unpredictable camping experience; sanctuary guidelines recommend that you bring a week of extra food in case your pick-up boat is delayed by poor weather.
MORE INFO http://wildlife.alaska.gov

(LEFT) ↗
Male walruses take advantage of the females' and cubs' absence to sunbathe on the beaches of Bristol Bay, Alaska.

(TOP RIGHT) ↗
The solitary maned wolf communicates with others of its kind by leaving distinctive-smelling urine spots.

(BOTTOM RIGHT) ↗
Golden rays traverse the Gulf of Mexico in schools of up to 10,000.

MANED WOLVES BRAZIL

LOCATION Caraça Natural Reserve, 120km east of Belo Horizonte **WHY NOW?** You can watch the wolves' nightly feeding **LEVEL OF DIFFICULTY** Low – they're easily viewed on the patio after dinner **STATUS** The population is vulnerable due to habitat loss and transmission of diseases from domestic dogs

Brazil's maned wolf is shy, nocturnal and rarely observed. Found on grasslands of southeast Brazil, this unique canid has the appearance of a very large fox standing on black stilt-like legs, but it is not closely related to any other dog breed in the world. You might never see one, but fortunately the priests at the seminary of Caraça have made the task a bit easier, because every evening for over 20 years they have been putting food out for wolves that come onto the patio in full view. Reserve guests get front-row seats for this increasingly popular event, and for almost everyone it will be their only chance of ever seeing this mysterious wolf.

Unlike other large canids of the world, the 1m-high maned wolf does not live or hunt in packs. At most, monogamous pairs may share a 30 sq km territory, though they seldom cross paths except to mate. Despite their solitary lives, wolves still communicate with each other by leaving distinctive urine spots (said to smell like hops or marijuana).

Because the Caraça Natural Reserve sits at the intersection of the Cerrado and Atlantic Forest ecosystems, it wouldn't hurt to stay for a couple of days to see the rich wildlife and increase your chances of seeing the wolves.
MORE INFO www.beautifulhorizons.net/photos/caraa_nature_at_her_best/index.html

GOLDEN RAYS MEXICO

LOCATION Yucatan Peninsula, Cancun, Mexico **WHY NOW?** You'll catch the ray migration **LEVEL OF DIFFICULTY** Low – finding the rays could be hard, but you'll have fun no matter what **STATUS** They're abundant and widespread

The massive migration of golden rays in the Gulf of Mexico will come as a shock to anyone who thinks of rays as solitary animals hiding in the sand and scooting along the ocean bottom. Each year these beautiful rays (also known as cownose rays) gather in schools of as many as 10,000 and swim a giant circular route around the Gulf of Mexico – a journey that takes them northward past the tip of the Yucatan Peninsula in late June.

Measuring up to 2m across, schools of thousands of golden rays are a stunning sight – their slow, rhythmic swimming is mesmerising and hauntingly graceful. Although it's rare to stumble across one of these legendary groups of rays, anyone who comes to the Yucatan to dive in its turquoise bathtub-warm waters is likely to run into smaller numbers of rays mingling with numerous reef fish, sea turtles, dolphins and the much larger manta rays.

Golden rays can be recognised by their colour and by the unique creased lobe in front of their domed heads that gives them an odd cowlike appearance. Rays eat clams and crabs that they expose by fluttering their long fins against the sandy ocean floor. They protect themselves with a poisonous stinger (think 'stingray') but during migration they are considered shy and unthreatening.
MORE INFO www.travelyucatan.com

WHAT YOU'LL SEE

WOLVES

BROWN BEARS

EUROPEAN BISON

WEST CAUCASIAN TURS

LYNXES

KAVKAZSKIY NATURE RESERVE
RUSSIA

WHY NOW? You'll access one of Europe's most pristine alpine mountain ranges The Western Caucasus Mountains of southwest Russia have been called the most biologically diverse and beautiful mountains in the northern hemisphere, and you'll see why when you visit. Large portions of these high rugged mountains on the Black Sea coast are extremely remote and have seen little human disturbance for centuries. This is fortunate because the Caucasus are the only place in the world where temperate deciduous forests have existed continuously for about 40 million years, creating stupendous old-growth forests and high levels of endemic plants and animals. Rare animals abound in this mountain stronghold, including (believe it or not) leopards and an endemic high-altitude goat called a tur.

The area's many rivers descend precipitously from 4000m peaks down rugged slopes to the Black Sea, passing glaciers, 130 mountain lakes, countless sheer gorges and

250m-high waterfalls. Along the way they pass through relict rhododendron forests, drop down into birch and maple forests, cross pine and fir forests and meander through ancient oak-chestnut woodlands.

This remarkable range of habitats provides homes for wolves, brown bears, newly reintroduced European bison, boars, lynxes and a host of localised species such as the Caucasian red deer and the Caucasian otter. You are most likely to see some of these larger animals if you hike into the alpine meadow zone, where bears gather to feast on bulbs and ungulates such as chamois and turs romp on towering cliffs. West Caucasian turs are particularly interesting because these 100kg goats with stunning curved horns are exhilarating to watch as they scamper fearlessly across sheer rock faces. All are widely poached and hunted elsewhere in their range, so scientists hope these animals can make their last stand in the Western Caucasus, although even here there is increasing pressure on their survival due to lack of enforcement.

Recently recognised as one of the top biodiversity hot spots in the world, the huge 2600 sq km Kavkazskiy Nature Reserve includes parts of Sochi National Park, four natural monuments and other protected areas. There are very few roads here and scarcely any visitors, but this will definitely change after the 2014 Winter Olympics in Sochi bring the area to the world's attention. Go now if you want to see this area before it's discovered.

MORE INFO www.wild-russia.org/html/tour.htm

HUMPBACK WHALES CANADA

LOCATION Avalon Peninsula, 100km southwest of St John's **WHY NOW?** The whales come near shore to feed on spawning capelin **LEVEL OF DIFFICULTY** Low – you can watch breaching whales from the comfort of a picnic blanket **STATUS** Their numbers are still diminished after a long era of hunting

Because humpback whales prefer to feed near coastlines, this species suffered at the hands of whale hunters almost more than any other whale. Now that their populations have staggered back from the brink of extinction, it is once again possible to watch their delightful shoreline feeding techniques and there may be no better destination for this activity than the southern coast of Newfoundland's Avalon Peninsula.

Several thousand humpback whales arrive here in June to feed on billions of spawning capelin, a small member of the smelt family that rides waves onto beaches and lays its eggs in the wet sand. Humpbacks only eat in summer, living off their fat reserves all winter, so it's vital that they spend the summer where there is abundant food. Newfoundland's vast capelin population attracts the largest gathering of humpback whales in the world.

One of Newfoundland's best viewing locations is St Vincent's Beach, between the towns of St Vincent's and St Mary's, where the sand drops off so steeply into deep water that these 36,000kg whales practically swim onto the beach (and sometimes do!) to grab mouthfuls of capelin. This makes for fantastic, up-close-and-personal whale-watching that's fun for kids and the whole family. St Vincent's also attracts minke and fin whales, along with thousands of gannets, shearwaters, terns and kittiwakes. Local naturalists and boat operators are making an effort to photograph and document every individual whale, so you can help out by taking your own photographs or by joining a boat trip.

MORE INFO www.atlanticwhales.com

[LEFT] ↗
Humpback whales gather on the south coast of Newfoundland's Avalon Peninsula in June to feed on capelin.

[TOP RIGHT] ↗
Little auk nests are located underground; some colonies have an estimated 15 to 20 million nesting pairs.

[BOTTOM RIGHT] ↗
The concentration of ladybird beetles in the Santa Catalina Mountains can reach 25,000 per sq metre.

LITTLE AUKS GREENLAND

LOCATION 1600km north of Nuuk **WHY NOW?** The parents are very actively feeding their chicks **LEVEL OF DIFFICULTY** Medium – independent travel is logistically challenging but cruise ships now visit the area **STATUS** They are abundant and in no immediate danger

Standing next to a little auk colony, you will be overwhelmed by sensory input. Although diminutive, these 160g seabirds (also called dovekies) are the most abundant seabirds in the Atlantic Ocean and they nest in immense colonies numbering in the millions of pairs. During the peak nesting season, from early to mid-July, adults are noisily flying back and forth bringing mouthfuls of plankton to their hungry chicks, and the air is full of deafening trills, chirps and shrieks. Since the nests are located underground, and much of the action is hidden from view, what makes this event so spectacular is the sight of endless squadrons of black-and-white adults winging past icebergs, jagged rock spires and snowfields in some of the most ethereal light that you will ever see.

The biggest little auk colonies are located on the northwest coast of Greenland, where an estimated 15 to 20 million pairs nest in the Avanersuaq (Thule) District alone. One colony of around a million pairs is located near Siorapaluk, the northernmost village in the world (1360km from the North Pole) and a popular stop for cruise ships. Little auk colonies are vulnerable to repeated disturbance, and their underground nests can be crushed if you walk over them, so be a careful observer as you take in this amazing experience.
MORE INFO www.greenland.com

DID YOU KNOW?

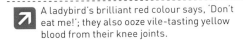

Humpbacks have unique patterns on their fins and tails that allow them to be individually identified and recognised.

A ladybird's brilliant red colour says, 'Don't eat me!'; they also ooze vile-tasting yellow blood from their knee joints.

LADYBIRD BEETLES USA

LOCATION Santa Catalina Mountains, 25km northeast of Tucson, Arizona, USA **WHY NOW?** The ladybirds are gathering to avoid the desert heat **LEVEL OF DIFFICULTY** Low – a trip to the mountains gets you out of the heat too **STATUS** They're abundant and under no serious threat

Common in gardens and much beloved because they eat aphids, scales and other destructive pests, ladybird beetles that live in the American Southwest have their own unique wildlife event that is worth seeing. These shiny red beetles spend their winters in cool mountain canyons but awaken each spring to fly down into the surrounding lowlands and lay their eggs on newly emerging wildflowers. Ladybird larvae eat copious quantities of aphids during the green flush of spring then hatch out as adults just as the deserts dry out and the sun cranks up the heat. When temperatures in the lowlands reach 40°C, the new generation of ladybirds flies back into the cooler mountains where they gather in such enormous numbers that they utterly carpet leaves, branches, rocks and tree trunks. Scientists once counted the ladybirds in one such congregation, and they gathered 2270 litres of ladybirds – 42 million in a single group. In some regularly used areas concentrations reach nearly 25,000 ladybirds per sq metre.

It's a favourite pastime, and a great excuse to escape the heat, for lowland residents to wander up to the high peaks around the desert towns to see this spectacle in mid-summer. Check out 2800m Mt Lemmon in the Santa Catalina Mountains, or any other Arizona mountain.
MORE INFO www.fs.fed.us/r3/coronado/forest/recreation/scenic_drives

↗ **JULY**

WEEK.02

WHAT YOU'LL SEE

- POLAR BEARS
- WALRUSES
- MUSK OXEN
- SNOWY OWLS
- GREY WHALES

WRANGEL ISLAND RESERVE
RUSSIA

WHY NOW? Wrangel Island is ice-free for only a short window of time

If you have ever wanted to go on an expedition to a remote, mysterious region that few people have visited then Wrangel Island, in the Chukchi Sea, might just be your ticket. Located far above the Arctic Circle and 140km north of Siberia, 7600 sq km Wrangel Island is basically off-limits to the outside world except for a few icebreakers that may or may not make it through the pack ice and fierce storms during the brief summer season. However, the rewards of a visit are off the charts, and provide just enough incentive that each summer a handful of tour companies book space on the couple of icebreakers powerful enough to make this arduous journey.

You will want to visit Wrangel because this is the only land mass in the incredibly productive Chukchi Sea and virtually every animal in the region comes here to breed or feed in its shallow waters. Wrangel Island boasts the greatest population of Pacific

walruses in the world, with up to 100,000 animals congregating at any given time on a single beach. It is also home to some of the highest concentrations of polar bear dens in the world, with six to 12 polar bears per sq km in some areas. Then there are the 200,000 nesting snow geese (the last remaining nesting population in Asia) and snowy owls, arctic foxes, lemmings, musk oxen and reindeer.

One other odd fact makes Wrangel unique: it was the only significant part of the Arctic region that was not covered in glaciers during the Pleistocene epoch, meaning that soils, plants and animals have survived unscathed here for millions of years, resulting in the highest biodiversity of any site in the entire Arctic region. In fact, it was recently discovered that woolly mammoths were still living here in 1700 BC, a mere 3600 years ago.

The idea of woolly mammoths roaming the island won't seem as far-fetched when you wander this haunting landscape amid an unexpected profusion of dryads, pasqueflowers, poppies and 380 other species of plant. You almost expect a mammoth to appear over those ancient eroded mountain peaks in the distance at any minute, but in the meantime there's that incredibly rare spoon-billed sandpiper to find.

MORE INFO www.wild-russia.org

BROWN BEARS USA

LOCATION Katmai National Park, 467km southwest of Anchorage, Alaska, USA **WHY NOW?** You can see bears catching salmon at the famous Brooks Falls **LEVEL OF DIFFICULTY** Medium – access to the park requires several flights, and the backcountry hikes require extensive planning **STATUS** The bears are not threatened in the park

If you've ever seen photographs of brown bears standing on the lip of a waterfall and catching leaping salmon with their mouths, you are seeing Brooks Falls in Alaska's Katmai National Park. This immense 14,500 sq km park is home to one of the densest populations of brown bears in the world (2000 are found here), as well as some of the world's largest salmon runs, so when the salmon are running in July and September this is a paradise for fat and happy bears.

These 700kg bears are so huge because they have access to abundant high-quality food. Fortunately, they generally don't bother humans, but they are still extremely dangerous and unpredictable, and backcountry hikers are well advised to exercise great caution in the park. Most visitors are content to watch bears from the viewing platform at Brook Falls near the main visitor centre, which leads to crowding during the July peak season, but many of the park's vast wilderness areas are rarely visited if you feel like getting away from the masses.

Katmai's diverse landscapes range from the volcanic Valley of Ten Thousand Smokes to endless alpine peaks, fertile coastal plains and complex coastlines of fiords and headlands. This is a great place to observe moose, caribou, wolves, lynxes, wolverines, sea otters, bald eagles and killer whales. Several commercial airlines offer flights into King Salmon from Anchorage, where a short hop on a float plane or boat takes you to Brooks Camp and the park headquarters. This is an expensive trip and needs to be booked as far in advance as possible. **MORE INFO** www.nps.gov/katm

(LEFT) ↗
Alaska's Katmai National Park has some of the world's largest salmon runs, which makes the 2000-strong brown bear population happy and heavy.

(TOP RIGHT) ↗
Ecuador's Tandayapa Valley offers sightings of more than 31 species of hummingbird.

(BOTTOM RIGHT) ↗
Great white shark viewing is a $30 million business in South Africa.

HUMMINGBIRDS ECUADOR

LOCATION Chocó Cloud Forest, 50km west of Quito **WHY NOW?** The dry season makes for easier travelling **LEVEL OF DIFFICULTY** Low to medium – unfortunately, roads allow access to the formerly pristine area, but it's still possible to venture into rugged rainforests **STATUS** The entire ecosystem and its inhabitants are under grave threat from logging

Sadly, it seems like the international attention focused on Ecuador's Galápagos Islands has allowed almost complete destruction of a far more biologically rich ecosystem – the Chocó cloud forests of the Ecuadorian Andes. These wet forests of unsurpassed biodiversity occur only in a narrow band between the high peaks of the Andes and the Pacific Ocean – and more endemic birds occur here than anywhere else in the New World.

One excellent example is the fabulous assortment of hummingbirds found in the Chocó. Just the names of some of these dainty, glowing jewels – sparkling violet-ear, empress brilliant, gorgeted sunangel, booted racket-tail and green-tailed trainbearer – are enough to make you drool for a visit. The Tandayapa Valley may be the easiest place to see these gorgeous creatures, with the hummingbird feeders at the Tandayapa Bird Lodge attracting an astounding 31 species of hummingbird, more than any other location in the world. Other reserves and lodges are scattered around the region, and there's still hope because a dozen Chocó communities in the surrounding province of Esmeraldas have not yet sold their timber to commercial loggers, accounting for 300 sq km of pristine rainforest. Tandayapa is reached off the main paved highway from Quito to Esmeraldas.

MORE INFO www.tandayapa.com

GREAT WHITE SHARKS SOUTH AFRICA

LOCATION 160km east of Cape Town **WHY NOW?** You'll see sharks feeding on young seals **LEVEL OF DIFFICULTY** Low – most of the viewing is down from fishing boats **STATUS** The population is in dire danger from overfishing

People flock to South Africa to see its many terrestrial predators, but the offshore waters are unrivalled for equally spectacular views of another super-predator in action. Here, great white sharks patrol deep waters around massive Cape-fur-seal colonies, where they launch ferocious attacks by accelerating vertically towards fat, subadult seals swimming on the surface, hitting – or missing – their targets with such explosive force that the sharks erupt completely out of the water several metres into the air. These 'predatory breaches' are absolutely stunning to witness.

So many great white sharks are seen here – sometimes 20 to 30 in a day – that the area between False Bay and Mossel Bay, and especially the area around Dyer Island, is considered the Great White Shark Capital of the World. Shark viewing has become a huge business in South Africa, bringing in more than $30 million dollars a year. Most boats put out bait to draw the sharks in for awesome deckside views, while the more courageous observers can descend in shark cages for heart-racing eye-to-eye views of 3m- to 6m-long sharks. In either case you'll find yourself staring straight into the toothy mouth of one of nature's most powerful creatures, an image you're not likely to forget any time soon.

MORE INFO www.whiteshark.co.za

DID YOU KNOW?

Despite their reputation as carnivores, brown bears derive 90% of their food from plant matter such as grasses, roots and berries.

Recent studies have revealed that great white sharks live within a system of intricate social relationships.

↗ JULY

WEEK.03

WHAT YOU'LL SEE

- MOUNTAIN GORILLAS
- CHIMPANZEES
- AFRICAN FOREST ELEPHANTS
- AFRICAN PARADISE FLYCATCHERS
- BLACK BEE-EATERS

BWINDI IMPENETRABLE NATIONAL PARK UGANDA

WHY NOW? The jungle trails are easiest to navigate during the dry season

This aptly named World Heritage Area is a place where isolation, rainfall and 'impenetrable' terrain have ensured preservation of large tracts of untouched rainforest. Very old, complexly layered lowland and montane rainforests are protected here, preserving a rare example of continuous habitats that allows free-ranging movements of its wildlife. The park's 120 species of mammal, including chimpanzees (150 to 250 individuals) plus six other diurnal monkey species – in addition to 251 butterfly species and 360 bird species – make this site home to the richest and most diverse mix of animals in East Africa.

Gorilla tracking is the park's main attraction and it is estimated that half of the world's population of mountain gorillas – some 340 individuals in 23 family units – live in Bwindi. Four groups (Mubare, Habinyanja, Rushegura and Nkuringo) have been

habituated to humans, giving you a nearly 100% chance of successfully tracking and seeing Bwindi's gorillas. These groups move daily and may be as close as 15 minutes from the park entrance, or several hours of hard walking away. Gorillas are usually seen between the park headquarters at 1450m and 2000m, but there can be a lot of steep hills and narrow valleys in between. Park rangers track gorillas each day and note where they sleep; then first thing in the morning guides and guests make a beeline for the nest site and the tracking begins, making for a pretty exciting experience no matter what happens.

Other wildlife – especially birds – is encountered on forest trails and the rainforest itself is magnificent: 200 species of tree, including giant buttressed mahoganies, as well as 105 species of fern and 86 species of orchid. Red-tailed and l'Hoest's monkeys crash through the foliage or scamper across your trail and disappear into a tangle of vines. Keep your eyes open for giant forest hogs, and antelope such as bushbuks or duikers. Expect to see dozens of new bird species each day, including Africa's most elusive bird, the African green broadbill.

Located 514km southwest of Kampala, the park is relatively easy to visit (except for its very rough roads) because gorilla-viewing is so popular that all major tour companies offer Bwindi tours; the tourist infrastructure is good to excellent.

MORE INFO www.uwa.or.ug/bwindi.html

BELUGAS CANADA

LOCATION Somerset Island, 2300km north of Ottawa **WHY NOW?** The belugas concentrate in great numbers at this time of year to moult and rear calves **LEVEL OF DIFFICULTY** Medium – Somerset Island is extremely remote and access requires a long flight **STATUS** The belugas are fairly stable and the population seems healthy

When you first see a beluga it's hard to imagine that this animal is for real. Not only are these 5m-long whales as white as Carrara marble, but they strike such expressive poses that you'd swear they're making faces at you. In fact, belugas are charming and curious animals and it's one of the reasons they are a popular attraction at sea parks around the world. But seeing them in the wild is an altogether different experience, and seeing hundreds of thousands on their summer moulting grounds is simply breathtaking.

Each summer, belugas migrate to traditional moulting and calving sites that they use year after year, nearly always around river mouths where the slightly warmer water is ideal for newborn calves. Adults also take advantage of shallow gravel bars at river mouths to rub old yellowed outer-skin layers off and reveal a fresh coat of pure white skin underneath. This is a very active time for belugas, who make shrill ringing calls heard for miles as they roll around excitedly and splash in the water.

These summer gatherings can be observed at the mouth of Canada's St Lawrence River, where about 1000 belugas can be found, or at the mouth of the Churchill River where there are about 3000. Both of these sites are easily accessed and fairly crowded with sightseers, but real adventurers can travel further north to see belugas in a pristine Arctic setting on the northern edge of Somerset Island. Fly from Ottawa to the Nunavut capital of Iqaluit, then by private plane to Cunningham River.

MORE INFO www.nunavuttourism.com

(LEFT) ↗
Adult beluga whales use the gravel bars at river mouths to exfoliate their old yellow skin, exposing the fresh white skin underneath.

(TOP RIGHT) ↗
The critically endangered Yunnan snub-nosed monkey lives high up in remote conifer forests.

(BOTTOM RIGHT) ↗
Short-tailed shearwaters migrate to Tasmania in Australia for their December breeding season before heading north to Unimak Pass for a feeding frenzy.

YUNNAN SNUB-NOSED MONKEYS CHINA

LOCATION Baima Snow Mountain Reserve, 450km northwest of Kunming, Yunnan **WHY NOW?** It's the season when babies are born **LEVEL OF DIFFICULTY** High – it's hard to find this animal in the exceedingly difficult terrain **STATUS** They are critically endangered

The Yunnan snub-nosed monkey (often called the golden monkey) is one of the world's most enigmatic and poorly known primates. Almost as soon as explorers described this odd monkey in the 1890s, it was lost to the world until being rediscovered in 1962, and even then it remained basically unknown until more detailed studies emerged in the 1990s. It is thought that only 1500 remain in the world in a very narrow range in southwest China and eastern Tibet. Named for their curious pug noses with upturned nostrils, snub-nosed monkeys reside in remote conifer forests from 3000m to 4700m, at the highest elevations of any nonhuman primate.

Feeding almost exclusively on tree lichens, these monkeys live in large, fast-moving troops that roam across extremely steep terrain full of impenetrable bamboo thickets and unremitting cold, damp weather. Finding these monkeys would be one of the hardest wildlife adventures of your life, and in no small part the problem is compounded by incredibly complicated language and logistical barriers in this enormously rugged boundary region around southwestern Yunnan and eastern Tibet. The Baima Snow Mountain Nature Reserve, with 20 peaks over 5000m, may be the easiest option because it's located on the Yunnan–Tibet Highway. Buses can get you there, but launching an expedition into the mountains will be another matter altogether.
MORE INFO www.chinatrekking.com/destinations/yunnan/baimang-snow -mountain

SHORT-TAILED SHEARWATERS USA

LOCATION Unimak Pass, 100km northeast of Unalaska, Alaska, USA **WHY NOW?** Immense numbers gather at this time to feed on krill **LEVEL OF DIFFICULTY** Medium – it can be logistically challenging to get a boat to Unimak Pass **STATUS** They are exceptionally abundant

Wherever the sun goes, so goes the plankton, the krill and then the fish, with predators not far behind – this simple equation explains the long-distance migrations of many marine mammals, including the tens of millions of short-tailed shearwaters that breed in December on small islands off the coast of Tasmania, Australia. Once their breeding season is over, these superabundant seabirds track the sun north towards Alaska's Aleutian Islands, where they gather again in July for one of earth's greatest and least-often observed bird events.

Drawn by phenomenally dense aggregations of krill and herring, shearwaters (along with hundreds of humpback whales that have migrated up from Hawaii) mass up in Unimak Pass, a wide channel that connects the Bering Sea and Pacific Ocean just east of Unalaska Island. The few naturalists who have seen this spectacle report fantastic images of whales lunge-feeding through schools of krill with flocks of millions of shearwaters carpeting the ocean black over many square kilometres. The sound of birds lifting into flight as your boat chugs through the rafts is almost deafening and the entire scene is totally surreal. You don't want to miss this one, but it only lasts a month or so before the shearwaters begin their journey south.
MORE INFO http://unalaska-ak.us

WHAT YOU'LL SEE

- BLACK CAIMANS
- YELLOW ANACONDAS
- JAGUARS
- CAPYBARAS
- HYACINTH MACAWS

PANTANAL NATIONAL PARK
BRAZIL

 **WHY NOW?** Things get crowded when the water levels start to drop at this time Established as a World Heritage Site in 2000, the Pantanal of Brazil, Bolivia, and Paraguay is easily one of the top five places in the world to see wildlife. First of all, from December to March, runoff from seven rivers transforms this 210,000 sq km area into an immensely productive wetland half the size of France. Then, starting in June, the tide literally turns as the waters begin to recede, trapping many of the region's 600 fish species in increasingly smaller ponds, lakes and channels. From July to December, the wildlife viewing is mind-blowing as ever-growing numbers of animals gather around shrinking bodies of water to drink and feed on the huge quantities of trapped fish.

This is when wading birds – 10 species of heron and egret, three species of stork, and six species of ibis and spoonbill – begin nesting in gigantic, noisy colonies that can

cover square kilometres. And almost more impressive is the sight of the region's 20 million black caimans massing around every water hole, reaching densities of 150 caimans per sq km (the highest levels in the world).

Equally drawn to water holes are capybaras, anacondas (reaching up to 7m in length), marsh deer and jaguars; but don't overlook the fact that this entire unique region is fabulously rich in wildlife. What distinguishes the Pantanal ecologically is that it combines elements of central Brazil's *cerrado* savannahs and Paraguay's *chaco* scrublands – along with an endless maze of ponds, lakes, rivers, forests and islands – to create a habitat for 200 species of mammal and 650 species of bird.

Annual flooding mostly saves this area from development and disturbance, and even to this day it remains sparsely populated by very large scattered ranches, *fazendas,* that have grazed cattle here during the dry season for over 200 years. This area is called 'South America's Wild West' and it is still a wild place where pumas, ocelots, maned wolves, giant anteaters and crowned eagles coexist peacefully with light human use.

The best way to approach the Pantanal is along the funky dirt Transpantaneira Road, which dries out in July enough that you can drive (or cycle!) the 150km from Poconé near Cuiabá, south to Porto Jofre on the Rio Cuiabá.

MORE INFO www.pantanal.com

BASKING SHARKS ENGLAND

LOCATION Isle of Man, 120km northwest of Liverpool **WHY NOW?** It's the beginning of the prime viewing season **LEVEL OF DIFFICULTY** Medium – viewing is easy but sightings are unpredictable **STATUS** They've been overfished in the past, and the population is still vulnerable

There was a time when huge summer gatherings of basking sharks were welcomed by the fishermen of Great Britain and Ireland because these giant 2000kg fish yielded a lot of meat and oil. Up to 1800 sharks were killed in a single season as late as 1952, but the fishery collapsed soon after and today they are staging a slow comeback. Fortunately, basking sharks still gather in July and August to feed among plankton swarms on productive sea coasts such as the Isle of Man, where a network of enthusiasts keep an eye out for every sighting.

It's obvious when these 8m- to 13m-long sharks show up because high dorsal fins signal their presence as they swim in slow circles with their massive mouths gaping open, filtering plankton from the water. Whenever they find a particularly productive patch of food they continue circling for several days until the food dissipates. Under ideal conditions, over 100 basking sharks can be seen at any one time, and their slow placid nature allows for extended viewing from the mainland or from boats at close range. It is thought that these highly social fish use these gatherings as a chance to look for mates, and since they have small eyes they sometimes approach boats to see if it might be a potential partner.

MORE INFO www.manxbaskingsharkwatch.com

[LEFT] ↗
Basking sharks gather on productive sea coasts, such as that of the Isle of Man, to feed on plankton.

[TOP RIGHT] ↗
If a wolverine were the size of a bear it would be the strongest creature on earth.

[BOTTOM RIGHT] ↗
The courtship displays of the bird of paradise are the most incredible of any animal.

WOLVERINES FINLAND

LOCATION Lieksa, 550km northeast of Helsinki **WHY NOW?** You can use the 24 hours of daylight to maximise your chances of seeing one **LEVEL OF DIFFICULTY** Medium – you can view them from comfortable blinds but sightings are unpredictable **STATUS** Little is known about the population size but it is probably stable in Finland

Few animals in the Northern Hemisphere are surrounded by as much mystique and legend as the incredibly powerful and fierce wolverine – a creature so nomadic and ornery that each individual requires a home range of 500 to 1500 sq km. It is said that if a wolverine was the size of a bear it would be the strongest creature on earth; even though it is no larger than a mid-sized family dog, a wolverine can single-handedly take down adult caribou, elk or moose.

So many stories abound of the intelligence, ferocity and strength of this formidable predator that it comes as no surprise that seeing wolverines has become a booming business in the self-proclaimed 'Wolverine Capital of the World'. This tradition seems to have originated when bait stations set up for wildlife photographers – who come to Finland for superb photographs of bears, wolves and lynxes – started attracting wolverines too. Around cities like Lieksa, Kuhmo and Oulu, and elsewhere in the country, there are now a wide variety of comfortable wildlife blinds (often complete with camp beds, toilets, heat and high-tech equipment) and a network of folks to help you find every animal you want to see. In most cases, bait stations have been run for years and animals are used to observers.

MORE INFO www.wolverinefoundation.org

BIRDS OF PARADISE PAPUA NEW GUINEA

LOCATION Tari Valley, 600km northwest of Port Moresby **WHY NOW?** There are male courtship displays at the start of the dry season **LEVEL OF DIFFICULTY** High – it's very expensive, dangerous and logistically challenging **STATUS** Very little land in Papua New Guinea is protected from logging interests

Papua New Guinea's birds of paradise are so gorgeous and bizarrely plumaged that early scientists could not believe these birds were for real. In fact, they were named not for their outrageous colours but because the first stuffed specimens that arrived in England were missing their legs, which led to the idea that these birds descended from heaven and lived entirely in the air. However, the reality is no less strange, because these birds are truly amazing in real life and have some of the most incredible courtship displays of any known animal.

Unfortunately, seeing these birds in their native habitat can be difficult. Papua New Guinea is notoriously lawless so most visitors rely on private flights and high-end lodges for safety, while independent travellers take matters into their own hands. Then, even under the best conditions, looking for displaying males can be frustrating and tedious. If this sounds inviting then head for Tari Valley in the Southern Highlands for more types of birds of paradise than any place on earth. Tavi can be reached by road from Mendi or by small chartered plane.

Tavi's 15 species include the blue bird of paradise, which hangs upside-down with its electric blue feathers spread like a tutu, making loud metallic humming sounds. Or the Lawe's parotia, which wears a war bonnet of six wiry plumes on its head and dances on the ground with high steps and a skirt created by its wings.

MORE INFO www.papuabirdclub.com

DID YOU KNOW?

The upper molars of wolverines are turned sideways to help them tear apart frozen meat and crush bones to extract marrow.

The basking shark's massive 1000kg liver is full of low-density oils that help the shark to float effortlessly.

↗ AUGUST

WEEK.01

AÏR & TÉNÉRÉ NATURAL RESERVES NIGER

WHAT YOU'LL SEE

- BARBARY SHEEP
- DORCAS GAZELLES
- FENNEC FOXES
- SAND CATS
- CHEETAHS

↘ **WHY NOW?** You can take advantage of the few rain showers seen all year

The Aïr and Ténéré Natural Reserves of northern Niger protect a fabulously desolate landscape of rugged mountains and immense sand seas considered the finest in the Sahara. At 77,300 sq km, this is the largest – and some might say most spectacular – protected area in all of Africa, and the scale of this place is stunning. Heading northeast from your base camp in Agadez you cross the Aïr Mountains ('eye-ear'), nine granite massifs the size of Switzerland, and travel 500km to reach the vast and stunning dune systems of the Ténéré Desert. It goes without saying that this scorching hot, completely arid region is the stuff of serious expeditions.

Almost overlooked amid this enormous landscape is an unanticipated diversity of wildlife that ekes out a living here. Although many large animals have been killed by poachers and Tuareg nomads who have roamed this desolate place in small numbers

for centuries, the region's sheer inaccessibility has allowed many animals to survive. This includes oddly out-of-place populations of hyenas, cheetahs, baboons and ostriches, remnants of a time when this part of the Sahara was lush and fertile.

More typical of arid rock and sand habitats are fennec foxes, sand cats, Addax antelope and Dorcas gazelles. The elegant scimitar-horned oryx, a true desert specialist, was last seen here in 1983 and may be extinct, but no one knows for sure. Birds are surprisingly abundant, in part because this is the first patch of green they see as they migrate south from the Mediterranean. Many of the 165 bird species are resident breeders in pockets of woodland that grow in slightly wetter mountain canyons and wadis.

If you want to see what happens when it rains here, your best bet is to visit in July or August when an average of 75mm of rain falls on the upper slopes of the Aïr Mountains. This is a gully-washer compared to desert regions further east in the reserve that average a mere 20mm a year, with some areas receiving a few millimetres once every 20 years. Anyone who ventures into the Aïr Mountains and Ténéré Desert is advised to travel in a caravan of 4WD vehicles or camels with local guides from Agadez or Arlit.

MORE INFO www.eoearth.org/article/

MEXICAN FREE-TAILED BATS USA

LOCATION Bracken Cave, 40km northeast of San Antonio, Texas, USA **WHY NOW?** You'll see 20 million bats **LEVEL OF DIFFICULTY** Low – there's easy access to the viewing area **STATUS** It's the world's most abundant bat

Long feared and misunderstood, bats are gaining new-found admiration at a time when they are increasingly threatened by pesticides and human disturbance. Even if you don't go into paroxysms of excitement over their tiny, mouse-like faces and kinetic personalities, expect to be awestruck by the bats of Bracken Cave.

The Mexican free-tailed bats at Bracken Cave form the largest gathering of mammals in the world – an astounding 20 million bats. The cave itself is off-limits because it is a maternity colony where millions of vulnerable new-born pups cling to the walls waiting for their mothers to return from their nightly feeding flights, but each evening at sunset the bats issue forth in a mighty torrent that rushes past you with the sound of wind.

The bats spend the next eight hours eating their weight in insects, with the entire colony eating an estimated 200 metric tonnes of insects each evening. Lactating females increase their food intake two to three times their normal rate, and the insects they gather are mostly agricultural pests collected above nearby fields. Amazingly, when females return to the cave at dawn they manage to find their own pup amid babies packed at up to 2000 per sq metre.

There are at least 10 major maternity caves in Texas, plus other sites like the colony of 1.5 million bats under the Congress Bridge in Austin, where you can sit and eat a picnic dinner on the park green each evening. Bracken Cave is privately owned by Bat Conservation International, but they offer viewing trips for their members and are currently developing a public visitor centre.

MORE INFO www.batcon.org

(LEFT) ↗
Texas is home to a population of 20 million Mexican free-tailed bats.

(TOP RIGHT) ↗
Coconut crabs are the world's largest terrestial crab.

(BOTTOM RIGHT) ↗
The intense colours of the carmine bee-eater are a striking contrast to the blue skies of Botswana.

COCONUT CRABS AUSTRALIA

LOCATION Christmas Island, 360km southwest of Java, Indonesia **WHY NOW?** You can catch the excitement of mating crabs **LEVEL OF DIFFICULTY** Low – they're easily found and observed **STATUS** The crabs are thought to be abundant and stable

These giants among land-living arthropods are a little creepy at close range, though once you get over your initial queasiness you'll find these slow-moving coconut crabs to be fairly gentle and harmless. About the most excited they get is in July and August, the mating season.

Coconut crabs grow to 40cm in length, and have a leg span up to 1m wide, but what you'll notice next are the large front claws. These powerful claws can lift 29kg, but they're used primarily for cracking open coconut husks to get at the juicy contents. You don't want to feel the pinch of these claws on your finger; it hurts a lot and the crab won't let go easily.

Most of the time, coconut crabs roam open forests near the ocean, searching for rotting bananas, coconuts or meat, and wandering down to the ocean to wet their 'gills' in the water. They have an excellent sense of smell and perhaps they use this to find potential partners during the breeding season. Once they cross paths a male and female fight each other, with a successful male flipping the female on her back so they can mate. Coconut crabs are found on islands from Africa eastward to the South Pacific, but they are particularly numerous on Christmas Island.

MORE INFO www.christmas.net.au

CARMINE BEE-EATERS BOTSWANA

LOCATION Okavango Delta, 250km northwest of Maun **WHY NOW?** You can check out the huge nesting colonies **LEVEL OF DIFFICULTY** Medium – getting around the flooded Okavango Delta can be challenging **STATUS** They're common and not threatened

The paradox of Botswana's Okavango Delta is that it floods during the dry season, when the parched land is in greatest need of water, because the waters arrive here after a glacial six-month river journey from Angola. As a result, the Okavango is not only an astoundingly rich inland river delta, but it is also home to over 300,000 large mammals ranging from herds of 3000 buffalo to a total of 35,000 elephants, making it one of the foremost wildlife viewing sites in the world.

It's likely that you'll come to see hippopotamuses swimming in crystal-clear waters, or cheetahs and giraffes tiptoeing around the edge, but one of the surprising memories you'll take home is the sight of carmine bee-eaters at their nesting colonies. These rosy pink birds with blue rumps and foreheads have such intense colour that they sizzle, and the effect when they're nesting by the hundreds or thousands is dazzling. Carmine bee-eaters nest in sand tunnels on steep riverbanks, gathering in noisy, boisterous colonies that can reach 10,000 birds. At times, especially before egg-laying, an entire colony launches into flight and swirls around dramatically. Look for them along the river in the Panhandle area, near the road that heads north towards the Namibia border near Shakawe.

MORE INFO www.okavango-delta.net

DID YOU KNOW?

→ Coconut crabs have breathing organs under their tails that can breathe on land but require occasional re-wetting with sea water.

→ Carmine bee-eaters will use large mammals, humans, moving vehicles or fires as 'beaters' to stir up the insects they eat.

↗ AUGUST
WEEK.02

KRONOTSKY NATURE RESERVE
RUSSIA

WHAT YOU'LL SEE

- BROWN BEARS
- SNOW SHEEP
- SEA OTTERS
- STELLER'S SEA EAGLES
- SALMON

WHY NOW? You'll see bears gathering to feast on salmon

One way to measure the unbelievable biological wealth of the Kamchatka Peninsula is to count the number of plants found here. Despite being covered in snow and ice for most of the year, this subarctic 1250km-long finger of land in Russia's Far East is home to over 1000 species of plant – and where there are a lot of different plants you know you're going to find a lot of animals.

Without a doubt Kamchatka is one of the top places on earth for pristine habitats and abundant wildlife, although only a few thousand tourists a year make it to this remote and little-known region. In fact, scarcely 400,000 people live on the entire 472,000 sq km peninsula, and half of those live in Petropavlovsk, the only major city and the base camp for every expedition on the peninsula. Little disturbed and scarcely explored, this area is instead populated with over 15,000 brown bears, 10,000 snow sheep, 1500

reindeer, wolves, foxes, wolverines and sables, not to mention half of the world's population of massive Steller's sea eagles. Coastal areas are home to nine species of whale, huge seabird colonies and thousands of sea otters.

Visitors to Kamchatka come for one of two reasons: to see the most impressive collection of volcanic features in the world, including the largest active volcano in the northern hemisphere; and to see abundant and remarkably peaceful brown bears feasting on millions of salmon. Fortunately, you can do both at the Kronotsky Nature Reserve, 200km northeast of Petropavlovsk and one of seven huge protected areas that together comprise the UNESCO Kamchatka Volcano Reserve. Explore Kronotsky's famous Valley of Geysers and the 10km-diameter Uzon Caldera. Or check out Yuzhno-Kamchatsky Reserve at the southern tip of the peninsula in August to witness the largest salmon run in the world and hundreds of bears at Kurilskoye Lake.

These unsurpassed wilderness areas remain protected by their inaccessibility, which also makes your journey logistically challenging unless you sign up with a tour company that takes care of paperwork, accommodation and the inevitable helicopter rides to remote locations. Independent travel is possible but requires self-confidence and knowledge of the Russian language and bureaucracy.

MORE INFO www.kamchatkatourism.com

LEOPARDS SRI LANKA

LOCATION Wilpattu National Park, 180km north of Colombo **WHY NOW?** You'll see relaxed and conspicuous leopards **LEVEL OF DIFFICULTY** Medium – if you're travelling independently stock up on supplies beforehand **STATUS** They are well protected in the park but their long-term future is uncertain

Ecotravellers rejoiced when the crown jewel of Sri Lankan parks reopened in 2003 after a 14-year closure due to political unrest. Steeped in ancient history and legend, this 1316 sq km national park is rich with the abundant animals that flock to its 60 'villus' – beautiful, sand-rimmed freshwater lakes in an otherwise dry zone. Everything from 1000kg water buffalo to mouse deer the size of rabbits are attracted to the water, but nothing beats the sight of leopards lazing in the shade of nearby umbrella trees.

There may be no better destination for guaranteed sightings of relaxed leopards, especially in August when you'll see them sprawled on tree limbs or taking a dust bath after wandering down to the water for a drink. This remarkable concentration of leopards greatly increases your chances of observing their interactions, whether you run across males fighting or pairs hanging out together.

You won't get bored while waiting for some leopard action because there are so many animals to watch – sambars, chitals, barking deer, elephants, sloth bears and other felines such as fishing and jungle cats or the endemic rust-spotted cat. The water is also a favourite hang-out spot for painted storks, white ibises, whistling teals and kingfishers, as well as mugger crocodiles, common cobras, Indian pythons and star tortoises.

Visitors can stay in bungalows or campsites in the park, or at nearby hotels, while exploring 240km of (mostly 4WD) roads within the protected area. There are a number of restrictions, however, and you're advised to purchase supplies in advance if you're staying in the park.

MORE INFO www.srilankatourism.org

(LEFT) ↗
Their relatively vast population increases the chance of seeing a leopard in the wild in Sri Lanka.

(TOP RIGHT) ↗
Jersey tiger moths adorn the flora in the Valley of the Butterflies.

(BOTTOM RIGHT) ↗
A battle-scarred male humpback whale protects its kin in the seas around Tonga.

JERSEY TIGER MOTHS GREECE

LOCATION Valley of the Butterflies, 27km southwest of Rhodes City, Rhodes **WHY NOW?** You'll avoid the summer heat with thousands of like-minded moths **LEVEL OF DIFFICULTY** Low – walk among shaded groves along a babbling brook **STATUS** They're common and widespread, although numbers are down at this site

On the sun-backed hillsides of Rhodes there is no better place to escape the heat than among the groves of huge trees in the deep canyon of the Pelekanos River. This lush patch of habitat is called the 'Valley of the Butterflies' because of the million or so Jersey tiger moths that gather each summer. In places they completely carpet tree trunks, boulders and rock walls with a stunning tapestry formed by their deep brown bodies. Their appearance is further accentuated by lovely cream-coloured lines on their forewings, but hidden from view are brilliant ochre-red hindwings that they flash when disturbed.

Jersey tiger moths are a common species, but nowhere do they occur as densely as they do on the Greek island of Rhodes. After eating all winter, tiger moth caterpillars hatch out of their cocoons as adults and wait out the summer's heat before mating in the fall. These adults are born without stomachs so they survive by sitting motionless and living off their fat reserves all summer. Unfortunately, their numbers are declining at this popular site because tourists frequently disturb the moths and make them fly in order to see their pretty orange wings, causing many adults to starve to death.
MORE INFO www.faliraki-info.com/sights/butterflies.htm

DID YOU KNOW?

 Kamchatka's 3528m-high Kronotsky volcano is perfectly symmetrical; some consider it the world's most beautiful volcano.

Between 1945 and 1972, nearly 50,000 humpbacks were killed by the Soviet fleet, but they only reported killing 2700.

HUMPBACK WHALES TONGA

LOCATION 350km north of Nuku'alofa **WHY NOW?** You can snorkel in crystal-clear waters with mothers and calves **LEVEL OF DIFFICULTY** Low – swimming and snorkelling in bathtub-warm water is required **STATUS** They're critically endangered

Southern hemisphere humpback whales, among the friendliest of all whales, suffered tremendous hunting pressure until the 1970s. Even today humpbacks are hunted illegally (confirmed by DNA testing of whale meat available in Japanese markets) and only 500 remain in the once mighty Tongan calving grounds. Given this history, it is remarkable that these gentle 15m-long giants readily approach and trust snorkellers and swimmers in the breathtakingly clear waters off Tonga, making an already incredible experience even more moving.

Humpbacks migrate from Antarctica to Tonga's Vava'u Group to give birth from July to September, when the warm waters are most ideal for their vulnerable young calves. Eight licensed whale-watch operators from Vava'u follow Tongan guidelines in approaching the whales, letting curious whales swim as close as they choose, but not approaching within 30m. Boat operators also bring along underwater microphones so you can hear one of the most complex and beautiful songs produced by any animal. If you'd rather watch from land, try the Toafa Lookout on west Vava'u island.

Amazingly, so few tourists visit Vava'u that you might feel like you're having this experience to yourself. The flip side is that the infrastructure is pretty basic and limited, but if swimming with whales in an unspoiled island paradise is your version of heaven you'll have no problem.
MORE INFO www.tonga-faqs.com

↗ AUGUST
WEEK.03

CAPE CLEAR ISLAND
IRELAND

WHAT YOU'LL SEE

- MANX SHEARWATERS
- GREAT SHEARWATERS
- FULMARS
- KITTIWAKES
- GUILLEMOTS

WHY NOW? You'll catch the peak movement of migrating seabirds

When the bird observatory at Cape Clear Island was established in 1959, this little island off the southwest coast of Ireland already had a reputation as a spot for seeing rare birds that had strayed over from North America or Asia. No one realised at the time that the island would soon become one of the top 'seawatching' sites in the world. This arcane exercise in watching the sea for migrating birds could only have been invented by fanatical birdwatchers, because some of the most stupendous viewing days come when there are gale-force winds with pelting raindrops, and it takes a stiff upper lip to find pleasure in a pastime like this.

But it's not really that bad, and the rewards of a visit to Cape Clear more than make up for any inconvenience experienced along the way. For starters, this utterly enchanting 5km-long island is home to 125 laid-back residents living in splendid

pastoral isolation within sight of mainland Ireland.
Due to the island's diminutive size and overall dearth
of vehicles, it is a pleasure to walk along country
lanes overlooking Roaringwater Bay and the Celtic
Sea.

However, the real reward is the spectacular seabird
migration that peaks in the third week of August as
countless birds from the immense North Atlantic
seabird colonies rush south towards the southern
hemisphere. On peak days, truly amazing counts
of 20,000 Manx shearwaters per hour have been
recorded, and counts of 1600 Cory's shearwaters and
800 great shearwaters per hour have also been noted,
along with a steady stream of razorbills, cormorants,
skuas, puffins, kittiwakes and fulmars.

These numbers do little justice to the incredible
visual energy of this event as birds race by in the fierce
pushing winds. Shearwaters are particularly stunning
to watch because they are fast, powerful fliers that arc
and swoop in the highest winds like three-dimensional
figure-skaters.

A daily ferry from Baltimore, southwest of Cork,
provides access to the island. There are a number
of accommodation options, including a self-catering
hostel at the island's famous bird observatory, plus
a pub, restaurant and a few markets. Bring along
rainproof gear, a foam pad for sitting on and a thermos
for hot drinks.

MORE INFO www.capeclearisland.com

INDIAN WILD ASSES INDIA

LOCATION Wild Ass Wildlife Sanctuary, 110km west of Ahmedabad **WHY NOW?** The stallions fight in the breeding season **LEVEL OF DIFFICULTY** Medium – the hot, shadeless and barren landscape doesn't make this a pleasure cruise **STATUS** They are critically endangered with numerous threats

Few tourists wander westward to the desolate saline clay deserts of India's Gujarat state. Little grows here, and the earth itself is blinding white from the soil's barren salty crust. Known as the Rann of Kutch, this desert floods for about a month during the monsoon season, but the rest of the year it's as dry as the inside of an oven.

This is also the site of India's largest wildlife sanctuary and the world's final refuge for Indian wild asses, a very lovely member of the horse family that once roamed as far west as Afghanistan and Iran. Even in the immense wildness of the 4954 sq km Wild Ass Wildlife Sanctuary, the asses have not fared well due to illegal salt mining, intense overgrazing by domestic livestock and the activities of soldiers on an Indian army base located within the sanctuary. In the 1960s there were just over 300 wild asses remaining but various reports put their current numbers at closer to 3000.

Tall, chestnut-brown and long-legged, these 230kg animals are exceptionally fast runners. Things get pretty exciting during the mating season when males fight viciously over access to fertile females, with combatants rearing up on their hind legs while kicking and biting savagely.

The sanctuary also supports thriving populations of many birds and 33 species of mammal including foxes, desert cats, wolves, blackbucks, nilgais and chinkaras. Visitors often enter the Rann of Kutch from Dasada village, where there is accommodation and you can get jeep excursions into the desert. Ask your driver not to chase the asses because that impacts their survival.

MORE INFO www.gujarattourism.com

(LEFT) ↗
Indian wild asses roam the vast, dry plains of Gujurat's Wild Ass Wildlife Sanctuary.

(TOP RIGHT) ↗
Atlantic puffins feast on the plentiful fish and eels on offer in the north Atlantic.

(BOTTOM RIGHT) ↗
Pollution and overfishing are contributing to the destruction of precious coral reefs.

ATLANTIC PUFFINS ICELAND

LOCATION Westmann Islands (Vestmannaeyjar), 100km southeast of Reykjavik **WHY NOW?** You'll help save 'pufflings' **LEVEL OF DIFFICULTY** Low – you'll be staying in a picturesque Icelandic fishing village **STATUS** They are abundant and not immediately threatened

With their oversized bills and goofy faces, Atlantic puffins are the clowns of the bird world, which explains why they are probably the most photographed of all birds. If you like puffins – and who doesn't? – then there is no better place to find them than Iceland, where about 10 million show up to nest each summer, over half of which descend on the Westmann Islands around the charming town of Heimay.

During the summer, puffins in breeding plumage have bright orange and yellow bills that clash vividly with their smart-looking black-and-white bodies. Pairs nest in underground burrows and if you listen carefully you can hear them make their soft moaning growls under the soil. Walk carefully around colonies so you don't hurt the nests.

Local tradition includes harvesting puffins for food from 1 July to 15 August, but if you show up shortly thereafter you can participate in the 'national sport' of saving baby pufflings as they fly out from their nests for the first time and crash-land into the streets of Heimay. Children launch a Puffin Patrol and roam the streets saving hundreds of pufflings by setting them free over the ocean. There are regular ferries from Porlakshofn on the mainland to Heimay, as well as flights from Reykjavik.

MORE INFO www.visiticeland.com

DID YOU KNOW?

 The puffin's scientific name means 'little friar'; the birds hold their feet together as they fly, giving the appearance of praying.

 When scientists drilled through a reef in Belize they found that over the course of 7000 years the reef had grown 18m deep.

SPAWNING CORAL REEFS CARIBBEAN

LOCATION Pick any tropical island between Florida and South America **WHY NOW?** See coral spawn **LEVEL OF DIFFICULTY** Medium – involves diving at night **STATUS** Seriously threatened

Coral reefs are among the most productive and diverse ecosystems on earth, comparable to tropical rainforests in terms of species richness and density – one Caribbean coral reef study counted 534 species of organism living on a single 5 sq metre plot. Unfortunately, these priceless reefs are dying off at a shocking rate due to pollution and overfishing.

Given the global importance of these habitats, and the countless people who love to dive reefs, it is astounding that the most important aspect of a coral's life was only discovered in the early 1980s when Australian scientists found that, over the space of a few hours on single nights around the full moon, an entire coral reef spawns (releases all of its eggs and sperm into the water). Witnessing a spawn is a haunting and life-changing experience; the water turns milky pink and fish of all sizes have an absolute feeding frenzy.

Spawning events occur on different nights according to the species involved and geographic location, but scientists are beginning to piece together site-specific spawning tables. Use their results to help plan a trip to the Caribbean for the best chance of catching one of these spectacular and rarely observed events. Dive companies in some parts of the Caribbean, such as Bonaire and Curaçao, have even begun offering specialised dives in search of spawning coral.

MORE INFO www.nova.edu/ncri/research/a21/caribbean_coral_spawning_table.pdf

↗ **AUGUST**
WEEK.04

TAMAN NEGARA NATIONAL PARK
MALAYSIA

WHAT YOU'LL SEE

- WHITE-HANDED GIBBONS
- BLACK GIANT SQUIRRELS
- BARKING DEER
- CHANGEABLE HAWK EAGLES
- MALAYSIAN PEACOCK PHEASANTS

WHY NOW? The dry season is when most animals breed

Since 1938 Taman Negara has been the definitive must-see park in Southeast Asia. In fact, Taman Negara simply means 'national park' in the Malay language because it is *the* park. At 4343 sq km, Taman Negara is the largest and finest tract of protected lowland rainforest in Southeast Asia, and one of the top parks in all of Asia.

Taman Negara is well known for its absolutely pristine habitats and full spectrum of native animals, including critically endangered Sumatran rhinos and tigers. Sightings of rhinos and tigers are exceptionally rare, but you are at least likely to see some of the park's 400 elephants or some oddly snouted Malayan tapirs. Part of the park's infrastructure includes a series of hides on stilts that overlook important waterholes and salt licks that give you an excellent chance of spotting unsuspecting wildlife, including muntjacs (barking

deer), seladang (wild oxen), serows, sambars, mouse deer and wild pigs.

When not staring into the dense jungle searching for large mammals, turn your eyes upward to look for monkeys, 1.5kg giant squirrels, yellow-throated martens or a sampling of the park's 360 colourful bird species. You can't help but notice the ponderous and remarkably noisy hornbills, one of the park's most distinctive animals. Another favourite are the ground-loving pittas, especially the stunning garnet pitta with a brilliant mix of red and blue colours. Meanwhile, bird experts seek out the Malaysian rail-babbler, a strange forest-floor bird with no clear taxonomic affinities to other birds.

The rainforests of Taman Negara are extremely rich because they have been growing and evolving without disturbance for over 130 million years. As a result, the diversity of trees is higher than nearly any other site in the world with 240 tree species and hundreds of epiphytes counted on a single 1-hectare plot.

Taman Negara's charm and curse is that it is so popular. It is an excellent introductory park, with numerous accommodation options around the park headquarters and an extensive trail system, but seasoned wildlife observers might prefer one of Malaysia's lesser known parks in order to avoid the crowds. Taman Negara is 300km northeast of Kuala Lumpur and easily reached by train, public bus or private car.

MORE INFO www.tamannegara.org

HIPPOPOTAMUSES TANZANIA

LOCATION Katavi National Park, 40km south of Mpanda **WHY NOW?** The hippos are packed check-to-jowl in tiny mud baths **LEVEL OF DIFFICULTY** Medium – it's off the beaten path **STATUS** The hippos are threatened by illegal upstream damming of the park's main river

If you imagine taking all the hippos you'd see at any famous East African park and cramming them together into a muddy trickle of water that you could almost jump across, you'd have a good sense of what it's like at Katavi National Park during the dry season. The best feature of this scarcely known and rarely visited national park is the series of mud baths along the Katuma River, where Katavi's 4000 hippos pack together like seal colonies during the height of the dry season. There's a lot of action under such crowded conditions, including territorial males engaging in dramatic bloody battles on a daily basis.

Too remote to be included on a typical vacation safari, Tanzania's third-largest park remains unknown despite having what may be the greatest game concentrations in the country. One visitor in 1992 was amazed to discover that he was the 18th party to visit the park in two years, and it's only become slightly busier in a place that feels more like wilderness than a national park. This leaves plenty of room for the park's 20,000 zebras, 17,000 topis, 15,000 buffalo, 4000 giraffes, 200 lions and large herds of impalas, reedbucks, duikers, elands and many other animals.

When combined with adjacent game reserves, the 4500 sq km Katavi National Park is part of an astounding 25,000 sq km natural area of immense importance for wildlife preservation. A number of lodging options are now available within the park, which can be accessed by train or public bus to nearby communities, or by plane to airstrips within the park.

MORE INFO www.katavipark.org

[LEFT] ↗
Katavi National Park in Tanzania has 4000 hippopotamuses, as well as zebras, giraffes, lions and impalas.

[TOP RIGHT] ↗
Storks often build their nests on roofs and chimneys.

[BOTTOM RIGHT] ↗
The resident killer whales in Johnstone Strait live in stable pods and display predicatable seasonal patterns.

WHITE STORKS BULGARIA

LOCATION Black Sea coast, 25km north of Varna **WHY NOW?** You'll catch the stork migration **LEVEL OF DIFFICULTY** Low – it's an easy and inexpensive place to travel **STATUS** They're in high numbers but are facing growing threats

Bulgaria is just being discovered by mainstream birdwatchers more than happy to find a little-known but inexpensive, welcoming country with huge numbers of birds. Explore Bulgaria during the autumn when several hundred thousand pelicans, storks and raptors migrate down the east coast in a narrow band between the Black Sea and the eastern tip of the Balkan Mountains. These migrants, especially expert gliders such as white and black storks, congregate here from all over Europe because this is their best route for migrating south around the eastern end of the Mediterranean Sea.

Upwards of 200,000 white storks, along with 20,000 white pelicans, 10,000 lesser spotted eagles, 20,000 common buzzards and many other birds use this route, with flocks of hundreds or thousands of birds seen per day. White storks are beloved because they nest on roofs and chimneys across Europe and figure in legends about storks bringing newborn babies, but it's another matter altogether to watch several thousand circling overhead at one time.

The sheer 100m-high limestone cliffs of Cape Kaliakra, just outside the seaside town of Albena, provide a spectacular platform for viewing passing birds, although plans to massively develop this site severely threaten the birds. Migration begins in late August and typically peaks during the third week in September, but the location and timing varies each year.

MORE INFO http://bspb.org/index.php

DID YOU KNOW?

White storks are expert gliders but tire when flapping their wings, so they migrate by following rising pockets of hot air (thermals).

The populations of resident and transient killer whales diverged two million years ago and haven't interbred for 100,000 years.

KILLER WHALES CANADA

LOCATION Johnstone Strait, 350km northwest of Victoria, British Columbia **WHY NOW?** The whales arrive to eat migrating salmon **LEVEL OF DIFFICULTY** Medium – getting close-up views involves sea kayaking **STATUS** Numbers are low and declining due to pollution and salmon fishing

From the water-level seat of a sea kayak your first impression of a fast-approaching 7m-long killer whale might range from heart-beating fear to all-out awe, but either way it's an experience you will never forget. Sightings like this are virtually guaranteed in British Columbia's Johnstone Strait, on the northeast shore of Vancouver Island, where the world's greatest concentration of killer whales gathers each summer to feed on migrating salmon. The 200 killer whales that assemble here are called 'residents' but in reality they roam from northern Vancouver Island to southern Alaska along thousands of kilometres of coastline.

Whale-watching, not only for killer whales but also for minke and humpback whales, is now a major draw for the tiny seaside town of Telegraph Cove. Kayakers are welcomed here, and the town even offers long-term parking for boaters taking extended sea camping trips along the coast. Fortunately for observers, the resident killer whales of Johnstone Strait live in large stable pods with fairly predictable seasonal patterns (as opposed to far-ranging transient pods) but even so, finding a pod might entail joining a tour group that is in radio contact with other groups. Most of these resident whales spend their entire lives in the same extended family groups and local naturalist guides will recognise many individual whales.

MORE INFO www.killerwhalecentre.org

↗ SEPTEMBER

WEEK.01

CHANG TANG NATURE RESERVE
TIBET, CHINA

WHAT YOU'LL SEE

- TIBETAN ANTELOPE
- WILD YAKS
- SNOW LEOPARDS
- BAR-HEADED GEESE
- BLACK-NECKED CRANES

↘ **WHY NOW?** Travel is easiest now as the ground starts to freeze again

Perched 4000m to 5000m above sea level in the desolate rain shadow on the north side of the Himalayas, the 700,000 sq km Tibetan Plateau is one of the harshest and least accessible places on earth. About 130,000 hardy, nomadic peoples live on the southern half of the plateau, but the entire northern region sees almost no people, which is not surprising since many areas barely receive 20cm of rain and see below-freezing temperatures for an average of 10 months of the year.

Given these austere, extreme conditions, it is surprising that the plateau is inhabited by a unique community of large mammals once numbering in the millions. Starting in the 1960s, gangs of poachers equipped with jeeps and high-powered rifles wreaked havoc on these wildlife populations, but in the face of impending extinction for several species, the Chinese government has done a remarkable job of setting aside vast

preserves totalling 500,000 sq km and enforcing harsh penalties against poaching, making this once again a potential world-class wildlife destination.

Not only is this place vast and uninhabited on a scale that's hard to comprehend, but some very interesting wildlife live here. At the top of everyone's list is the highly endangered Tibetan antelope (chiru), whose ultra-fine wool is used in making *shahtoosh* scarves valued at $15,000. Tens of thousands of these antelope (once a million) make an annual migration north to high, remote calving grounds, then return south in time for the autumn rut. The plateau is also home to yaks. Thought to be extinct in the wild until they were rediscovered here in the 1980s, their population has now rebounded to around 15,000.

Chang Tang, the largest of five major reserves on the Tibetan Plateau, is also home to Tibetan wild asses (kiang), Tibetan gazelles, Tibetan brown bears, Tibetan argalis, dwarf blue sheep, snow leopards, wolves and lynxes. To the south there are 500 lakes where thousands of birds nest, including rare black-necked cranes, bar-headed geese and brown-headed gulls.

Travel in this region is exceedingly challenging, although there is now a highway from Lhasa to Golmud, and another route across the southern plateau. Snow, mud and river washouts make road travel very difficult and almost every journey requires a major expedition.
MORE INFO www.tew.org

↗ SEPTEMBER
WEEK.01

AFRICAN ELEPHANTS BOTSWANA

LOCATION Chobe National Park, 80km west of Victoria Falls **WHY NOW?** At the peak of the dry season elephants line up along the Chobe River to drink **LEVEL OF DIFFICULTY** Low – it's a popular and well-organised park **STATUS** They are well protected and abundant

At the water holes and riversides of Chobe National Park, African elephants use their bulk to dominate access to precious water during the season when everything dries up. With a population of 60,000 to 120,000 elephants, things get pretty exciting as the dry season reaches its peak in September and October and everything from equally bossy water buffalo to irritated lions tries to crowd in for a drink.

Although Chobe is famous for its fantastic concentrations of elephants, they are a big problem for the park's ecosystems because there are so many that they eat all the foliage and topple trees to get leaves that are otherwise out-of-reach. While the destruction is severe and not attractive, this is still unquestionably the best time to see thousands of elephants lining up along the river each morning and evening. They are exceptionally tolerant of vehicles (but be sure to maintain a respectful distance); the close-up views of elephants interacting, swimming in the river and feeding on riverside trees are unsurpassed.

Another great sighting at Chobe are the hungry lions taking advantage of the daily drinking routine of buffalo by hiding in the vegetation and targeting vulnerable calves as they approach the brush-lined rivers. Choose a riverside viewing location and you might get to see a lion kill. While you're waiting you'll be endlessly entertained by a ceaseless parade of bushbucks, red lechwe, zebras, sables and other antelope.

Chobe National Park has a well-established network of roads and lookout points, while local operators offer river cruises and motorboat hires for a perspective from the Chobe River.

MORE INFO www.botswanatourism.co.bw/attractions/chobe_national_park.html

[LEFT] ↗
Elephants own the waterholes, and their presence makes other herbivores feel safe from predators.

[TOP RIGHT] ↗
Manta rays can measure up to 7.6m wide and weigh 2300kg.

[BOTTOM RIGHT] ↗
The white plumes of the male Wallace's standard-wing are a key component of courtship displays.

MANTA RAYS MALDIVES

LOCATION Lankanfinolhu Faru (Manta Point), North Male' Atoll **WHY NOW?** The water is murky but it's the best time of year for manta rays **LEVEL OF DIFFICULTY** Medium – it's considered an intermediate dive site due to the strong currents **STATUS** They are widespread in the world's tropical oceans but near-threatened

With some research you could find a variety of sites throughout the world's tropical oceans to watch manta rays, but Manta Point just north of the Maldive Islands' capital of Male' is well known for the predictable appearance of mantas at a traditional reef-side 'cleaning station'. This refers to a common manta behaviour in which these 2m- to 3m-wide giants rise up out of the ocean's depths and congregate at a site where wrasses and angelfish gather to swim inside the mantas' gills and all over their bodies to pick off parasites and bits of dead skin.

At Manta Point divers descend about 18m, hold onto rocks in the strong current and wait for mantas to show up for their cleaning sessions. Patience is required, and if you remain still when the mantas arrive and don't try to touch them you may be treated to a half-hour session of incredible close-up manta views. Manta rays are known to reach 7.6m in width and weigh an incredible 2300kg, but few at the Maldives even remotely approach this size.

The Maldives are an expensive and rather limited destination because you are basically required to stay at the private resorts that own almost all the land, but the diving is excellent.

MORE INFO www.visitmaldives.com

WALLACE'S STANDARD-WINGS INDONESIA

LOCATION Aketajawe-Lolobata National Park, 10km east of Dodaga, Halmahera Island **WHY NOW?** You should go at the beginning of the dry season to see their courtship practices **LEVEL OF DIFFICULTY** Medium – the park infrastructure and local guidance available may be minimal **STATUS** They are common but face high levels of habitat loss

The Moluccan Island of Halmahera is an excellent and rarely visited destination for nature-lovers, with its first national park (established in 2004) perhaps the least visited and least known of any park in Indonesia. This is a fantastic site for one of the island's most interesting birds, the Wallace's standard-wing. At first glance the olive-brown standard-wing falls far short of its outrageously coloured bird of paradise kin on the nearby island of New Guinea, but closer inspection reveals a violet crown, iridescent emerald breast and bizarre white plumes that stand high above the bend of the wing on males.

These plumes figure prominently in a spectacular courtship display that occurs when a female approaches a group of as many as 40 males who cooperate to make a cacophony of enticing noises. Upon the female's approach each male leaps 2m to 11m in the air, then descends on spread vibrating wings with his wing-plumes flaring outwards before landing to show off his emerald breast. These lek sites are used year after year so a local guide might help you find this seldom-observed event.

Access the island by flying to Ternate, where the park headquarters may provide additional details on visiting this area that few tourists venture into.

MORE INFO www.indonesia-tourism.com/north-maluku

↗ **SEPTEMBER**

WEEK.02

SHARK BAY WORLD HERITAGE SITE AUSTRALIA

WHAT YOU'LL SEE

- DUGONGS
- BOTTLE-NOSED DOLPHINS
- SEA TURTLES
- TIGER SHARKS
- AUSTRALIAN PELICANS

WHY NOW? In September, dugongs move into nearshore seagrass beds where seeing them is a certainty

Yes, it's true that Western Australia's Shark Bay has sharks, but don't let the name scare you away – Shark Bay is one of the world's great natural wonders. In fact, this UNESCO World Heritage Site is one of only a few sites in the world that meets every one of the program's criteria.

Located 800km north of Western Australia's capital city of Perth, Shark Bay is a shallow 13,500 sq km lagoon fabulously rich in marine resources, including the world's most extensive seagrass beds and countless sea turtles, dolphins and whales. The placid 300kg dugong, a sea creature of mythic proportions that gave rise to mermaid tales, occurs in huge numbers – with 10,000 congregating along the shoreline to give birth in September.

(LEFT) ↖
Shark Bay is rich in
marine life, including
bottlenose dolphins.

Drawn by crystal-clear waters and 320 days of sunshine annually, visitors to Shark Bay might have a hard time deciding what to see first – but given Shark Bay's status as a premier marine mammal location, consider starting your visit with the famous dolphins that come to Monkey Mia to nuzzle visitors and receive snacks from rangers. Standing in shallow surf surrounded by curious dolphins is an experience you'll never forget, and if one visit with the dolphins isn't enough you can volunteer at Monkey Mia and stay for up to two weeks.

Whether you bring your own 4WD or join a 4WD tour, be prepared for a thrill if you travel the rough sandy roads northward to the remote lookouts and beaches of Francois Peron National Park. This is a paradise for wilderness camping and for encounters with rare wildlife including highly endangered western barred bandicoots and boodies, which thrive here because the park has been fenced to keep out non-native foxes and cats. Between August and October many of the region's 700 wildflower species will also be in full bloom, creating an unparalleled riot of colours.

Further south at Hamelin Pool, marvel at one of the region's most significant treasures, a collection of ancient microbial colonies that grow into cauliflower-like columns in shallow salt water. Known as stromatolites, these colonies should not be missed because they are living examples of the first life forms that populated the earth 3.5 billion years ago.

MORE INFO www.sharkbay.org

ELK USA

LOCATION Yellowstone National Park, northwest corner of Wyoming, USA **WHY NOW?** The males are bugling and fighting **LEVEL OF DIFFICULTY** Low – the best viewing is from roadside lay-bys **STATUS** They are common

Autumn is an awesome time to visit Yellowstone National Park, one of the largest and oldest parks in the US. The aspens, maples, huckleberries and serviceberries turn yellow and orange amid the dark green conifer forests, creating a dramatic mix of colours, while early-morning mists hover over frosty meadows as the sun rises through the trees. And best of all, this is the season when the elk are bugling and rutting.

This is an event that the 300kg males have been preparing for all year, eating up to 32kg of food a day in order to grow massive racks of antlers. By mid-August the antlers are at full size and males toughen up their neck muscles by thrashing their antlers against bushes and small trees. The biggest and strongest males soon begin sizing each other up by making shrill strangled 'bugling' calls that ring through the forest and make your hair stand on end. From mid- to late September the males are in full rut – urinating, wallowing in mud and fighting fierce battles with antlers clanging together. Females gather in harems under the protection of the dominant males, but rival males are constantly issuing challenges and stampeding the females. Between the battles, running around and endless bugling it's a very exciting event to watch – just stay clear of the hormone-crazed males because they are quite aggressive.

Most action happens in valley bottoms where protective forests surround riverside meadows. Professional photographers often look first along the stretch of road between the Madison and Norris junctions, but elk are widespread throughout the park.

MORE INFO www.nps.gov/yell

(LEFT) ↗
To grow their huge racks of antlers, bull elk need to consume up to 32kg of food a day.

(TOP RIGHT) ↗
There are 12 species of bat in Gunung Mulu National Park's Deer Cave.

(BOTTOM RIGHT) ↗
African wild dogs compete to be the most submissive, which fosters group cohesion.

WRINKLE-LIPPED BATS MALAYSIAN BORNEO

LOCATION Gunung Mulu National Park, 100km southeast of Miri, Sarawak, Borneo **WHY NOW?** You'll get to see three million bats **LEVEL OF DIFFICULTY** Low – travelling to the park requires a short plane flight or a long boat trip **STATUS** They are potentially threatened by the destruction of their feeding habitats

Scientists were stunned in 1977 when they began exploring the limestone massifs around Gunung Mulu and discovered one record-shattering cave after another. In one cave the Sarawak Chamber was large enough to hold 47 jumbo jets, while the Clearwater Cave was 108km long, and the Deer Cave had the world's largest cave passage and an immense population of bats. When Gunung Mulu National Park was established in 1985 and word leaked out about the astounding nightly exodus of bats from Deer Cave, the site became one of Sarawak's top tourist attractions.

The cave's 12 bat species (the largest variety for a single cave) are estimated to number in the millions, guaranteeing that the observer will be entranced by the ceaseless river of bats that begin pouring from the cave's mouth around 5pm each evening. Dark clouds of bats ascend into the air and spin over your head in giant doughnut-shaped rings in order to confuse hunting bat hawks, while day-flying swiftlets pour back into the cave at the same time. Guided hikes into the cave reveal another sight not for the faint of heart – vast mounds of bat guano covered in so many cockroaches that the mounds look like living seething creatures. Access is from Miri via a 30-minute flight or 12-hour boat ride.

MORE INFO www.mulupark.com

DID YOU KNOW?

Ammonia fumes released by bat guano can be toxic to humans, but Deer Cave is big enough that the fumes have a chance to dissipate.

It might be a sign of their adaptability that wild dogs have been observed on the summit of Mt Kilimanjaro, 5895m above sea level.

AFRICAN WILD DOGS BOTSWANA

LOCATION Moremi Game Reserve, 90km north of Maun **WHY NOW?** The emergence of pups is timed to the dry season **LEVEL OF DIFFICULTY** Medium – the park roads require 4WD and safari preparations **STATUS** They are stable and well protected

The Moremi Game Reserve encompasses many of the most productive portions of one of Africa's top game areas – the massive Okavango Delta of northern Botswana. And it is here that abundant red lechwe (over 30,000) and extremely high densities of impalas contribute to making this the ideal habitat for the African wild dog, Southern Africa's most endangered large carnivore. Not only is this home for one of the largest remaining populations of these highly charismatic dogs, but they have become inured to the constant presence of vehicles and their relative indifference permits rare encounters, including witnessing hunts and watching young pups at den sites.

Pups are born in midwinter to take advantage of peak prey concentrations around water sources, and by September you'll have the chance of watching them make their first playful excursions outside the den. Watch the packs closely and you will discover some of the behaviours that foster group cohesion, including intensely submissive greeting displays in which each individual strives to outdo the others to be the underdog. Cooperation helps these highly social dogs bring down midsized antelope and hold their own against lions, hyenas and leopards at kills. See all this and more from an extensive network of roads and boat trips at Botswana's most diverse and prolific reserve.

MORE INFO www.botswanatourism.co.bw

↗ SEPTEMBER
WEEK.03

LAPLAND
NORTHERN EUROPE

WHAT YOU'LL SEE

REINDEER
WOLVERINES
ARCTIC FOX
WHITE-TAILED EAGLES
GOLDEN EAGLES

WHY NOW? You'll catch the spectacular autumn colours

Lapland is a unique and ambiguously defined area in the northernmost reaches of mainland Europe, encompassing parts of Norway, Sweden, Finland and the northwest corner of Russia. It is understood to be the region inhabited by ethnic Sami (Lapp) people and their reindeer, or everything above the Arctic Circle. However it is defined, this is a remote and little-trodden wilderness with few people.

Throughout Lapland and its numerous national parks and preserves there are large populations of charismatic boreal animals such as wolverines, elk, reindeer, lynxes, arctic foxes and brown bears living among endless vistas of forests, lakes, bogs, glacier-covered mountains and fast-flowing streams.

Travel here in September when the biting insects are gone and you can search for wildlife among the stunning backdrop of autumn colours that Lapland is famous for. Not

only are the forests of birch trees simply breathtaking in their dazzling show of red and orange leaves, but ground-hugging plants are equally colourful too.

In this season most of the migrant breeding birds have left, but there is still a lot of activity as resident animals scurry around fattening up in preparation for the long, harsh winter ahead. Nights are already getting cold but snow won't cover the ground until October.

Some species have faced pressure from heavy hunting until recent decades so they can be skittish and will require careful tracking and observation skills, but so many parts of the landscape are open and exposed that you will have excellent chances of spotting wildlife. Depending on your goals and timeline, you can hire local guides to help you find the rarest animals. Visiting one of the national parks on your own would be fairly easy because of the excellent trail systems and networks of overnight huts, but some parks are remote wilderness areas of the highest calibre and require a lot of expertise and planning.

The Lemmenjoki and Urho Kekkonen National Parks in Finland (www.outdoors.fi) are both huge protected areas with a wide range of habitats and wildlife and excellent autumn colours. Padjelanta and Sarek National Parks in Sweden (ww.naturvardsverket.se/en/In-English) are seldom-visited mountain areas of extreme beauty and challenge. Check out Øvre Pasvik National Park to discover the animals found in the largest virgin pine forest left in Norway.

MORE INFO www.english.dirnat.no

GIANT ANTEATERS BRAZIL

LOCATION Emas National Park, 480km southwest of Brasilia **WHY NOW?** There's a spectacular emergence of flying termites in the first rains **LEVEL OF DIFFICULTY** Medium – the park is remote and rarely visited so it has a limited infrastructure **STATUS** Only 2% of the *cerrado* grasslands are protected

Deep in Brazil's southern highland is a vast, sprawling grassland habitat known as *cerrado*. Few people visit the region or Emas National Park, so maned wolves, greater rheas, peccaries, coatimundis and armadillos roam freely in numbers that aren't found anywhere else in South America. Unlike the Serengeti with its antelope and wildebeests, or the North American prairie with its herds of bison, the grazing niche at Emas is uniquely filled by termites whose 2m- to 3m-tall brick-red mounds are scattered across the plains as far as you can see. There are literally hundreds of thousands of termite mounds over hundreds of square kilometres, providing a boundless food supply for the giant anteater.

Rarely seen elsewhere, giant anteaters are 2m-long with stiff-haired tails and an attractive black sash of colour around their necks and shoulders. They use their long front claws to tear open termite mounds and eat up to 30,000 termites a day with their sticky 60cm-long tongues.

With the first rains in September or October an even more exciting event happens when winged termites emerge from the mounds at night. At this time hundreds of bioluminescent predatory beetle larvae cover each mound, using their lights to attract termites. For a few magical evenings it is possible to wander among termite mounds covered in glowing lights as far as you can see.

Visitors typically drive from Brasilia or Cuiabá, bringing their own food and 4WD vehicles for travelling along grassland tracks. There are few accommodation options at the park headquarters or local ranches.

MORE INFO www.enjoybrazil.net/amazon-brazil-national-park-das-emas.php

[LEFT] ↗
Giant anteaters open up termite mounds with their long claws, consuming up to 30,000 termites a day.

[TOP RIGHT] ↗
Female and young mandrills live in large groups numbering as many as 1350; when females are in oestrus, solitary males arrive and fight for the female's attention.

[BOTTOM RIGHT] ↗
Fifty thousand birds, including barnacle geese, migrate through Estonia each year.

MANDRILLS GABON

LOCATION Lopé National Park, 350km east of Libreville **WHY NOW?** It's the best time to see the widest range of wildlife **LEVEL OF DIFFICULTY** Medium – it's a rigorous jungle environment **STATUS** They are highly threatened by the bushmeat trade and habitat loss

Although widely recognised in popular culture for their extremely colourful faces and rear ends, there is actually little known about mandrills in the wild. Many aspects of their unique social system have been learned about in the past 10 years, and only recently was it discovered that they are not related to baboons as was once believed. Mandrills are actually the largest monkey, and could be considered the most flamboyantly coloured mammal on earth.

Mandrills live in the tropical forests of Gabon, Cameroon and Congo, although they are best known and easiest to see in Lopé. Unlike other primates, females and their young stick together in lively groups that can number up to 1350 individuals. When females go into oestrus, between June and early November, solitary males show up in large numbers, flush with brilliant colour and ready to engage in noisy and fierce bloodied battles for access to the fertile females.

The best way to see mandrills is to join researchers who are radio-tracking mandrills in the park. In September you're likely to have excellent sightings of mandrills, in addition to forest elephants, forest buffalo, sitatungas and red river hogs. Many visitors use the Lopé Hotel as a base camp for game drives into the park, then stay at the Mikongo Camp run by the Zoological Society of London.
MORE INFO www.ecofac.org/Ecotourisme/_EN/Lope/Presentation.htm

WATERFOWL MIGRATION ESTONIA

LOCATION Lahemaa National Park, 50km east of Tallinn **WHY NOW?** You'll catch the peak of the migration **LEVEL OF DIFFICULTY** Low – Estonia is enjoyable and welcoming **STATUS** The waterfowl are not threatened

Once part of the Soviet bloc and largely unknown to the outside world, Estonia is only recently being discovered for the phenomenal migrations of birds that use the country as a key stepping stone on their annual journeys to and from the Arctic. It is now thought that 50 million birds travel through Estonia each year, with vast numbers of birds stopping at sites along Estonia's enchanting coastline of bays, estuaries and 1500 islands. Most tourists head southwest from Tallinn to the famous Matsalu National Park, which attracts 10,000 to 20,000 common cranes and has seven watchtowers for wildlife watching, but why not strike out on your own instead by travelling east to the new Lahemaa National Park on the Parispea Peninsula.

The park is one of the best places to observe migrating Arctic waterfowl in northern Europe, and single day counts have reached 100,000 geese, 250,000 long-tailed ducks and tens of thousands of scaups and scoters. When not staring at the endless streams of waterfowl coming in over the Gulf of Finland, check out nearby bushes and fields for migrating songbirds such as the shore lark, the red-throated pipit and the Lapland bunting (longspur).

Take time to check out as much of the Estonian coast as possible; other incredible sites include the area around the Virtsu Harbour, the bay at Kurressaare and Ristna at the western tip of Hiiumaa Island.
MORE INFO www.lahemaa.ee

↗ SEPTEMBER
WEEK.04

MANU NATIONAL PARK
PERU

WHAT YOU'LL SEE

- SCARLET MACAWS
- ANDEAN COCKS-OF-THE-ROCK
- EMPEROR TAMARINS
- GIANT OTTERS
- ANACONDAS

WHY NOW? Travelling in the dry season is easiest

Manu is awesome; the massive park and biosphere reserve in southeast Peru has the greatest biodiversity of any protected area on earth and its statistics are staggering. The park is home to 1000 bird species, 15% of the world's total, making it the richest bird locality on earth. Biologists have also documented 41,000 species of invertebrate on a 1-hectare plot and 43 species of ant in a single tree. But beyond some of these preliminary numbers, scientists scarcely know how to survey the biodiversity of a site that is so extraordinarily rich.

A visitor will be completely overwhelmed by the ceaseless noise and movement of animals here. The rainforests of Manu pulse with so much life that this place feels like the heartbeat of the planet, and the experience is overwhelming, awe-inspiring and even a little scary. The animals here have never been hunted so many exhibit no fear

as you walk by, and it feels like you've stumbled into paradise on earth.

Whether you are a scientist or a casual visitor, it's difficult to begin describing this incredible place. Peru's 7 million sq km corner of the Amazon basin is the largest area of continuous tropical forest in the world, and Manu is a core 15,350 sq km slice of this immensely important area. This is home to 200 species of mammal, including jaguars, ocelots, giant otters, tapirs, pygmy marmosets and red howler monkeys – all fairly common at Manu, but rare and scarcely encountered anywhere else.

Among many unique animals such as hoatzins, sungrebes, piranhas and electric eels, there are two wildlife events that symbolise Manu. One is the spectacular gathering of hundreds of colourful macaws at riverside clay licks; the other is the courtship display of the flamboyant Andean cock-of-the-rock, an outrageous scarlet-orange bird with a strange helmet-like crest. Both events reach their peak activity around September, making this an excellent month to visit the park.

You can fly from Cuzco to the mouth of the Manu River and take a canoe into the park, but the alternate route is a fantastic and unforgettable two-day drive over the Andes on a single-lane dirt road. A handful of lodges and tour companies can help you explore this incredible area.

MORE INFO www.andeantravelweb.com/peru

HAWK HILL USA

LOCATION Golden Gate National Recreation Area, 4km north of San Francisco, California, USA **WHY NOW?** You'll see upwards of 2000 hawks in a single day **LEVEL OF DIFFICULTY** Low – it'll be the easiest hawk-watching experience of your life **STATUS** They are not threatened

While there are several hundred raptor migration sites in the world, and many with higher numbers of birds, none beat San Francisco's Hawk Hill for sheer ambience and excitement. This world-famous migration site sits atop a 286m-high peak on the north side of San Francisco Bay, with absolutely stunning views of the Golden Gate Bridge, downtown San Francisco and the entire Bay Area. No other raptor migration site in the world is so close to a major city or so accessible to people of all ages and abilities.

Under the leadership of the nonprofit Golden Gate Raptor Observatory, this migration site is monitored daily from late August to early December by a cadre of 280 exceptionally enthusiastic volunteers. Enduring cold winds, numbing fog and blazing sun, teams of volunteers count over 30,000 migrating hawks, eagles and falcons each season. Nineteen species of raptor are seen annually, with upwards of 2000 birds a day possible during peak migration from late September to early October.

Visitors are more than welcome to stop by and participate in the excitement of the count, and on a good day even people who've never watched a bird in their lives get caught up in the thrill as hawk after hawk soars directly overhead, circling and banking dramatically against the incredibly scenic backdrop of the city. Every Saturday and Sunday in September and October volunteers offer daily Hawk Talks and Banding Demonstrations, so you'll not only get a chance to watch migrating raptors but you'll learn about raptor identification, their life history and research being conducted at the site.

MORE INFO www.ggro.org

[LEFT] ↗
San Francisco's Hawk Hill is monitored by 280 volunteers who will count upwards of 30,000 hawks, eagles and falcons during the migration season.

[TOP RIGHT] ↗
In the old city of Harar, hyenas are kept well fed by villagers to prevent attacks on livestock and humans.

[BOTTOM RIGHT] ↗
It's believed that sharks can get enough oxygen without even moving in the Cave of Sleeping Sharks because it has unusually high levels of oxygen and low levels of saline.

SPOTTED HYENAS ETHIOPIA

LOCATION Harar, 500km east of Addis Ababa **WHY NOW?** Go at the end of the rainy season to see greenery and flowers **LEVEL OF DIFFICULTY** Low – the ancient city of Harar is a popular tourist destination **STATUS** Hyenas are vulnerable to persecution outside of the parks

Founded sometime in the 7th century, the ancient city of Harar, Ethiopia, is a glimpse back in time. Along with hundreds of mosques and shrines, and echoes of its cultural flowering in the 16th century, Harar preserves a wildlife tradition not found anywhere else in the world: the feeding of spotted hyenas outside the city gates each night. It is said that this practice started during a time of drought over 100 years ago as a way of satiating hyenas so they would not attack humans and livestock. Today there are only one or two older men who carry on this ritual, but they are training young boys so the practice doesn't die out.

Show up around 7pm to watch the Hyena Man begin calling hyenas out of the shadowy night with his strange high-pitched chanting. One by one, hyena eyes start glowing in the dark until there are about 20 hyenas circling at a distance. They yip and 'laugh' and quarrel as the feeder tosses out chunks of meat and bone, luring in the tamest ones by dangling strips of meat from a stick held in his jaws. It's a savage and dangerous offering, but the Hyena Man trusts the animals completely.

MORE INFO www.selamta.net/harar.htm

DID YOU KNOW?

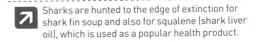

Despite a reputation for cowardice and brute strength, hyenas have intelligence on a par with primates and a complex social system.

Sharks are hunted to the edge of extinction for shark fin soup and also for squalene (shark liver oil), which is used as a popular health product.

CAVE OF THE SLEEPING SHARKS MEXICO

LOCATION Isla Mujeres, 13km east of Cancun **WHY NOW?** You should go after the hurricane season **LEVEL OF DIFFICULTY** Medium – it requires diving to depths of 20m to 30m **STATUS** They are highly threatened by the global fishing industry

It was once thought that sharks had to swim in order to breathe, but in 1969 a local diver from Isla Mujeres, just offshore from Cancun, discovered a cave of 'sleeping sharks'. Further investigations by a National Geographic team in 1972 revealed that Caribbean reef sharks, along with tiger, lemon and blue sharks, come to this unusual cave to 'sleep' for hours at a time. Other research teams later found sleeping sharks in caves at Japan's Izu Oceanic Park, at Costa Rica's Cocos Island, at Bimini in the Bahamas and at a few other sites.

It remains unclear if the sharks are technically sleeping because divers report that the sharks' eyes follow the divers as they swim about – a rather unnerving experience, to say the least. The Cave of Sleeping Sharks at Isla Mujeres has uniquely high levels of oxygen and low levels of saline so it's thought that the sharks get enough oxygen without moving, while the relatively fresh water loosens the grip of saltwater parasites on their skin.

Unfortunately, hurricanes have damaged the reefs somewhat, and it's possible that overfishing has diminished the sharks' food supply because shark numbers have been down in recent years. Finding the best place to see sharks sleeping on top of each other like passed-out drunks may require some up-to-date research.

MORE INFO www.isla-mujeres.net

↗ OCTOBER
WEEK.01

FALKLAND ISLANDS
SOUTH ATLANTIC OCEAN

WHAT YOU'LL SEE

- BLACK-BROWED ALBATROSS
- GENTOO PENGUINS
- KING PENGUINS
- FALKLAND STEAMER DUCKS
- SOUTHERN ELEPHANT SEALS

WHY NOW? It's the beginning of the albatross mating season

These remarkable islands 645km off the coast of South America were visited by Charles Darwin in the 19th century, but have been largely overlooked by naturalists ever since. Today, only 2500 people live on the 778 islands, which cover 12,173 sq km, and 80% of the population lives in the capital city of Stanley, leaving a lot of open space for wildlife. The land is beautiful and wild, and Falklanders are rightly proud of their natural heritage.

Although remote and fairly expensive, the islands are finally gaining the attention of birdwatchers, naturalists and cruise ship tours who come to see endemic birds and large seal and seabird colonies at the confluence of Antarctic and subantarctic waters. This is the most important breeding site in the world for rockhopper penguins, the second most important site for gentoo penguins, and the easiest place in the world to

see king penguins. But the islands are most famous for their immense black-browed albatross colonies, a total of 800,000 birds comprising 80% of the world's population.

The albatross arrive on their breeding grounds in October, with mated pairs from the year before greeting each other ecstatically after a year-long absence. Their subsequent courtship displays are loud and elaborate, as males and females face each other, spread their 2.5m wings, point their bills skyward and moo and bray together. The largest of the 12 albatross colonies is on uninhabited Steeple Jason Island, which is not easily reached, but they can be observed on other islands and they are widespread over the ocean.

October is also an excellent month for seeing new-born southern elephant seals. Intensely hunted in the 19th century, this species is making a slow comeback and over 5000 pups are born each year on the islands now. Two other seal species and about a dozen species of whale are regularly observed or common in these waters.

The Falklands runs an excellent interisland flight service, plus charter boats to numerous wildlife-rich sites along the coast, making it straightforward to see the best localities. No matter where you travel you are likely to see seals, penguins, giant petrels, caracaras and endemic flightless Falkland steamer ducks. Native land birds are best found wherever the dense native tussac grass still survives.

MORE INFO www.visitorfalklands.com

WHITE RHINOCEROSES SOUTH AFRICA

LOCATION Hluhluwe-Umfolozi Game Reserve, 250km northwest of Durban **WHY NOW?** You'll see rhinos buried up to their eyeballs in mud **LEVEL OF DIFFICULTY** Low – the best viewing happens while sitting inside a hide **STATUS** The population is again healthy, but still faces pressure from poaching

Hluhluwe-Umfolozi was set aside with the specific purpose of protecting Africa's tiny relict population of southern white rhinos, an action which saved the species from certain extinction. In the sanctuary of this single location, white rhino numbers have blossomed; from only 25 at the end of the 19th century, there are now over 16,000 in South Africa alone, all of them descended from Hluhluwe-Umfolozi stock. Hluhluwe-Umfolozi itself is home to 1800 of these magnificent creatures – far more than the combined total of all other African countries – and visitors are virtually guaranteed to see some.

Rhinos are more or less evenly distributed throughout the reserve, favouring low-lying wooded grasslands and 'vleis' (seasonally flooded wetlands) rather than the park's many hills and high points. Among the best spots to look are the chain of grassland water holes along the main route from Memorial Gate to Hilltops Camp, while in the dry season a good bet is to set up shop inside the Thiyeni Hide to observe rhinos as they come down to the river to wallow in the mud and scratch up against trees – two activities which play an important role in controlling ticks and other external parasites.

Due to its permanent rivers and high-quality vegetation, this reserve is also home to large populations of giraffes, wildebeests, zebras, impalas and greater kudus, in addition to lions, leopards, elephants, buffalo and both rhino species. Another speciality of the reserve is its three resident packs of African wild dogs, the only protected population in the KwaZulu-Natal province.

MORE INFO www.game-reserve.com/south-africa_hluhluwe-umfolozi.html

(LEFT) ↗
Rhinos don't just wallow in the mud for fun – it also helps them control ticks and external parasites.

(TOP RIGHT) ↗
Kali Gandaki Valley in Nepal helps funnel flocks of demoiselle cranes over the Himalayas during their winter migation.

(BOTTOM RIGHT) ↗
Many of the eggs laid by Olive Ridley sea turtles at Ostional Beach are destroyed by the digging of neighbouring turtles.

DEMOISELLE CRANES NEPAL

LOCATION Kali Gandaki Gorge, 40km northwest of Pokhara **WHY NOW?** You'll catch peak crane migration **LEVEL OF DIFFICULTY** Medium – you can reach the nearest village, Jomsom, via plane or a long trek **STATUS** The demoiselle is the second most abundant crane in the world

The demoiselle crane is a study in grace and beauty, an incredibly elegant blue-grey bird with a plume of white feathers on its head. These statuesque birds breed in remote arid areas of Mongolia, Siberia and China, but in order to reach their Indian wintering grounds they must first cross over the Himalayas on an epic high-altitude journey in which many perish.

If you wish to witness this perilous crossing, head for the Kali Gandaki Valley, a gigantic gorge between the Annapurna and Dhaulagiri massifs (the 10th-highest and 7th-highest mountains in the world) that naturally funnels the cranes over the mountains during the first week of October. It is thought that a majority of the world's demoiselle cranes follow this route, with over 60,000 cranes observed in a 12-day period by one biologist. The setting is particularly spectacular as the exhausted cranes cross snowy peaks and descend into Kali Gandaki, the world's deepest gorge (6800m from the highest peak to the bottom).

The base camp in this region is the village of Jomsom, accessible from Pokhara via small plane. Many Himalayan treks begin here, including expeditions into the ancient kingdom of Mustang, and it is possible to see a wide range of Himalayan birds and mammals while trekking around Jomsom.
MORE INFO www.south-asia.com/Kingmah/tonproj.htm

DID YOU KNOW?

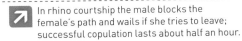

Albatross fly continuously for months or years; in their 70- to 80-year lifetime they fly several million miles.

In rhino courtship the male blocks the female's path and wails if she tries to leave; successful copulation lasts about half an hour.

OLIVE RIDLEY TURTLES COSTA RICA

LOCATION Refugio Nacional de Fauna Silvestre Ostional, 50km southwest of Nicoya **WHY NOW?** The rainy season is your best bet for seeing *la arribada* **LEVEL OF DIFFICULTY** Low – they're easy to see but difficult to predict **STATUS** The turtles are numerous but still endangered

There is no predicting *la arribada*, 'the arrival' of mass numbers of olive ridley turtles on the Pacific coast beaches of Mexico and Central America. After a year at sea, these 36kg sea turtles lumber ashore over the course of several days and nights – 200,000 to 500,000 at a time – to lay their eggs. It starts slowly, a few skittish turtles coming ashore one night, then on successive nights several dozen show up, then the next day at high tide hundreds of thousands suddenly arrive. The peak period occurs around September and October, and is most likely to occur around the first and the last quarter of the moon. If you are lucky enough to witness this event you will never forget the experience of seeing thousands of female turtles simultaneously digging holes and laying eggs.

Famous turtle beaches include Escobilla Beach in Oaxaca and Nancite Beach in Costa Rica, but best of all may be Costa Rica's Ostional Beach, where as many as 500,000 turtles have been counted. It's hard to understand why so many would come ashore at once, especially because a good proportion of the 20 million eggs they lay are destroyed by the digging of neighbouring turtles, but it's a strategy that's worked for 190 million years.
MORE INFO www.costarica-nationalparks.com/ostionalwildliferefuge.html

↗ OCTOBER
WEEK.02

NGORONGORO CRATER
TANZANIA

WHAT YOU'LL SEE

- AFRICAN LIONS
- PLAINS ZEBRAS
- BLACK RHINOS
- HIPPOS
- LESSER FLAMINGOS

↘ **WHY NOW?** Wildlife is concentrated around water holes at the end of the dry season

Located on the eastern Serengeti Plain, the Ngorongoro Crater is one of East Africa's best-known landmarks and most famous wildlife hot spots. It is also the world's largest unbroken caldera (collapsed volcanic cone), with a circular rim perched 600m over the wildlife-rich caldera floor. From viewpoints on the rim you can, if the weather is clear, see right across the 20km-wide crater and identify its main habitat features – the Gorigor Swamp, Lake Magadi, Lerai Forest and the open plains.

Only one major road descends into the crater and one climbs out; both are one way and steep, and a 4WD is compulsory. Access can be impossible in the wet season (especially from April to May), but in the dry season (July to October) there are 120km of roads to explore and the animals are so used to vehicles that they pay no attention

to observers, resulting in fabulous wildlife-watching opportunities.

The crater is believed to have the highest density of predators in Africa and provides one of the best places to see them in action. Lions and spotted hyenas are abundant, totalling around 450 altogether; cheetahs are occasionally seen; and leopards are present, although they are more confined to the forested rim. Scan the plains with binoculars and you can make out columns of the predator's prey animals in the distance – plains zebras, wildebeests, gazelles and buffalo. You'll also spot Masai ostriches, kori bustards, secretary birds and grey-crowned cranes.

The Lerai Forest, rich with fever trees, is the place to look for vervet monkeys, olive baboons, elephants, elands, bushbucks and waterbucks. Nearby shrubby areas are the best places in Tanzania to see otherwise elusive black rhinos – there are about 20 in the crater and you should have little difficulty seeing one or more. East of the Lerai Forest, look for hippos at the Hippo Pool and lesser flamingos at Lake Magadi.

Located 165km west of Arusha, Ngorongoro Crater comprises a mere 3% of the easily overlooked Ngorongoro Conservation Area. Expand your journey outside the crater to see the world-famous Olduvai Gorge or to organise an adventurous trek into the seldom-visited Crater Highlands. From November to April the western part of the Conservation Area hosts Serengeti's massive wildebeest population.

MORE INFO www.ngorongoro-crater-africa.org

RIVER OF RAPTORS MEXICO

LOCATION 30km north of Veracruz City, Veracruz **WHY NOW?** It's the peak of the raptor migration **LEVEL OF DIFFICULTY** Low – they even offer cold beers and shade for the hawk-watchers **STATUS** Raptors are vulnerable to various threats

It is cause for wonder and hope that the greatest raptor migration on earth was only discovered in 1991. And if people can overlook four to six million migrating hawks, imagine how many other great discoveries are yet to be made! In hindsight, this discovery was sitting under everyone's noses because it was well known that virtually all the migrating raptors of North America funnel broadly across the coastal plains of Texas and head south along eastern Mexico's Gulf Coast. Just north of Veracruz City, this wide coastal plain is pinched to a narrow passageway by a spur of the Sierra Madre mountains, and here the small gritty town of Cardel, Veracruz, has become the focus for hawk-watchers all over the world.

So many birds of prey pass over Cardel that the phenomenon has been given the name 'River of Raptors'. Even in a quiet period, more hawks pass over here (an average of 75,000) than other raptor migration sites in the world see during an entire season, but during the peak of the season it is possible to see 150,000 or more hawks per hour, and totals for a day of counting can be half a million to a million birds! There are so many that distant columns of thermalling hawks look like dark thumbprints on the sky, and between each column there are sheets and rivers of hawks like an endless canopy of birds across the entire sky. Public buses can take you to Cardel, then head for the highest building in town, the Bienvenido Hotel. Look for hawk-watchers on the roof.

MORE INFO www.pronaturaveracruz.org

[LEFT] ↗
During peak migration up to 150,000 hawks per hour pass over Cardel.

[TOP RIGHT] ↗
The colourful Augrabies flat lizard scampers over rock faces in the Orange River Gorge.

[BOTTOM RIGHT] ↗
Glow-worms lower strands of sticky mucus from their abdomens to which insects stick, providing a food source.

AUGRABIES FLAT LIZARDS SOUTH AFRICA

LOCATION Augrabies Falls National Park, 130km west of Uppington
WHY NOW? The emerging black flies trigger lizard courtship **LEVEL OF DIFFICULTY** Low – the roads are paved and accessible year-round **STATUS** They are not threatened

Named Aukoerebis, 'the place of great noise', by the indigenous Khoi people, the 56m-high Augrabies Waterfall is a thundering torrent during the rains of January to April, but for the wildlife enthusiast an even more impressive spectacle unfolds during the September-to-October breeding season of the Augrabies (Broadley's) flat lizard. These slender and extremely colourful lizards can't be missed because they scamper up and down sheer rock faces everywhere you look in the Orange River Gorge below the waterfall. In fact, there are so many flat lizards that this is considered the densest population of lizards in the world because they completely cover riverside boulders.

Only the males are draped in colour, with brilliant red, yellow and blue patches designed to show off their status and health to other males and to the plainly attired females. Males are most densely packed and most active along fast-flowing stretches of water where black flies (muggies) emerge from the river by the millions. Here the lizards feed almost constantly, leaping acrobatically into the air to catch passing flies over and over again, leaving the ground with each leap and even making somersaults in midair; it's like watching rainbow-coloured popcorn. Female lizards are attracted to the activity at prime feeding spots. The lizards ignore tourists so you'll see everything at close range.

MORE INFO www.sanparks.org/parks/augrabies

CAVE GLOW-WORMS NEW ZEALAND

LOCATION Waitomo Caves, 160km south of Auckland **WHY NOW?** It's an excellent time of year to see wildflowers too **LEVEL OF DIFFICULTY** Low – it's only accessible on carefully managed tours **STATUS** The caves are stable and well protected

It doesn't feel like you're in a cave when you enter the Glow-worm Grotto in the Waitomo Caves on New Zealand's North Island. The walls and ceiling are covered with thousands of tiny sparkling lights and it's more like standing under a starry sky. Well known to the local Māori people long before it was officially 'discovered' in the late 1800s, this site has been one of New Zealand's most popular attractions for over 100 years.

Glow-worms are the larvae of tiny gnats that have developed a unique strategy for catching insects in the cave's perpetual darkness. From the ceiling they lower 5cm- to 20cm-long silk strands lined with balls of sticky mucus, then wait for flying insects to be drawn to their glowing abdomens. Insects get trapped among the sticky threads and the larvae reel in their prey and eat it, whether it's a stray insect blown into the cave, a newly emerged mayfly from the river below or one of their own adults.

Because the cave environment is a fragile resource, the site is carefully monitored so the crowds of visitors don't alter the cave's temperature, humidity or levels of carbon dioxide. Your 45-minute guided tour of the cave includes a boat ride down the Waitomo River through the Glow-worm Grotto.

MORE INFO www.waitomo.com

DID YOU KNOW?

The colours on flat lizards reflect UV light, with the dominant males glowing more brightly in the eyes of rivals and females.

Glow-worm larvae almost certainly occur in other, less-publicised caves – there are 300 to choose from in the Waitomo region alone.

⬈ OCTOBER
WEEK.03

MADAGASCAR

WHY NOW? You can enjoy mild weather while looking for baby lemurs and breeding birds

Madagascar is the most highly ranked conservation priority in the world, and it's probably true that more conservation projects and dollars are focused on this island than at any other site on earth. Separated from the African mainland more than 160 million years ago, over 75% of the island's 200,000-plus species are endemic to Madagascar. If you exclude birds and bats, 97% of the island's animals are found nowhere else in the world and nearly all of them are threatened or in dire danger of extinction.

When humans arrived 2000 years ago, Madagascar was home to extraordinary, now-extinct creatures including a lemur the size of a gorilla, a pygmy hippo, giant tortoises and a 500kg giant bird. Surviving creatures are no less bizarre, such as the ghoulish aye-aye, the agile cat-like fossa (nicknamed the Madagascar pink panther) or the tenrec (a shrew-hedgehog hybrid). Best known are Madagascar's amazing lemurs – 50 species

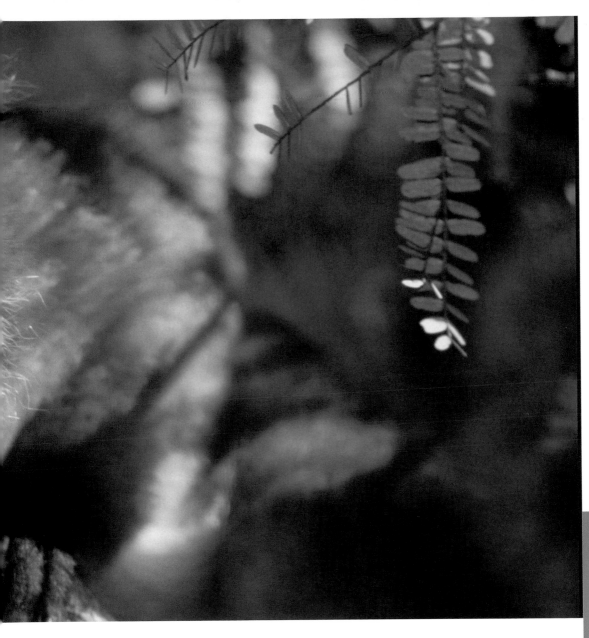

(LEFT) ↖
Madagascar is home
to 51 species of lemur,
including the black
lemur, but most species
are critically threatened.

in all – ranging from dwarf lemurs that weigh 175g, to popular and jaunty ring-tailed lemurs, to giant leaping indri lemurs that weigh 7kg. At least 16 species of lemur are already extinct and nearly all remaining lemurs are critically threatened. The golden bamboo lemur was discovered in 1986 and it's possible other species are yet to be found.

Of Madagascar's 260 species of bird, at least 115 are endemic and five families of birds are found nowhere else in the world. These include some of the world's most endangered raptors – the Madagascar red owl, the Madagascar fish eagle and the Madagascar serpent eagle.

Exploring this novel landscape of rare plants and animals is both fascinating and depressing because vast areas of forest have been converted into highly degraded scrub land and remaining pockets of intact forest are relentlessly whittled away despite strict protection and international attention. From the air, the island's rivers look like they're bleeding the land away because rates of erosion on denuded hillsides is so extreme. If you had to pick one place where your volunteer energy is needed, this might be it (check out www.mwc-info.net/en/information/volunteer2.htm for more info).

There are still a lot of great parks to visit, including areas that have been scarcely explored. Go now and see if you can make a difference.
MORE INFO www.wildmadagascar.org

RED DEER SCOTLAND

LOCATION Isle of Rum, 27km west of Mallaig **WHY NOW?** The males are in full rut **LEVEL OF DIFFICULTY** Medium – it involves walking over rough, wet terrain **STATUS** They are no longer threatened

The Isle of Rum, located in the Inner Hebrides off the northwest coast of Scotland, is best known for its sizable and well-studied population of red deer. This 104 sq km island is rugged and mountainous with sweeping views of the Sea of the Hebrides, and it's a fantastic place to see these impressive deer; when carrying a giant rack of antlers, the males can weigh 240kg. Much of the year red deer roam the island in large, single-sex groups, but this changes in mid-September when the males develop shaggy ruffs, sharpen up their antlers and prepare for battle. There are few sights as majestic as a bull red deer silhouetted against the ocean, roaring with the lust of the breeding season.

The rutting season is a noisy, highly energised time of year. Males rarely eat during the two-month rut, and expend tremendous amounts of energy bellowing at each other, copulating with females in their harems, and battling any other male that challenges their authority. Only males in the prime of their life are up for the effort, and they may only have one good mating season in their life because it is so taxing on their health. In fact, surviving the winter is a huge challenge for these exhausted males.

This beautiful island is owned and managed by the Scottish Natural Heritage, which operates a hostel in the Kinloch Castle where you can stay, unless you want to camp out in the inevitable rain and wind. Ferries travel regularly to the island, but be sure to bring everything you'll need including strong waterproof clothing and stout footwear if you want to explore the island.
MORE INFO www.isleofrum.com

(LEFT) ↗
The red deer mating season is so taxing on the stags that they may only have one good mating season in their prime before their health deteriorates.

(TOP RIGHT) ↗
The Rio Trombetas Biological Reserve is home to around 5000 giant river turtles.

(BOTTOM RIGHT) ↗
The African buffalo communicates using smell and lowing calls, as it has poor eyesight.

GIANT RIVER TURTLES BRAZIL

LOCATION Rio Trombetas Biological Reserve, 250km northwest of Santarém **WHY NOW?** Egg-laying occurs in the dry season **LEVEL OF DIFFICULTY** Medium – seeing the turtles requires exploration of a tropical wilderness with few facilities **STATUS** They are highly threatened but have high reproductive potential

Giant river turtles of the Amazon once numbered in the millions and their annual egg-laying events were one of the foremost wildlife spectacles in South America. Even today, with populations reduced to mere thousands, these egg-laying events are still described as overwhelming and awe-inspiring. Recent attempts to farm turtles commercially with captive-bred adults provide a glimmer of hope for the species, but their last wild stronghold is a 150km stretch of sandy beaches along the Rio Trombetas in the far north of the Amazon Basin, where about 5000 turtles remain.

As big as sea turtles, these 90kg turtles with 1m-long shells are distinguished in having feet instead of flippers and by their long, sideways-bending necks. During the wet season they swim widely among flooded forests, but at the height of the dry season when sandy riverbanks are fully exposed they haul out at night and lay 70 to 80 eggs, with thousands of turtles laying at a time. They are exceedingly skittish while laying and any disturbance ruins their nesting effort, so extreme caution is required during the breeding season. Rangers may keep you away during this time, but turtles are easily viewed basking in the sun by day. You can now fly from Manaus or Belém directly to Porto Trombetas, situated on the southeast edge of the reserve. **MORE INFO** www.worldwildlife.org/wildworld/profiles/terrestrial/nt/nt0173 _full.html

AFRICAN BUFFALO KENYA

LOCATION Masai Mara National Reserve, 270km west of Nairobi **WHY NOW?** The beginning of the rains brings the buffalo together **LEVEL OF DIFFICULTY** Medium – some safari preparation is required **STATUS** They are well protected in the park

Perhaps no other large animal has the African buffalo's reputation: an 850kg bull stands 1.7m tall at the shoulder and can reputedly push around a 4WD. Lone bulls can be extremely dangerous, and even blind or injured buffalo might survive for years because of their size and bellicosity. Fortunately, with the arrival of the rains after mid-October, buffalo on the Masai Mara begin gathering in large herds among abundantly growing grasses. During this time they are pretty inactive and move in docile, grazing herds like their domestic counterparts.

Highly social, buffalo form large nonterritorial herds that can number as many as 1500 (or even higher in especially productive areas) whenever there is enough food to support such large numbers. At this time, cows in oestrus attract the attention of bulls who posture for dominance, circling, pawing the dirt, thrashing bushes and sometimes charging head-on in brief violent clashes that can send males cartwheeling onto their backs. Because they presumably evolved from forest buffalo, their eyesight is poor and much of their communication is done with lowing calls and smells rather than vision.

This greening of the plains after the first rains is a beautiful time to visit Masai Mara. The massive herds of wildebeests, zebras and gazelles are now heading southward towards the Serengeti and there's a lot of excitement everywhere. **MORE INFO** www.maasaimara.com

DID YOU KNOW?

 Madagascar was home to 500kg land birds only 200 years ago; an omelette made from one of their 9kg eggs would feed 150 people.

In the 1800s as many as 48 million giant river turtle eggs were harvested annually from the Amazon Basin.

⬀ OCTOBER
WEEK.04

WHAT YOU'LL SEE

- BLACK WALLAROOS
- SUGAR GLIDERS
- SOUTHERN BOOBOOKS
- LEICHHARDT'S GRASSHOPPERS
- SALTWATER CROCODILES

KAKADU NATIONAL PARK
AUSTRALIA

WHY NOW? The first sprinkles of rain signal the end of the dry season

The Aborigines call this time in northern Australia the Gunumeleng, the time to pack up floodplain campsites and move towards high ground because the violent thunderstorms of the wet season are on their way. The weather is still hot, and increasingly humid, but sprinkles of rain start to soften up the parched earth and the paperbark trees are heavy with strongly scented blossoms. Everywhere you look, the land is gently turning green and trees are full of fruit bats that have come to feed on the tree blossoms.

Kakadu is a large and diverse park, with habitats ranging from rocky plateaus to mangrove salt marshes. On the east it is bounded by a stunning 500km-long sandstone escarpment with waterfalls, deeply cut formations and the world's foremost collection of Aboriginal rock paintings dating back 40,000 years. The centre of the park is

[LEFT] ↖
South Alligator River in
Kakadu National Park
was misnamed by a
19th-century explorer
who didn't recognise
this reptile as being
a crocodile.

dominated by the flat grasslands and floodplains of
the South Alligator River, so named by a 19th-century
explorer who thought the resident crocodiles were
alligators. Billabongs, some of them lasting year-round,
dot the floodplain with pockets of vitally important
water, providing homes for countless water birds and
crocodiles. Woodlands and tropical rainforest fill large
portions of the park and resound with the screeches of
red-collared lorikeet flocks.

As water returns to Kakadu after a seven-month
drought, the land springs back to life. Insects emerge
in great numbers, including the orange-and-blue
Leichhardt's grasshoppers that Aborigines call Alyurr –
the Lightning Man's children – because they presage
the fierce electrical storms that dump masses of water

over the land as the year comes to an end. This is a
great time to be in the park because courting resident
birds are joined by migrant koels and giant channel-
billed cuckoos calling stridently to attract mates.

Head out at night to spotlight for creatures such
as northern quolls and sugar gliders, or birds such
as southern boobooks and barking owls (giving their
wroof-wroof calls). Night walks in escarpment country
could yield rock ringtail possums and northern dibblers;
for easy walking terrain try the Bardedjilidji Sandstone
Walk just below the Border Store.

Kakadu has an excellent visitor centre (Bowali) and
cultural centre, along with campgrounds, resorts,
walking trails and observation hides.
MORE INFO www.environment.gov.au/parks/kakadu

POLAR BEARS CANADA

LOCATION Churchill, 1000km north of Winnipeg, Manitoba **WHY NOW?** The polar bears gather while waiting for ice to form **LEVEL OF DIFFICULTY** Low – it's expensive and remote but easy to reach **STATUS** They are potentially doomed to local extinction due to global warming

Churchill calls itself the 'Polar Bear Capital of the World' for good reason: each year for about six weeks starting in mid-October, over 1000 polar bears gather on the frozen tundra outside of town while waiting for the sea to freeze up. And immediately southwest of town is the 11,475 sq km Wapusk National Park, site of the largest polar bear maternity denning area in the world. All told, there are more polar bears than humans here, so the residents of Churchill shape their lives around keeping an eye out for bears and practising 'bear safe' behaviour.

Polar bears spend the summer wandering along the forest edges and shorelines of Churchill, eating very little and living off their fat reserves in what is called 'walking hibernation'. By late October they are gaunt and lethargic, saving their remaining energy until they can get onto the ice and start hunting seals. This is the season when thousands of tourists descend on Churchill for custom 'tundra buggy' tours that take them out onto the tundra into the midst of waiting bears. At this time the bears are fearless and curious, easily approached by vehicles and allowing fantastic close-up views. The bears seem almost docile but they are actually very hungry and exceedingly dangerous, so the experience of riding in the buggy is like being inside a cage among sharks, although a lot more comfortable. Churchill is reached by plane or train from Winnipeg. Book tours in advance, and check out the Churchill Northern Studies Centre for ecology classes or to volunteer in exchange for room and board.

MORE INFO www.chem.ucla.edu/~alice/explorations/churchill/cindex.html

[LEFT] ↗
Southwest of Churchill in Manitoba, Canada, is the largest polar bear maternity denning area in the world.

[TOP RIGHT] ↗
Spiny lobsters migrate to reefs in single file for 30-50km, touching heads to tails.

[BOTTOM RIGHT] ↗
Described as cat-sized rats, quokkas are most active during the cooler hours of the day.

SPINY LOBSTERS USA

LOCATION Bimini Islands, 79km east of Miami, Florida, USA **WHY NOW?** You'll see an amazing underwater migration **LEVEL OF DIFFICULTY** Medium – it requires some diving skill **STATUS** They are common

Spiny lobsters are best known as a choice, highly popular food item. There are 45 species of spiny lobster around the world, and in some countries they are a commercially significant resource, with record lobsters reaching 1m in length and weighing nearly 12kg. However, one species found on the Bimini Islands – a group of tropical islands that are part of the Bahamas – also has a remarkable behaviour.

Until early autumn, juvenile and young lobsters forage broadly over thousands of square kilometres of 3m- to 10m-deep shallows on the Great Bahama Bank. Sometime from late October to early November, the calm, stable conditions found on the banks are upset by the arrival of autumn storm systems with winds that lower water temperatures and stir up strong swells and sediment. This change triggers the lobsters to line up in long columns and begin a mass movement that lasts several days. What's particularly fascinating about this mass migration of tens of thousands of lobsters is that they line up single-file with each lobster closely touching the lobster in front and behind. They walk like this for 30-50km until they reach the edge of the banks where the shallows drop off into deeper, less disturbed reefs and here they disperse for the winter.

South Bimini is easily reached by small plane from Miami. The main settlement of Alice Town is located on North Bimini and there are numerous dive operations.

MORE INFO www.biminicruisingguide.com

QUOKKAS AUSTRALIA

LOCATION Rottnest Island, 30km west of Perth **WHY NOW?** You'll see babies on their first forays out of their mother's pouch **LEVEL OF DIFFICULTY** Low – they have no fear of humans, which allows for close viewing **STATUS** They are common but still vulnerable because they only live on a few small islands

Described as cat-sized rats by an early explorer, it's no surprise that quokkas gave this island its name Rottnest, the 'rat nest'. Visitors to the island today don't need to be quiet and cautious to experience this unique marsupial – in fact it helps if you are as conspicuous as possible because quokkas will amiably hop over like tiny kangaroos in search of handouts (don't feed them under any circumstances). They are bouncy, inquisitive and have no fear of humans, and it would be hard not to find them adorable and cute.

Unfortunately, their confiding, easy-going nature was their downfall in the face of introduced predators, and as a result they disappeared from their original range, except for a handful of predator-free islands. Luckily for wildlife-watchers, it is almost impossible to escape from quokkas on 'Rotto', where the island's 10,000 quokkas gather around freshwater pools and hide under scrub and roadside bushes waiting to waylay passers-by. They are most active during the cooler hours, sheltering from the midday heat inside the maze of passages they tunnel through dense undergrowth. Rottnest is Western Australia's most popular island getaway, with all the tourist trappings you'd expect, but it's still a perfect place for the whole family.

MORE INFO www.rottnestisland.com

DID YOU KNOW?

Polar bear hairs are actually clear, rather than white, but they appear white when they reflect sunlight, as snow does.

The name Bimini comes from an indigenous Caribbean language and is derived from Bibi (mother) and Mini (waters).

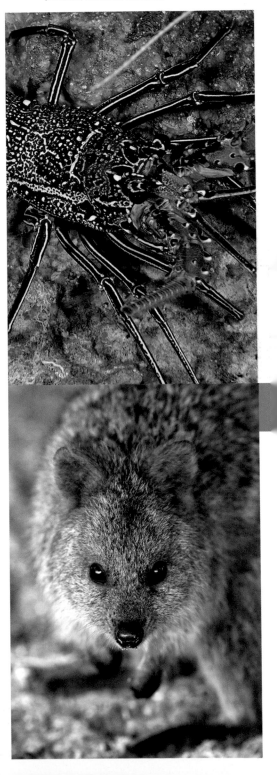

↗ NOVEMBER

WEEK.01

WHAT YOU'LL SEE

- GIANT CLAMS
- MANTA RAYS
- HAWKSBILL TURTLES
- BLACK-TIP REEF SHARKS
- DWARF MINKE WHALES

GREAT BARRIER REEF MARINE PARK AUSTRALIA

WHY NOW? You can try to catch the coral spawn

Stretching 2300km along the Queensland coast, the Great Barrier Reef is the largest network of coral reefs, cays and islands in the world. It is not a single entity, rather a disjointed chain of 2600 individual reefs and 300 coral cays along the edge of eastern Australia's continental shelf, but considered together these individual units form the largest living structure on earth, visible even from the moon.

It is amazing that this massive structure is built by tiny colonial organisms that secrete hard limestone skeletons, and rely on single-celled algae that live in their tissues to photosynthesise and provide them with food. Colonial corals form many fantastic shapes ranging from waving fan corals to treelike staghorn corals, and living among the corals is a phenomenal diversity of animals and plants, from giant whales to micro-organisms. More than 2000 species of fish have been found on the Great Barrier

Reef, with up to 860 living on a single reef, along with 4000 species of mollusc, 300 species of coral and countless invertebrates and plants.

The best way to see the reef is to take a day trip to snorkel or dive at one of dozens of sites commonly visited by boat operators from major centres. One excellent strategy is to snorkel along slowly, focusing on the countless smaller fish and animals and letting the larger animals come to you. Some larger animals seen while snorkelling could include six species of sea turtle, shark and ray. Sea turtles are often encountered, and if you don't chase them they are likely to approach and check you out. Manta rays are common inhabitants of the Outer Reef, and they are often seen flying birdlike through the water as they filter zooplankton.

Dolphins and whales are best seen by boat, with unique and newly recognised dwarf minke whales fairly common in the Far Northern Section, while humpback whales gather in the central reef area every summer to breed.

If you time your visit for the week after the first full moon in November, you have a chance of catching the awesome and rarely seen spawning of the coral reef, a nocturnal event in which all the corals release their eggs and sperm at once.
MORE INFO www.greatbarrierreef.org

BALD EAGLES USA

LOCATION Chilkat River, 125km northwest of Juneau, Alaska, USA **WHY NOW?** See wintering eagles **LEVEL OF DIFFICULTY** Low – there's easy roadside viewing along the Haines Highway **STATUS** Bald eagles are one of North America's great conservation success stories

It's no surprise that bald eagles were chosen as the national symbol for the US. With 2.5m-wingspans, ponderous confident flight, piercing cries and a bold white-headed appearance, they are one of the most majestic birds in North America. Seeing a bald eagle is a memorable experience, especially because their populations plummeted dramatically in the late 20th century and crossing paths with one of these huge raptors was a rarity for many decades.

Now, imagine yourself on the banks of Alaska's Chilkat River on an early November morning. What you're seeing is truly incredible – so many bald eagles perched on the branches of riverside cottonwoods that they look like Christmas tree ornaments. Here is the grandest gathering of bald eagles in North America (often called the 'Bald Eagle Council Grounds'), with up to 3500 birds congregating along one short ice-free stretch of the Chilkat River near Haines, Alaska.

All day long, eagles fly back and forth from perches on riverside trees to gravel bars along the river, alternately resting and feeding on dead and decaying salmon, with sporadic breaks for a little squabbling between neighbours.

From its quirky frontier lifestyle to its dramatic views of North America's longest fiord and soaring snow-covered peaks, Haines offers a taste of everything uniquely Alaskan, not to mention an astounding variety of restaurants, hotels, museums, galleries and even a local microbrewery. You might think the town shuts down in winter but in fact one of its finest events of the year is the annual Alaska Bald Eagle Festival, held in the first week of November. **MORE INFO** www.baldeaglefestival.org

[LEFT] ↗
Up to 3500 bald eagles, America's national bird, will gather on a single ice-free stretch of the Chilkat River in Alaska.

[TOP RIGHT] ↗
Dinoflagellates produce a blue-green flash when disturbed.

[BOTTOM RIGHT] ↗
The Siberian ibex rut creates herds of up to 170 ibexes; the males court the females with various behaviours, including allowing the femles to urinate on the male's face.

BIOLUMINESCENT BAY PUERTO RICO

LOCATION Island of Vieques, 80km southeast of San Juan
WHY NOW? You'll pay off-season prices and get some respite from high temperatures **LEVEL OF DIFFICULTY** Low – visit the bay on boats or kayaks **STATUS** The bay is threatened by light and water pollution

What you see at Bioluminescent Bay (also known as Mosquito Bay) are not the tiny dinoflagellates in the water but the incredible effect they create in their vast numbers. This amazing place is a 'biobay', a partially enclosed lagoon with the perfect set of conditions for cultivating bioluminescent micro-organisms, and the one on Vieques is considered the finest and brightest display left in the world. Sadly, many of the world's biobays have had their delicate ecological balances destroyed by pollution, development or dredging of the lagoon opening, which permanently alters the fragile mix of warm lagoon water and colder ocean water.

The waters of Bioluminescent Bay contain several hundred thousand dinoflagellates per litre, and in response to disturbance each one produces a brilliant blue-green flash. The effect when you swim or kayak in the water is dazzling because your every movement is traced in ethereal light. You can see the show any night of the year but it's particularly fun to visit in the night or two after the full moon because you can play in the bioluminescent water for a while then watch the moon rise over the bay.

Vieques is a 20-minute flight from San Juan, and this small island is worth visiting for a couple days.
MORE INFO www.biobay.com

DID YOU KNOW?

 The dinoflagellate's flash attracts larger predators, which devour small predators that might eat the dinoflagellate.

 Ibexes have 3cm-thick calluses on their knees and webbing between their toes to help them scramble up and down rock faces.

SIBERIAN IBEXES KAZAKHSTAN

LOCATION Aksu-Dzhabagly Nature Reserve, 70km east of Shymkent
WHY NOW? It's the best time to see herds of ibexes and rutting behaviour **LEVEL OF DIFFICULTY** Medium – it's easy to visit but harder in November **STATUS** They're common but vulnerable to poaching

You've probably never heard of Aksu-Dzhabagly but it is the oldest nature reserve in Central Asia, and the first in the world to receive status as a UNESCO biosphere reserve. This rugged mountain area on the borders of Kazakhstan, Uzbekistan and Kyrgyzstan is an absolutely stunning mix of green valleys and alpine peaks with abundant wildlife. It is the only place in Kazakhstan where snow leopards are regularly observed, and you can expect wolves, bears, porcupines, marmots and numerous birds. This is a magnificent setting for observing the autumn rutting behaviour of the Siberian ibex, a 130kg mountain-loving goat with huge sweeping horns.

Ibexes are exquisitely adapted for life on rocky cliffs, where they easily outclimb potential predators that they could not otherwise outrun (you try carrying that rack of horns!). In summer they wander up to 5000m in search of grasses, but with the coming winter they head downslope in preparation for the November rut. At this time of year they bunch up in herds of as many as 170, with males actively courting females by letting a female urinate on their faces, licking her shoulders and uttering screams. Males occasionally face off and crash together with resounding cracks of their horns. Travel here from Shymkent, where you can arrange homestays near the reserve.
MORE INFO www.lonelyplanet.com/kazakhstan/southern-kazakhstan

↗ NOVEMBER
WEEK.02

NAMIBIA

WHAT YOU'LL SEE

- ELEPHANTS
- BLACK RHINOS
- CAPE FUR SEALS
- DAMARA DIK-DIKS
- FLAMINGOS

WHY NOW? There are many dynamic changes as the rains arrive on this parched landscape

What a fascinating time to visit a fascinating country. It's the tail end of a long dry winter and the first rains are on their way; not the heavy drenching rains that occur from January to March, but the first light sprinkles that awaken green grasses, flowers, frogs and insects. Visit in November on the cusp of this incredible transformation: arrive before the rains and you'll find huge numbers of big game animals clustered around remnant water holes; arrive after the rains and you'll find big game starting to disperse into a newly rejuvenated landscape.

Namibia is the driest country in Southern Africa and one of the driest in the world, so it's surprising how much wildlife can be found here. In fact, Etosha National Park is considered one of the best wildlife reserves in the world. Although the park is dominated by the arid Etosha Pan, it is surrounded by sweetgrass plains and mopane woodlands

that sustain large numbers of lions, leopards, elephants and black rhinos, as well as huge gatherings of blue wildebeests, Burchell's zebras, springboks, gemsboks and elands. Water is precious here, especially during the dry season, so a single day at a water hole such as Okaukueujo can reveal literally thousands of animals. These dense concentrations lead to constant interesting behaviours, from mating and fighting among zebras and antelope to predators making a kill.

Also drawn to the first rains, at sites all over Namibia, are a flood of migrating birds, especially waders such as sanderlings, Caspian plovers and marsh sandpipers, plus water birds including storks and herons. As water levels rise on the Etosha Pan, up to a million lesser and greater flamingos arrive and begin nesting.

Similar movements of birds are recorded along the desolate Skeleton Coast National Park and, in November, Cape fur seals at an immense colony at Cape Cross Seal Reserve are giving birth to pups. Between 80,000 and 110,000 fur seals live here in a dense seething mass, and, unlike other seals that huddle together, fur seals vigorously and noisily defend their space, creating a staggering din that never subsides.

Despite the arid and barren nature of much of the landscape, Namibia is a surprisingly welcoming place to travel.

MORE INFO www.namibiatourism.com.na

JAGUARS BRAZIL

LOCATION Pantanal, 75km south of Poconé **WHY NOW?** It's the tail end of the dry season **LEVEL OF DIFFICULTY** Medium – it's not difficult to visit but involves multiple flights, plus land and boat travel **STATUS** The population is stable and well protected in this area

If you've ever wanted to see a jaguar you could do no better than travelling to the Pantanal in Brazil's Mato Grosso State. This vast wetland on the upper waters of the Paraguay River system is fed by the Cuiabá, Taquari and Miranda Rivers, and floods extensively for more than six months of the year. When water levels drop in the dry season jaguars love to sunbathe on riverbanks, where they are relaxed and allow superb viewing from passing boats. In some areas it is not uncommon for visitors to see upwards of 10 jaguars a day, although sightings are by no means guaranteed.

The wildlife-rich Pantanal is thought to shelter the largest jaguar population in the world, and a growing number of cattle ranchers on the Pantanal have opened their ranches to ecotourists and no longer kill jaguars, resulting in higher numbers of these big cats. Almost any boat trip down one of the Pantanal's rivers might reveal a couple of the magnificent 100kg big cats, but your odds improve dramatically if you take advantage of one of the several lodges specialising in viewing jaguars.

MORE INFO www.jaguarreserve.com, www.jaguarresearchcenter.com

[LEFT] ↗
The largest jaguar population in the world can be found at Pantanal in Brazil.

[TOP RIGHT] ↗
The 3500 grey seals at Donna Nook share their space with an RAF bombing range.

[BOTTOM RIGHT] ↗
The highly endangered kagu has no clear affinities with any other living bird.

GREY SEALS ENGLAND

LOCATION Donna Nook, 3km north of North Somercotes **WHY NOW?** It's the peak time to see calving and mating **LEVEL OF DIFFICULTY** Low – it's one of the easiest grey seal colonies to access **STATUS** They are not in danger

The grey seal colony at Donna Nook is unusual in many ways, including the fact that the site is part of an active RAF bombing range, but the seals don't seem to mind as they go about raising their newborn pups. Who knows, maybe the seals feel extra safe here; only half as many pups die here as at a typical breeding colony.

Fifty per cent of the world's grey seals breed on the British Isles, but most of the enormous 'grey seal cities' of breeding seals are found on rugged uninhabited islands in the Hebrides and Orkney. The colony of 3500 seals at Donna Nook, on the east-central coast of England, is unusual in that it is extraordinarily accessible, being located on a gentle sandy beach where people have first hand views of the seal's many behaviours. This is a fantastic place to watch males squabbling over their territories, females giving birth, or active mating just before the females leave for the season in December.

It is amazing that neither seals nor enthusiastic seal-watchers are bothered by the air-force planes. Both the staff of the Royal Air Force and the folks at Lincolnshire Wildlife Trust, who manage the site, work hard to minimise disturbance to the seals during this critical phase of their life cycle.
MORE INFO www.lincstrust.org.uk

KAGUS NEW CALEDONIA

LOCATION Rivière Bleue Provincial Park, 35km east of Nouméa **WHY NOW?** There is a lot of birdsong at the beginning of the rainy season **LEVEL OF DIFFICULTY** Low – the park is a pleasant jaunt from the capital city **STATUS** They are highly endangered as their habitats are cleared for nickel mines

The first thing that puts New Caledonia on the radar for wildlife enthusiasts is the extremely peculiar kagu, which looks like a cross between a heron and a rail but has no clear affinities to any other living bird. Found nowhere else in the world, and scarcely holding on outside of the park due to habitat destruction and introduced predators, the chicken-sized kagu is a stunning silver-grey bird with a towering crest of feathers, huge red eyes and coral-red beak and legs. Everything about the way this bird acts, sounds (it makes very loud yelping barks) and looks is far from ordinary; birdwatchers fly from all over the world to see this singular bird in its final stronghold. Although there may be no more than 500 remaining in the world, you will almost certainly see them at Rivière Bleue, and you may even have them strutting around the picnic grounds while you eat lunch.

But the kagu is only one reason to visit this isolated sliver of land that split off from Australia 85 million years ago. There are 19 other endemic birds to be found in New Caledonia, all but one occurring at Rivière Bleue. Look for the goliath imperial pigeon, the world's largest arboreal pigeon, or for the rare cloven-feathered dove, a green pigeon that appears to be wearing white woolly leggings. And if you love a challenge, there are three species of bird that are considered extinct but have been tentatively sighted and might still exist.
MORE INFO www.newcaledoniatourism-south.com

DID YOU KNOW?

Captive kagus have been observed holding the tip of their wing or tail in their beak and whirling around in circles, but it's unclear why.

The jaguar's powerful bite is thought to be a special adaptation for biting through turtles' shells so they can eat them.

↗ NOVEMBER
WEEK.03

WHAT YOU'LL SEE

- INDIAN RHINOS
- BENGAL TIGERS
- INDIAN ELEPHANTS
- BENGAL FLORICANS
- GANGETIC DOLPHINS

KAZIRANGA NATIONAL PARK
INDIA

WHY NOW? The park typically opens in mid-November as the floodwaters recede

Indian (one-horned) rhinos owe their existence to this vast expanse of riverside forest and grassland that was first set aside in 1905 after the wife of the Viceroy of India visited the area and didn't see a single one of its famous rhinos. At the time there were only a dozen or so left and her forward-thinking action couldn't have come any later. Today, Kaziranga is home to two-thirds of the Indian rhinos in the world (about 1250 live in the park) and the park also boasts the world's greatest density of tigers (86, according to the most recent census).

Kaziranga is a landmark in India's conservation history, and this is due in no small part to the park's staff, many of whom are Mikir people who have coexisted with this ecosystem for centuries, and who are utterly devoted to patrolling the park despite

their low pay and lack of recognition from government authorities. Poachers still kill a few rhinos, but enforcement of local game laws is pretty strict.

Another problem for park animals are the high floodwaters when the Brahmaputra River breaks its banks from May to October. Wildlife survives by retreating to the Miri Hills or the Karbi Plateau, but the 1998 floods drowned 38 rhinos, three elephants, two tigers and many other animals. As the floodwaters retreat, the grasslands that cover over half the park green up and animals happily disperse across the park in November.

For the safety of visitors all wildlife-watching is done from the backs of guided elephants or from jeeps, with observation towers scattered around the park providing other opportunities. All travellers must be accompanied by authorised guides; many tours on offer are booked up in advance so make reservations early.

It may sound like a hassle but this park is well worth the effort. There's something exotic about riding on the back of an elephant through the park's rich matrix of towering elephant grass, marshland and tropical forests, knowing that at any moment you could spot a tiger hiding in the grass or run across a water buffalo, swamp deer, leopard, jungle cat, pangolin or sloth bear. Access Kaziranga by bus from Jorhat, which is reached by regular flights from Delhi or Kolkata.

MORE INFO www.kaziranga-national-park.com

RED CRABS AUSTRALIA

LOCATION Christmas Island, 360km southwest of Java **WHY NOW?** The great crab migration begins soon **LEVEL OF DIFFICULTY** Low – once you get to the island you can't avoid the crabs **STATUS** They are abundant

The annual migration of red crabs on Christmas Island is one of nature's most bizarre events – there's no other word to describe the mass movement of 120 million fluorescent red crabs that completely carpet the landscape. Although the high rainfall (2000mm a year) and high humidity (80% to 90%) on Christmas Island allows these unusual crabs to live year-round on land, they are still tied to water for their reproduction, so once a year they leave their burrows on the forest floor and walk for nine to18 days to reach the ocean.

It's a perilous journey with a million or so crabs dying en route due to heat and dehydration, not to mention the many that are crushed on the island's roads. In fact the crabs pose such a hazard to traffic that there are daily news bulletins about the crabs' movements that are listened to as closely as rush hour updates in Los Angeles. Even though crabs get into every nook and cranny, and enter open houses in great numbers, the island's residents have somehow learned to take it all with a grain of salt.

Males and females mate at the coast, with females holing up for 12 days in burrows until their eggs develop, then at night around the high tide they dash down to the water and shake their eggs into the ocean, where the larval crabs remain until they are 5mm long and begin their own miniature migration back onto the island. Much of this activity happens from mid-November to mid-December, with their migration tied to the last quarter of the moon. Check prior to visiting for updates.

MORE INFO www.christmas.net.au

[LEFT] ↗
Up to a million red crabs die each year on Christmas Island during their annual migration to the ocean.

[TOP RIGHT] ↗
The fruiting trees in Kasanka National Park attract straw-coloured fruit bats every November and December.

[BOTTOM RIGHT] ↗
Destruction of the forest habitats of the golden lion tamarin are endangering the population.

STRAW-COLOURED FRUIT BATS ZAMBIA

LOCATION Kasanka National Park, 520km northwest of Lusaka
WHY NOW? There are huge numbers of bats during the fruiting season
LEVEL OF DIFFICULTY Low – this private park seems particularly inviting
STATUS They will remain stable unless feeding areas are deforested

It's funny how some of the greatest wildlife spectacles on earth go unnoticed for years, and this is certainly the case with the recent discovery of straw-coloured fruit bats in central Zambia's little-known Kasanka National Park. These large (80cm wingspan) bats of equatorial Africa migrate great distances in search of fruiting trees, a journey that brings them to Kasanka every November and December, coinciding with peak production of musuku fruit. An estimated five million fruit bats gather here on a single hectare of swamp forest, with so many roosting at once that large tree branches are known to break under their combined weight.

Each evening at sunset the entire roost lifts off, and for a solid 25 minutes observers at the park's Fibwe Hide will be treated to the unforgettable image of giant bats spreading across the sky as far as they can see in all directions. Fruit bats spend the night flying over many square kilometres eating fruits and spitting out seeds everywhere they go, playing an ecologically significant role as seed-dispersers for these trees. During the day, bats can be watched as they huddle many deep on tree trunks and branches. Fortunately, Kasanka has built its fame around protecting these bats and the park has a very active volunteer program.

MORE INFO www.kasanka.com

GOLDEN LION TAMARINS BRAZIL

LOCATION Poço das Antas Biological Reserve, 100km northeast of Rio de Janeiro **WHY NOW?** It's the season when you might see babies **LEVEL OF DIFFICULTY** Medium – you can see them with reserve biologists **STATUS** They are endangered but are hovering on the edge of being critically so

Although the stunning golden lion tamarin, a diminutive primate with flaming reddish orange hair and flamboyant mane, has become a source of pride and a symbol of conservation in Brazil, its forested habitats are still being cut at an alarming rate. Even with international and local attention, over 5000 sq km of intact Atlantic forest was cut between 1985 and 1990 alone, further reducing one of the world's most threatened high-priority habitats. Poço das Antas Biological Reserve was set aside in the 1990s when it was realised how critically endangered the lion tamarin was becoming.

Golden lion tamarins live in small groups among tangled vines in the forest canopy, where they are safe from predators and find fruits and small animals to eat. Only the dominant female gives birth each year, but all the males in the group cooperate to take care of the youngsters. Most births occur from September to March. Amazingly, even though there are only 1000 golden lion tamarins left in the wild, they are doing very well compared to the black lion tamarin, which was feared extinct until rediscovered in 1970, or in comparison to the black-faced lion tamarin, which was discovered in 1990 and is down to 260 individuals.

MORE INFO www.micoleao.org.br

↗ NOVEMBER

WEEK.04

WHAT YOU'LL SEE

- KING PENGUINS
- MACARONI PENGUINS
- WANDERING ALBATROSS
- SOUTHERN ELEPHANT SEALS
- ANTARCTIC FUR SEALS

SOUTH GEORGIA ISLAND
SOUTH ATLANTIC OCEAN

WHY NOW? It's the beginning of one of the most fabulous wildlife gatherings on earth

Plunked down in the vastness of the South Atlantic, some 2150km off the southern tip of South America, South Georgia Island is one of the world's loneliest and most challenging outposts. Buffeted by fierce, unpredictable subantarctic storms and thrashed by choppy seas, this rugged island is difficult to visit and receives few visitors. Fortunately (for wildlife enthusiasts at least), it is increasingly being added to the itineraries of specialised cruise ship tours, bringing this remote destination within reach of anyone willing to pay the price.

South Georgia Island holds a special mystique for the sheer size of its wildlife populations and for the ethereal beauty of the island's towering cliffs and snow-capped mountains rising majestically out of crashing waves. Located at the edge of the

Antarctic Convergence, a phenomenally productive upwelling of nutrients, this is one of the Antarctic region's premier destinations for millions of breeding seabirds and marine mammals. You might come for the 400,000 nesting king penguins and not even realise that three to five million macaroni penguins raise their chicks here as well, or that the island is also home for two million white-chinned petrels, four million common diving-petrels and 22 million Antarctic prions. Add in vast numbers of another dozen seabirds, plus 300,000 southern elephant seals and three million Antarctic fur seals, and what you end up with could be the greatest concentration of wildlife in the world. The density in some areas has been measured at one bird or seal for every 1.5 sq metres.

Visitors are not allowed to stay on the island due to highly unpredictable weather, but even on a short shore visit it's possible to sense the incredible energy among these vast aggregations of nesting birds and calving seals. Without a doubt the two show-stoppers are the king penguins and the wandering albatross. King penguins are the second-largest and most beautiful of all penguins, with stunning burnt orange cheek patches that the male flashes at the female as he struts gracefully before her to win her love. Wandering albatross are one of the world's great birds and half of their total population nests here starting in mid-November, when they fly in on their 3.5m wingspans to perform their own elaborate courtship displays.
MORE INFO www.sgisland.gs

BIGHORN SHEEP USA

LOCATION Whiskey Mountain, 15km southeast of Dubois, Wyoming, USA **WHY NOW?** The rams are in full battle **LEVEL OF DIFFICULTY** Medium – seeing them is easy but may involve some hiking in cold and snow **STATUS** This population has dwindled dramatically in the past decade

Bighorn sheep are one of the most majestic and iconic large mammals in North America. These stocky sheep live on remote mountain slopes and remain wary of humans because relentless persecution brought them from a historic high of two million down to a few thousand around 1900. In modern times Wyoming's Whiskey Mountain has been the site of the largest remaining wintering herd in the country. This herd, numbering over 1400 in the 1990s but now only half that due to disease and predators, has been a major tourist attraction and the source population for dozens of transplants to five other western states.

Seeing a bighorn sheep in the wild mountain wildernesses of western Wyoming is a thrill, and it's especially exciting to show up in November when the sounds of 200kg males squaring off and fighting for dominance echo like gunshots through the hills. Sporting massive curled horns that can weigh up to 14kg, males first back up, then stand on their hind legs and crash into each other head-first with a combined speed of 80kph to 100kph. Rams have been observed ramming each other like this for 20 hours straight, over and over again until one gives up. You would think this hurts, but the males have double layers of bone in their skull with a spongy layer in between acting as a shock absorber.

You'll find them along the upper reaches of the Trail Lake Road, which starts a few kilometres east of Dubois. Check for details at the Bighorn Sheep Interpretative Center.
MORE INFO www.bighorn.org

(LEFT) ↗
The population of bighorn sheep on Whiskey Mountain has suffered the effects of predation and disease.

(TOP RIGHT) ↗
The critically endangered goliath bullfrog weighs around 3.3kg and measures 30cm in length.

(BOTTOM RIGHT) ↗
The Mt Moreland Reedbeds in South Africa attract up to 8% of Europe's barn swallows during the Northern Hemisphere winter.

GOLIATH BULLFROGS EQUATORIAL GUINEA

LOCATION Monte Alen National Park, 60km east of Bata **WHY NOW?** It's the beginning of the short dry season, which lasts until February **LEVEL OF DIFFICULTY** Medium – you can expect malarial mosquitoes and little tourist infrastructure **STATUS** They are critically endangered and could soon bcome extinct

Now here is a real adventure plan: travel to one of the least known areas in Africa in search of the world's largest frog, of which even less is known. With populations plummeting by 50% between 1989 and 2004, and expected to fall even faster in the near future, the 3.3kg goliath bullfrog is destined for extinction. These 30cm-long frogs were once found in the coastal mountains of Cameroon and Equatorial Guinea, but there are now few known sites where they can still be found.

One place is the fast-flowing rivers in the outstanding Monte Alen National Park, considered one of the finest but most underrated parks in Africa. Although illegal hunting for the bushmeat trade is occurring on a staggering scale, it is still one of the top places in Central Africa for forest elephants, lowland gorillas, mandrills, leopards and other large animals. A survey in 2005 discovered that this park had the highest levels of tree diversity in the Congo Basin and is one of the epicentres for plant diversity in all of Africa, yet nearby logging is quickly turning the park into an isolated island of habitat. Hiking is considered strenuous but top-notch. Bring your own food and supplies from Bata; there is simple accommodation in the park.
MORE INFO www.ecofac.org/Ecotourisme/_EN/MonteAlen/Presentation.htm

BARN SWALLOWS SOUTH AFRICA

LOCATION Mt Moreland Reedbed, 30km north of Durban **WHY NOW?** You'll see a huge nonbreeding roost **LEVEL OF DIFFICULTY** Low – it's on easily reached and popular site **STATUS** They are not threatened globally

In a country of star-studded big-game parks, it's surprising that one of the most stunning wildlife attractions involves the humble barn swallow. Even though there are 74 species of swallow in the world, this small shimmering blue bird is so familiar and highly regarded that it is simply called the swallow in Europe, or the barn swallow or house swallow because it lives in constant close association with humans. During the northern hemisphere winter swallows head south to warmer climes, and in South Africa's KwaZulu-Natal province 8% of Europe's barn swallows gather each evening to sleep in the Mt Moreland Reedbeds.

Tourists and sightseers from all over the world come to witness the phenomenal congregation of swallows in these marshlands at the edge of La Mercy Airport. For about 45 minutes, a staggering five million swallows circle and swoop over the marshes while catching their last insects of the day and waiting until the time is right to descend en masse and settle among the protective reeds, where they are safe from predators at night. The conversion of this small airport into the new King Shaka International Airport for the 2010 World Cup is controversial because it could impact this massive roost site despite mitigation efforts.
MORE INFO www.kzn.org.za

DID YOU KNOW?

Bighorn sheep crossed the Bering land bridge from Siberia about 750,000 years ago, then wandered south to northern Mexico.

Goliath frog tadpoles are not much bigger than other frog tadpoles, but grow enormously fast when they are two months old.

↗ **DECEMBER**

WEEK.01

KANGAROO ISLAND
AUSTRALIA

WHAT YOU'LL SEE

- NEW ZEALAND FUR SEALS
- KOALAS
- COMMON BRUSHTAIL POSSUMS
- GLOSSY BLACK COCKATOOS
- CAPE BARREN GEESE

WHY NOW? You can see young fur seals and northern hemisphere migrants

Skirted by high cliffs and sculpted dunes, the tilted plateau that is Kangaroo Island (Australia's third-largest island) offers some of the best wildlife-watching in Australia. Over half the original native mallee, heath and woodland remains, while 30% of the island is protected in 21 parks, including Flinders Chase National Park. Most importantly, there are no foxes or dingoes to prey on, nor introduced rabbits to compete with, native wildlife. As a result, the abundant wildlife on Kangaroo Island is striking when compared to the mainland. Unique subspecies and several rare species also thrive on this isolated island.

For many visitors, the island's most famous residents are its fur seals and sea lions. New Zealand fur seals rest at Admirals Arch, one of their 'haul-outs' to which they retire between feeding trips. There are 6000 or so fur seals living and breeding here and

at Cape du Couedic. While most lie prostrate in the sunshine, scuffles break out continuously and there are always seals heading into the surf to frolic, or weaving through the colony in search of a place to sprawl. Check out Seal Bay Conservation Park on the south shore for the world's only known colony of Australian sea lions that can be seen at close range.

Koalas, platypuses and ringtail possums have been introduced to the island, and in Flinders Chase the koalas are doing so well they're overgrazing some areas. Wildlife enthusiasts are more likely to get excited about the local subspecies of tammar wallabies, western grey kangaroos, the endemic dunnart, or the rarely encountered western pygmy-possums and southern brown bandicoots.

Enticing birds living on the island include Cape Barren geese (once nearly extinct) on the south coast and endangered bush stone-curlews that cry loudly from the forests at night. Western River Conservation Park is a good place to start looking for the local subspecies of the endangered glossy black cockatoo. Fewer than 300 of these hollow-dependent birds exist on the island. As you walk through stands of she-oaks, listen for crunching sounds overhead as cockatoos crack open cones and drop fragments to the ground while they eat the seeds.

There are numerous tour operators and starting points for exploring this wildlife-rich island and its many protected areas.

MORE INFO www.tourkangarooisland.com.au

LESSER FLAMINGOS KENYA

LOCATION Lake Bogoria National Reserve, 38km north of Nakuru **WHY NOW?** It's your best chance of seeing one to two million flamingos **LEVEL OF DIFFICULTY** Low – it's a short drive from a major city **STATUS** They are superficially numerous but the population hangs by a fragile thread

The great lakes of East Africa's Rift Valley run like a string of pearls from Lake Natron in Tanzania to Lake Turkana in northern Kenya. Some lakes, such as Nakuru, Bogoria, Natron and Magadi, are high in minerals that promote algae and tiny crustaceans but create a hostile environment for fish and other aquatic life. These conditions favour a few specialised species but what these saline (also called alkaline or soda) lakes lack in diversity, they more than make up for in sheer numbers.

Nothing symbolises this unique ecological balance better than jaw-dropping views of one to two million flamingos ringing Lake Bogoria's shoreline. This shimmering carpet of pink flamingos, all striding and moving with the grace of ballerinas, creates one of East Africa's most unforgettable images. Most are lesser flamingos, with their dazzling red legs, and there's a scattering of taller greater flamingos with pale pink or whitish legs. Both types of flamingo survive by straining algae and crustaceans out of the water with sievelike edges on their bills, but they have different-sized 'sieves', so they don't compete for food. Flamingos occasionally move between lakes to seek out the most productive spots because conditions vary from year to year.

The reserve was originally established in 1981 to protect 200 to 250 greater kudus found in the surrounding woodlands, but the vast flocks of flamingos that were then living at Lake Nakuru decided they liked Bogoria better and took advantage of this newly protected area. Access to the southern end of the lake requires a 4WD, but you can view the northern part from a sealed road.

MORE INFO www.magicalkenya.com

(LEFT) ↗
Lesser flamingos have red legs, while greater flamingos have pale pink or whitish legs.

(TOP RIGHT) ↗
Cocos Island National Park has the largest schools of scalloped hammerheads in the world; they are largely made up of females.

(BOTTOM RIGHT) ↗
Each dominant male proboscis monkey has a harem of up to eight females and their young.

SCALLOPED HAMMERHEADS COSTA RICA

LOCATION Cocos Island National Park, 500km southwest of Costa Rica **WHY NOW?** You'll see hundreds of hammerhead sharks **LEVEL OF DIFFICULTY** Medium – it requires a long boat trip and advanced diving skills **STATUS** They are near-threatened and declining rapidly

There seems to be no end to the accolades for Cocos Island. The famous oceanographer Jacques Cousteau called it 'the most beautiful island in the world', the Professional Association of Diving Instructors ranks it among the top 10 diving spots in the world, and in January 2009 it was short-listed as a candidate to be one of the new 'Seven Natural Wonders of the World'. There are many reasons to visit Cocos, from its notable geology to its unique flora and fauna, but most visitors make the very long trip to the island for the breathtaking diving among countless sharks, dolphins, manta rays, tuna and numerous other marine species.

Here you get a sense of the earth's original abundance when you see 500 scalloped hammerheads schooling together in the serene blue waters at the edge of the island's seamount. These schools are the largest gatherings of hammerhead sharks in the world, and they mostly consist of females. Males wander into the schools to seek out the dominant females who occupy the centre of these colossal groups. Sadly, this outstanding event is highly threatened by illegal shark fishing that has gone largely unchecked.

There are trails on the island but no accommodation options, so visitors must stay on their boats at night.
MORE INFO www.costarica-nationalparks.com

PROBOSCIS MONKEYS MALAYSIAN BORNEO

LOCATION Bako National Park, Sarawak, 37km northeast of Kuching **WHY NOW?** The climate is constant year-round so any time is good **LEVEL OF DIFFICULTY** Low – it's an excellent park for first-time visitors **STATUS** They are endangered and the population is declining sharply

The first time you observe proboscis monkeys you'll have one of several strong reactions: you'll find them either ridiculous, grotesque or endearing. The male's giant pendulous nose and huge pot belly make this one of the oddest animals you'll ever see. Scientists aren't sure what function the 'nose' serves (perhaps it adds to the male's sexual charm), but the pot belly contains a large multichambered stomach full of bacteria to help the monkeys process the tough leaves they eat.

Proboscis monkeys live only in mangrove and riverside forests in the lowlands of Borneo; there are no more than 7000 left and they're under great threat from habitat destruction. At night they sleep in riverside trees but move to adjacent mangrove forests during the day, readily leaping 10m between trees, swimming across channels or walking upright across mudflats as they travel. Groups consist of a dominant male with his harem of up to eight females and their babies. They communicate with a broad range of roars, grunts, groans, squeals and honks and are especially noisy during courtship and territorial disputes.

The best place to see them is at Bako National Park, which has an excellent trail system and where the animals are relatively tame because they've been protected here since 1957.
MORE INFO www.forestry.sarawak.gov.my/forweb/np/np/bako.htm

DID YOU KNOW?

 A hammerhead's eyes, nostrils and sensory organs are at the ends of its head 'branches', so it has stereoscopic vision and can tri-angulate smells and electromagnetic signals.

 Proboscis monkeys are the only primate with partially webbed feet.

DECEMBER
WEEK.02

NOUABALÉ-NDOKI NATIONAL PARK CONGO

WHAT YOU'LL SEE

- LOWLAND GORILLAS
- FOREST ELEPHANTS
- FOREST BUFFALO
- SITATUNGAS
- BONGOS

WHY NOW? It's the beginning of the short dry season

Shrouded in mystery and the ever-shifting vagaries of war and political unrest, the heart of the Congo Basin sees very few visitors from the outside world. Yet a vast area on the border of Congo and the Central African Republic promises one of the premier wildlife experiences in all of Africa for those who make the journey into this uncertain region. Together, the Nouabalé-Ndoki National Park in Congo and the neighbouring Dzanga-Sangha Dense Forest Reserve in the Central African Republic protect 14,000 sq km of the most impenetrable and wildlife-rich habitats on earth. Because immense stretches of dense swamp vegetation have kept human intrusion at bay, there are still very large populations of lowland gorillas and forest elephants here. Many portions of these parks remain unexplored, and in some areas animals are so unfamiliar with humans that they approach out of curiosity.

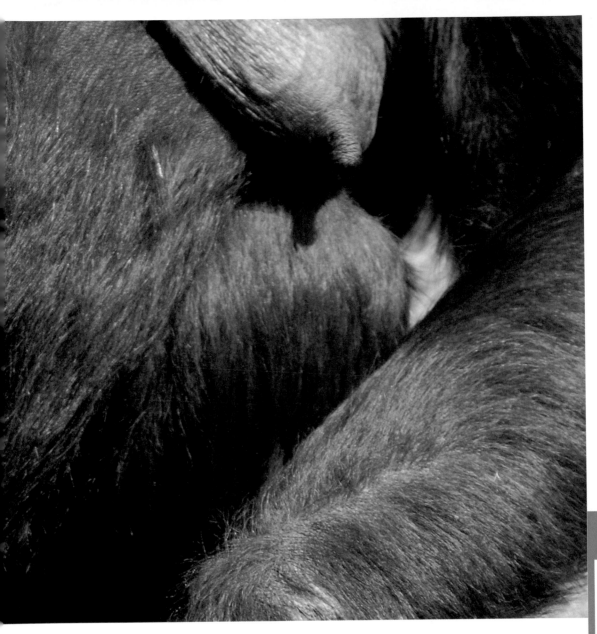

Since 2001 the Wildlife Conservation Society and government of Congo have done a particularly fine job of protecting wildlife populations and building a fledgling tourist infrastructure in Nouabalé-Ndoki. Trails, viewing platforms and high-quality rustic lodging are now available at the fabulous Mbeli Bai forest clearing, where as many as 180 habituated lowland gorillas gather in the open to feed on aquatic vegetation, along with numerous elephants, buffalo, giant forest hogs, bongos and sitatungas. Although this single 15-hectare clearing is one of the world's foremost wildlife sites, fewer than 600 tourists visited in 2006.

Increasingly, Nouabalé-Ndoki is part of a transboundary tourism circuit that includes the Dzanga-Sangha Reserve, so there is hope of piecing together a plan to see both amazing parks in one visit. International and national tour operators offer a few packages, which are probably your best bet because an independent expedition into one or both parks could be a major undertaking.

Sadly, these last refuges are under intense pressure from an increasing human population, poaching and foreign logging companies. Elephants have been nearly eliminated in the Central African Republic except at Dzanga-Sangha, but only in Nouabalé-Ndoki National Park are wildlife populations secure for the moment.

Visitors to Dzanga-Sangha are encouraged to check at the WWF office in Bangui, 525km northeast of the reserve, before visiting.
MORE INFO www.wcscongo.org).

ELEPHANT SEALS USA

LOCATION Año Nuevo State Natural Reserve, 88km south of San Francisco, California, USA **WHY NOW?** The males are battling for dominance **LEVEL OF DIFFICULTY** Low – you can see them on short guided tours **STATUS** They are stable and protected

Seeing elephant seals on their breeding grounds is an experience you'll never forget. Starting in mid-December, male elephant seals, weighing 2700kg and looking like giant blubbery sausages with flippers, haul onto the beach at Año Nuevo and immediately start some of the fiercest battles in the animal kingdom. Rearing 2m to 3m in the air, males slash repeatedly at each other with dangerous canines and thunderous blows. These ferocious, bloody battles may last 45 minutes and continue until combatants can barely move from exhaustion.

Males spend all year preparing for this spectacle, building up layers of blubber because they will not eat or drink during the three months they stay on land. Despite these preparations, only one in 10 males will ever reach the status of an alpha male, and the energy drain of the effort is so great that alpha males only have one successful breeding season as 'top seal'. Grand prize is a dominant position within the breeding colony and access to harems of 50 to 1000 females that start coming ashore in late December to give birth and mate. Until the 19th century, elephant seals were abundant from San Francisco to Baja California. However, by 1884 they were considered extinct after decades of excessive hunting, then in 1892 a colony of eight was discovered on a remote island by a biologist who killed seven of them and sent their bodies to the Smithsonian. From this terrifying low point, they have recovered to a population of 160,000 today, with about 5000 hauling up at Año Nuevo, the largest mainland breeding colony in the world. You can see them on guided walks at the reserve from mid-December to the end of March.

MORE INFO www.parks.ca.gov/?page_id=523

(LEFT) ↗
Elephant seals fight for the alpha male position; being 'top seal' requires so much energy that they may only hold that position for one mating season.

(TOP RIGHT) ↗
Swifts protect themselves from predators by roosting behind waterfalls.

(BOTTOM RIGHT) ↗
Flying lizards get airborne by popping out their ribs, which are connected by loose flaps of skin.

GREAT DUSKY SWIFTS ARGENTINA

LOCATION Iguazú National Park, 1350km north of Buenos Aires
WHY NOW? It's the best time to see waterfalls **LEVEL OF DIFFICULTY**
Low – it's a very popular, easily accessed park **STATUS** They are common and
widespread

Iguazú means 'big water' in the indigenous Guarani language, and there might
be no better way to describe the world's most spectacular waterfall. Here
on the border of Argentina and Brazil (with Paraguay a few kilometres away),
the Iguazú River turns south then north as it spreads out and plummets over
an immense U-shaped 80m-high lip of hard basalt. At this point the river is
1500m wide and, depending on water levels, forms anywhere from 160 to
260 separate waterfalls around a huge thundering bowl of mist, rainbows and
tropical rainforest.

The stunning visual presence of this place is nicely accentuated by a
bird that no one misses on a visit to the falls – the great dusky swift. With
incredible energy and great athletic grace, flocks of several hundred swifts arc
and wheel like daredevils through the billowing clouds of foam and mist. The
best time to see the swifts is towards the end of the day when they return
from their daily feeding flights over the 2200 sq km of rainforest protected by
Argentina's Iguazú National Park and Brazil's cross-border Iguaçu National Park.
It's hard to believe, but the swifts' goal is to roost behind the veil of waterfalls
where they are safe from predators; watch them cut through waterfalls and
disappear behind the water.

MORE INFO www.iguazuargentina.com

FLYING LIZARDS MALAYSIAN BORNEO

LOCATION Sarawak, northern Borneo **WHY NOW?** The courtship displays
in December and January bring out the best in these lizards **LEVEL OF
DIFFICULTY** Low to medium – it involves jungle travel and access varies from
site to site **STATUS** The lizards are common but their jungle homes are being
cleared at an alarming rate

Visit any national park in Sarawak and you can't help but notice that one of the
forest's most common and remarkable creatures is a flying lizard, with up to
six species at some locations. Slender as a pencil and camouflaged to look like
tree bark, the draco flying lizard isn't something you'd write home about, until it
launches into flight right before your eyes.

The lizard accomplishes this nifty trick by pivoting out its ribs, which are
connected by loose flaps of skin – sproing! Out pop the ribs and off the lizard
glides like a paper plane. This is where being so lightweight comes in handy,
because these little lizards glide effortlessly for as much as 50m between
trees. Not only is this a clever way of getting away from predatory snakes, but
scientists believe that the brightly coloured 'wings' help attract the attention
of potential mates during their excited breeding displays in December and
January.

One of the most fascinating experiences is having flying lizards land on you
while you're walking along a jungle trail. If you're quick, and careful, you can
catch one and gently toss it into the air and watch it fly away.

MORE INFO www.forestry.sarawak.gov.my

↗ DECEMBER

WEEK.03

PAPAHĀNAUMOKUĀKEA MARINE NATIONAL MONUMENT USA

WHAT YOU'LL SEE

LAYSAN ALBATROSS
GREAT FRIGATEBIRDS
RED-TAILED TROPICBIRDS
MONK SEALS
HAWAIIAN SPINNER DOLPHINS

WHY NOW? The albatross are courting and nesting in December

This mouthful of syllables is a Hawaiian name honouring the birth of the Hawaiian Islands (Papahānaumoku is the goddess who birthed the islands; her husband was Wakea) and it's been given to a part of the Hawaiian archipelago that very few people ever see – a sprawling line of 10 islands that lie far to the west of the main Hawaiian Islands: Nihoa, Necker, French Frigate Shoals, Gardner Pinnacles, Laysan, Lisianski, Pearl and Hermes Reef, Midway and Kure.

In fact, this is the most remote archipelago in the world, sitting smack-dab in the centre of the Pacific Ocean, with San Francisco 4500km to the east and Japan 3500km to the west. Even the Big Island of Hawaii is 1900km away, scarcely an afterthought beyond the curve of the earth. This intense isolation translates into one stellar quality: superabundant wildlife on a scale that the imagination can scarcely comprehend. It's far

easier to point out the islands' 14 million seabirds, but hidden beneath the surface of the ocean is a tropical marine environment that's been scarcely touched or fished. These superlative qualities are what lie behind the establishment of this 360,000 sq km national monument in 2007.

The best place to explore the wonders of this new monument is at the tiny spit of sand called Midway Island, where a million albatross and a million other seabirds come to breed. Albatross nests cover much of the island, including the lawns of Midway's decommissioned naval base. Once you hear courting albatross moan like lovesick cows and utter shrill repeated whistles, you'll see why they've been given the affectionate nickname 'gooney birds'.

Papahānaumokuākea Marine National Monument may be one of the most difficult and challenging places to visit in the world. Midway Island was opened to a few visitors in 2008, and it's the only island open to the public. The best way to visit is to sign up for a natural history expedition offered by the Oceanic Society (www.oceanic-society.org). Groups are limited to 16 visitors, so these six-day expeditions allow for a remarkably intimate experience. Another option is to volunteer with the Fish & Wildlife Service to help with wildlife surveys and habitat restoration projects (www.fws.gov/midway/volunteer.html).
MORE INFO www.hawaiireef.noaa.gov

BIRDWATCHING PANAMA

↘ **LOCATION** Canopy Tower, 25km northwest of Panama City **WHY NOW?** You can enjoy the best mix of resident and migrant birds **LEVEL OF DIFFICULTY** Low – it's pure birding bliss **STATUS** The birds are well protected

Imagine waking in the morning with canopy-level birds scolding you right outside your hotel window. You roll out of bed, wander up a flight of stairs, grab a coffee and some breakfast and take in one of Panama's best views looking over the treetops down onto the Canal Zone and the beautiful jungles of Soberanía National Park. Mornings like this have made the Canopy Tower one of the most memorable birding sites in the world, and one of Panama's most famous hotels. Although this once-abandoned radar tower is a very strange building, you can't argue with the fact that it puts you right up there in the jungle canopy with hundreds of birds that are otherwise very difficult to observe.

The close-up views of blue cotingas, green-shrike vireos, golden-hooded tanagers, red-legged honeycreepers and countless other colourful birds will outshine anything else you see in Panama, but if you get a hankering to see more birds, you're in the right country at the right time of year. For 20 years running, Panama led the world in having the highest numbers of any Christmas Bird Count, posting counts of around 350 species seen in a single 24-hour period. Check out the famous Pipeline Road and other well-known sites and you'll head home with a big list of your own.

MORE INFO www.canopytower.com

(LEFT) ↗
Panama is home to many species of bird, including blue cotingas, green-shrike vireos, golden-hooded tanagers and red-legged honeycreepers.

(TOP RIGHT) ↗
Male markhor antelope use their 2m-long corkscrew horns to fight by locking them and then using the leverage to twist their opponent onto the ground.

(BOTTOM RIGHT) ↗
Warthogs scatter their home ranges with up to 10 burrows, providing multiple escape routes should they be threatened by a predator.

MARKHOR ANTELOPE PAKISTAN

LOCATION Chitral Gol National Park, 240km northwest of Islamabad, 90 minutes' drive from Chitral **WHY NOW?** It's the rutting season for markhor and there's a chance of seeing snow leopards **LEVEL OF DIFFICULTY** Medium – snow and political unrest make this an adventure **STATUS** They are endangered

The 320km-long Chitral Valley in the Northwest Frontier Province of Pakistan, only 50km from the Afghanistan border and winding between soaring peaks of the Hindu Kush, is an awesomely beautiful place. At the same time, it is tucked between frontier tribal areas in one of the world's most volatile regions so it has dropped from the radar of most travellers. This is unfortunate because recent visitors (see lonelyplanet.com/thorntree for updates) report feeling safe and welcomed in an area that the media has not always presented positively.

Chitral Gol National Park has some of the most endangered wildlife in the western Himalayas, including snow leopards, Siberian ibexes, Ladakh urials, black bears, Tibetan wolves and Himalayan otters. You can visit anytime after late spring, but a December visit guarantees sightings of markhor antelope. Cold temperatures and impending snowfall drives them out of the alpine zone onto the park's lower slopes, and the males fight, locking their 2m-long corkscrewed horns together and twisting each other onto their backs. This may also be your best chance to spot snow leopards following their primary prey out of the high mountains. Sadly, their numbers have declined precipitously and it is now extremely difficult to see either the leopards or their signs; ask local rangers if they've seen anything recently. Chitral Gol also has the largest gathering of these odd Himalayan goats on earth – about 650, according to one recent estimate. The park has two lodges and astounding trekking.
MORE INFO www.travel-culture.com/pakistan/chitral.shtml

WARTHOGS KENYA

LOCATION Amboseli National Park, 265km southeast of Nairobi **WHY NOW?** It's the best time to see youngsters **LEVEL OF DIFFICULTY** Low – there are many guided tours and walks **STATUS** They are common and well protected

Despite their looks and reputation, warthogs are one of the more fascinating characters on the African plains. They are especially fun to watch when they have youngsters and you spot a whole line of babies trotting along behind their mother with heads high, manes flowing and skinny tails aloft. Sounders (a female and her brood) depend on burrows for their survival; they use up to 10 burrows in their home range and knowing where the nearest one is located can be a matter of life and death. When pursued by lions, cheetahs or hyenas, they bolt with astonishing speed for the nearest hole, babies heading in first and the mother backing in while slashing viciously with her tusks.

These wildly protruding tusks (actually greatly elongated upper canines) may be their most conspicuous weapons, but it's the lower canines, which are continually sharpened by rubbing against the upper canines, that deliver savage blows to their enemies. Big boars have three prominent fatty warts on the sides of their faces to help protect them from the blows of their competitors during mating-season fights.

You can catch warthog antics at many of Kenya's parks and reserves, but why not watch them at Amboseli against the extremely picturesque backdrop of Mt Kilimanjaro? This park has easy access and an excellent infrastructure.
MORE INFO www.kws.org/amboseli.html

DID YOU KNOW?

Smugglers have discovered that snow leopard fat smeared on drugs prevents drug-sniffing dogs from finding the contraband.

Warthogs lack fur and fat so they keep warm by lining their burrows with grass and huddling together.

↗ DECEMBER
WEEK.04

CORCOVADO NATIONAL PARK
COSTA RICA

WHAT YOU'LL SEE

SCARLET MACAWS

FIERY-BILLED ARACARIS

BAIRD'S TAPIRS

CENTRAL AMERICAN
SQUIRREL MONKEYS

OCELOTS

↘ **WHY NOW?** Travel is easiest in the dry season

Projecting into the Pacific like a bony thumb bent down towards the Panama, the Osa Peninsula ranks among the wettest and most rugged of Costa Rica's lowlands. It was also one of the most inaccessible, so logging has been held at bay until fairly recently. With much of its original rainforest intact, the peninsula is one of the premier sanctuaries for wildlife in the country and Corcovado National Park is its unspoiled wilderness core.

The best wildlife-watching in Corcovado is found around the Sirena Research Station at the heart of the park, but you have to get there first. It's possible to fly or boat in, but most people hike in from one of three trailheads and are rarely disappointed by the experience. Two coastal trails follow beaches where crashing waves mask the sound of your approach and allow excellent viewing of white-faced capuchins, collared peccaries, white-nosed

[LEFT] ↖
Corcovado National
Park's coastal trails
allow good vantage
points for viewing
capuchin monkeys.

coatis and northern tamanduas. Coastal trails also produce an endless pageant of birds, with guaranteed sightings of scarlet macaws at the top of the list.

Real rainforest fans can approach Sirena via the Los Patos trail, which abounds with birds such as great currasows, chestnut-mandibled toucans and turquoise cotingas. If you're lucky, you'll run across multiple mixed-species flocks with so many birds you'll have a hard time identifying all of them.

Staying at the research station is a must because the long-term presence of researchers has habituated customarily shy species to the comings and goings of people and makes mammal-spotting uncommonly easy. Finding the extremely elusive Baird's tapir is practically guaranteed, and there are even chances of observing one of several jaguars that frequent the open area along the airstrip. Corcovado is also the only national park in Costa Rica that has all four species of monkey found in the country – Central American spider monkeys, Central American squirrel monkeys, mantled howlers and white-faced capuchins – and even better, they are all common and easily approached here.

This park is a budget-traveller's paradise because cheap campsites and dorm-style rooms are available at Sirena. Excellent, inexpensive meals are available and it is recommended that you take advantage of this offering rather than bringing your own food because it generates a small profit for the park.

MORE INFO www.corcovado.org; www.osa conservation.org

SNOW MONKEYS JAPAN

↘ **LOCATION** Jigokudani Monkey Park, 170km northwest of Tokyo **WHY NOW?** You'll see monkeys 'hot-tubbing' on a snowy winter day **LEVEL OF DIFFICULTY** Medium – it's easier if you speak Japanese but still involves a long hike in the snow **STATUS** They are not currently threatened

Amid the steep mountain slopes, ski resorts and volcanoes northwest of Tokyo, there lurks a lesser-known natural attraction: the snow monkeys of Jigokudani Yaen Koen ('Jigokudani Monkey Park'). Known scientifically as Japanese macaques, snow monkeys live further north and at far colder temperatures than any other nonhuman primate. During northern Japan's frigid winters these 5kg to 15kg monkeys survive on a meagre diet of bark and tree buds, and struggle to stay warm.

However, snow monkeys possess an uncanny capacity for passing on new ideas. In fact, the famous '100th monkey' dictum that new ideas spread spontaneously once they reach critical mass arose from a scientific study in which a single snow monkey started washing her food in the ocean and within a few generations every monkey was doing the same thing. This same behaviour led a snow monkey to plunk herself courageously into one of Nagano's steaming hot springs in 1963. On a bitterly cold day, those 50°C waters must have felt like heaven because it wasn't long before this 'hot-tubbing' behaviour spread to all 270 monkeys that live in Jigokudani ('hell valley').

This lovely collection of hot springs is located outside the resort town of Yudanaka, the site of ancient architecture, cobblestone streets and 19 hot spring spas and guesthouses.

MORE INFO www.jigokudani-yaenkoen.co.jp/english/top/english.html

[LEFT] ↗
In the struggle to stay warm in northern Japan's freezing winters, snow monkeys make intelligent use of Jigokudani's hot springs

[TOP RIGHT] ↗
When being chased by a predator, the semi-aquatic lechwe runs into the safety of shallow water, where the predator can move with less speed

[BOTTOM RIGHT] ↗
Tikal National Park in Guatemala allows excellent views of the morning flyout of parrots

KAFUE LECHWE ZAMBIA

LOCATION Lochinvar National Park, 180km southwest of Lusaka
WHY NOW? You can see a real show during the brief breeding season
LEVEL OF DIFFICULTY Medium – most roads require a 4WD, but walking is encouraged **STATUS** Numbers are down significantly

Lechwe are unusual semi-aquatic antelope with a rather limited range in south-central Africa. With beefed-up hindquarters designed for high galloping bounds rather than all-out sprints, plus extra-long splayed hooves, lechwe excel in racing through shallow waters to escape predators that could otherwise catch them easily on dry ground. It is a spectacular sight to witness herds of lechwe startled by a predator because they leap frantically in all directions, splashing wildly and creating mass confusion.

Lechwe are uniquely adapted for the zone where shallow lake waters stretch across flat floodplains. This zone fluctuates widely between dry and wet seasons so lechwe are highly mobile. Prime examples of this habitat are found along Zambia's Kafue River, with one 22,480 sq km area protected at Kafue National Park, and another tiny pocket at Lochinvar National Park. Because of its size and dense lechwe populations (about 40,000), Lochinvar is the best place in the world to witness this antelope's remarkable breeding behaviour.

For a very brief window in December or January, males gather on temporary leks where they fiercely defend minuscule territories, with each male standing about 15m from its neighbours. Males in the prime locations attract high numbers of fertile females (find the action by looking for gaggles of females standing near one or two males) but the effort of mating with all these females and fighting off the competition quickly drains dominant males of their energy.

Lochinvar is reached via 4WD or charter plane; accommodation is available at a WWF campsite near the southern gate.
MORE INFO www.zambiatourism.com/travel/nationalparks/lochinva.htm

MORNING FLYOUT GUATEMALA

LOCATION Tikal National Park, 320km northeast of Guatemala City
WHY NOW? It's easiest to visit in the dry season **LEVEL OF DIFFICULTY** Low – it's a very popular and easily accessible park **STATUS** The parrot population is stable and well protected

Watching the morning flyout of parrots at Tikal National Park is a fitting conclusion to our year of watching wildlife. Here, amid the shattered ruins of one of history's greatest civilisations, the irrepressible triumph of the natural world is both majestic and humbling.

When we travel around the planet it feels like humans are wreaking havoc on the natural world in every place we visit, yet Tikal is a sobering (or hopeful) reminder that human civilisations are ephemeral and nature ultimately arises from the ashes like a mythical phoenix. Despite its past as the greatest city of the Mayan empire, Tikal is today home to abundant, relatively fearless wildlife and vast stretches of pristine rainforest. As you wander among Tikal's ancient towering pyramids you'll encounter many iridescent ocellated turkeys, great currasows and crested guans, along with magnificent predators such as orange-breasted falcons and ornate hawk-eagles.

Climb the steps of Tikal's tallest temple at sunrise and you'll witness the exuberant morning flyout of hundreds of noisy parrots winging across the misty tops of an astounding 5-million-hectare forest that stretches unbroken into Mexico and Belize. In this one moment, all the pieces of our year's journey are here – sadness, loss, resurrection, preservation and hope.
MORE INFO www.tikalpark.com

DID YOU KNOW?

Snow-monkey society is led by long-standing mother–daughter lineages; males must move from group to group because females won't mate with an overstaying male.

Tikal was once a royal city that covered 120 sq km; only a tiny fraction has been excavated.

WILDLIFE VOLUNTEERING

EARTHWATCH INSTITUTE

www.earthwatch.org

This global conservation charity places volunteers on scientific research expeditions in over 50 countries, with the aim of promoting the understanding and action necessary for a sustainable environment. Past volunteer expeditions have included projects as diverse as looking at climate change in the Arctic, researching the habitat of the cheetah in Namibia, studying elephant behaviour and protecting turtle hatchlings.

Timing & Length of Projects: Expedition lengths vary from two days to three weeks, with departure dates throughout the year. You can opt to go on two consecutive expeditions, at different locations within the same country.

Destinations: Worldwide.

Eligibility: Depending on the project, volunteers need to be aged at least 16 or 18. There are also some family teams which can include children 10 years and older. There are no required skills or experience. Earthwatch tries to accommodate all disabilities.

Selection & Interview Process: A telephone discussion is held with each participant to ensure an appropriate match between volunteers and projects.

GREENPEACE

www.greenpeace.org

Started as a small, campaigning organisation in Vancouver, Greenpeace is now an international organisation with offices around the globe. Its mission has remained unchanged: to use non-violent, creative confrontation to expose global environmental problems and force solutions. All offices offer plenty of volunteering opportunities, from stuffing envelopes to public outreach, and from lobbying to Amazon survival training. Many offices also offer intern positions to applicants with appropriate skills. Contact the international office for current openings or get in touch with your local office.

Timing & Length of Projects: There are various opportunities within numerous countries, including short- and long-term placements.

Destinations: Worldwide, including aboard Greenpeace's ships.

Eligibility: Depending on the project, volunteers can be unskilled or may need specific training and expertise. A commitment to the aims of Greenpeace is essential.

Selection & Interview Process: This varies between countries and on what the placement entails.

BIOSPHERE EXPEDITIONS

www.biosphere-expeditions.org

This group offers volunteers the chance to be involved in hands-on wildlife and conservation research alongside local scientists in locations around the globe. Promoting sustainable conservation, the group doles out 'adventures with a purpose'. Past projects have included snow-leopard research in the Altai mountains, whale studies on the Azores, human–elephant conflict resolution in Sri Lanka and chamois, bear and wolf conservation projects in the Tatra mountains.

Timing & Length of Projects: From two to 10 weeks, starting every two weeks.

Destinations: Project locations vary, depending on where there is a need, however they generally include Oman, Honduras, Azores Archipelago, Peru, Slovakia, Sri Lanka, Namibia, Brazil and the Altai Republic.

Costs: Between £990 to £1250 including all food, lodging and in-country transportation. At least two-thirds of this contribution goes directly into the conservation project to fund long-term sustainability.

Eligibility: Biosphere aims to be inclusive and there are no age or physical restrictions (the oldest participant was 87!). Expeditions vary in the amount of physical ability required and you must be confident that you can cope with the demands. Volunteers under the age of 18 must have parental consent.

Selection & Interview Process: As long as you meet the rather open criteria, you can join an expedition instantaneously online.

BLUE VENTURES

www.blueventures.org

Blue Ventures runs projects and expeditions to research and conserve global marine life. Its volunteer programme is popular and has won a number of prestigious eco-awards. Volunteers carry out research with scientists and camp staff in southwest Madagascar. This includes diving to collect data, monitoring sites, surveying coral reef habitats and identifying new sites. Onshore, volunteers assist with social-research activities, surveys, community environmental education, awareness-raising initiatives and teaching English or French in local schools. Placements can be focused towards volunteers' interests.

Timing & Length of Projects: Six weeks, although there are options to stay for three weeks or over six weeks. Projects begin year-round.

Destinations: Madagascar.

Eligibility: Minimum age is 18. There are no skills or experience required. Those with disabilities are accepted whenever possible.

Selection & Interview Process: Application form followed by a telephone interview.

ORANGUTAN FOUNDATION

www.orangutan.org.uk
This well-respected charity actively conserves the orang-utan and its Indonesian rainforest habitat. Volunteer placements are generally construction based, such as building release camps or conservation health centres. While volunteers do not have hands-on contact with orang-utans, they do encounter some of the free ranging, ex-captive orang-utans in the locality and will have the opportunity to accompany resident assistants into the forest to search for wild orang-utans. They're also given the chance to visit the orang-utan care centre.

Timing & Length of Projects: Six weeks between April and November with set starting dates.

Destinations: Indonesian Borneo.

Eligibility: Previous field experience is desirable but not necessary. Volunteers must be at least 18, physically fit, in good health and a member of the Orangutan Foundation. Applications should note that the placements require a great deal of physical exertion. Due to the nature of the work, placements are not open to those with physical disabilities.

Selection & Interview Process: Apply online. Interviews held in London.

OCEANIC SOCIETY

www.oceanic-society.org
The Oceanic Society is a nonprofit organisation dedicated to protecting wildlife and marine biodiversity. Research projects are sponsored in cooperation with selected universities; volunteers help fund and conduct fieldwork.

Timing & Length of Projects: Projects last seven to 10 days; volunteers may also register for back-to-back sessions lasting up to a month. Some projects (such as humpback whale migration research) have seasonal departure dates, but others operate year-round.

Destinations: Belize, Costa Rica, Suriname and Brazil.

Eligibility: Minimum age is 16. Fieldwork is often physically demanding, and a doctor's approval may be required.

Selection & Interview Process: The organisation commissions the fieldwork conducted by its Partner Programmes, which must share a responsible and sincere interest in conservation education and research. Volunteer openings for each project are limited.

CONSERVATION VOLUNTEERS AUSTRALIA – WORLD CONSERVATION PROGRAMMES

www.conservationvolunteers.com.au
From wildlife surveys to tree planting, Conservation Volunteers Australia is renowned for its work in urban, regional and remote Australia but also offers World Conservation Programmes enabling volunteers to join team-based conservation programmes around the globe. The organisation is a founding member of the Conservation Volunteers Alliance (www.cvalliance .org) bringing together worldwide organisations which promote and manage conservation volunteer projects. In 2006 Conservation Volunteers New Zealand (www .conservationvolunteers.co.nz) was launched.

Timing & Length of Assignments: Projects take place year-round; set departure dates are advertised on the website.

Destinations: California, Costa Rica, Ecuador, France, Galápagos Islands, Greece, Italy, Japan, New Zealand, South Africa and Turkey (the Gallipoli project).

Eligibility: Volunteers must be aged between 18 and 70 and should be in good health. Volunteers with disabilities are catered for where possible.

Selection & Interview Process: A short application form covering pre-existing medical conditions, allergies or injuries that may affect participation must be completed.

FUNDACIÓN JATUN SACHA

www.jatunsacha.org
This environmental conservation organisation offers volunteers a placement in one of eight biological stations, including one on the Galápagos Islands and others in tropical rainforests and highlands. Volunteers are involved in reforestation, seed collection, developing and teaching classes in environmental education, agroforestry, reserve maintenance and the development of organic agriculture.

Timing & Length of Projects: Volunteers can join projects year-round, and participate from two weeks to a year.

Destinations: Ecuador.

Eligibility: An interest in conservation, community development or environmental teaching.

Selection & Interview Process: Volunteers should apply with a letter indicating experience in relevant activities, reasons for applying, future interests, preferred station and preferred dates, a CV, a doctor's note of fitness, two passport-sized photos and the application fee.

INDEX

LOCATION INDEX ↗

PHOTO CREDITS

In order: clockwise on spread, from top left

JANUARY WEEK 1
Hira Punjabi, Lonely Planet Images
Manfred Gottschalk, Lonely Planet Images
Tom Boyden, Lonely Planet Images
Tim Laman, National Geographic Stock

JANUARY WEEK 2
Mike Tercek, Alamy
Michael Aw, Lonely Planet Images
Krzysztof Dydynski, Lonely Planet Images
Ray Tipper, Lonely Planet Images

JANUARY WEEK 3
Shannon Nace, Lonely Planet Images
Richard Mittleman/Gon2Foto, Photolibrary
Martin Cohen, Lonely Planet Images
Luke Hunter, Lonely Planet Images

JANUARY WEEK 4
Heinrich van den Berg, Getty Images
Christer Fredriksson, Lonely Planet Images
Peter Bennetts, Lonely Planet Images
John Hay, Lonely Planet Images

FEBRUARY WEEK 1
TimLaman, Getty Images
Dave Hamman, Lonely Planet Images
Alexander Safonov
Johannes Gerhardus Swanepoel, Dreamstime

FEBRUARY WEEK 2
Jeff Greenberg, Lonely Planet Images
Grant Dixon, Lonely Planet Images
Frances Linzee Gordon, Lonely Planet Images
Dave Watts, Nature Picture Library

FEBRUARY WEEK 3
Beverly Joubert, Getty Images
Guillermo Velez, iStock
Douglas Steakley, Lonely Planet Images
Andrew Parkinson, Lonely Planet Images

FEBRUARY WEEK 4
Bob Halstead, Lonely Planet Images
Toohoku Color Agency, Getty Images
Mark Carwardine, Nature Picture Library
John Branagan, Lonely Planet Images

MARCH WEEK 1
KPA/Hakenberg, Alamy
Vladimir Melnik, Dreamstime
Ralph Hopkins, Lonely Planet Images
Flip Nicklin / Minden Pictures, National Geographic Stock

MARCH WEEK 2
Andrew Brownbill, Lonely Planet Images
David Tipling, Lonely Planet Images
Tim Rock, Lonely Planet Images
Heinrich van den Berg, Getty Images

MARCH WEEK 3
Mark Newman, Lonely Planet Images
Theo Allofs, Corbis
Mark Daffey, Lonely Planet Images
David Tipling, Lonely Planet Images

MARCH WEEK 4
Jeff Rotman, Nature Picture Library
Andrew MacColl, Lonely Planet Images
Christer Fredriksson, Lonely Planet Images
Mitch Reardon, Lonely Planet Images

APRIL WEEK 1
Untamed, Photolibrary
Mark Newman, Lonely Planet Images
Rick & Nora Bowers, Alamy
Solvin Zankl, Nature Picture Library

APRIL WEEK 2
Tom Boyden, Lonely Planet Images
WorldFoto, Photolibrary
Jeffrey Beacom, Lonely Planet Images
David Tipling, Lonely Planet Images

APRIL WEEK 3
Blickwinkel/Meyers, Photolibrary
Jason Edwards, Lonely Planet Images
Stephen Saks, Lonely Planet Images
Rolf Nussbaumer, Nature Picture Library

APRIL WEEK 4
Clark Wheeler, iStock
Franco Banfi, Photolibrary
Rusty Dodson, Dreamstime
Beverly Joubert, National Geographic Stock

MAY WEEK 1
Natural Selection David Ponton, Photolibrary
Lorraine Swanson, iStock
Mitch Reardon, Lonely Planet Images
Tim Laman, Nature Picture Library

MAY WEEK 2
Jeff Greenberg, Lonely Planet Images
David Tipling, Lonely Planet Images
Dr Morley Read, Photolibrary
Karen Harrison, iStock

MAY WEEK 3
WILDLIFE GmbH, Alamy
David Fleetham, Alamy
John Cancalosi, Photolibrary
Bob Halstead, Lonely Planet Images

MAY WEEK 4
INTERFOTO/Zoology, Alamy
Robert F. Sisson, Getty Images
Judy Bellah, Lonely Planet Images
Ralph Hopkins, Lonely Planet Images

JUNE WEEK 1
David E. Meyers, Getty Images
Carol Polich, Lonely Planet Images
Keren Su, Lonely Planet Images
Jozsef Szentpeteri, National Geographic Stock

JUNE WEEK 2
Alexander Safonov
Serdar Uckun, iStock
Horst Jegen, Photolibrary
Er. Degginger, Photolibrary

JUNE WEEK 3
Nicholas Reuss, Lonely Planet Images
Andrew Parkinson, Lonely Planet Images
Mark Newman, Lonely Planet Images
Martin Cohen, Lonely Planet Images

JUNE WEEK 4
Adrian Bailey, Lonely Planet Images
Mark Newman, Lonely Planet Images
Pete Oxford, Nature Picture Library
Birgitte Wilms, National Geographic Stock

JULY WEEK 1
JTB Photo, Photolibrary
Bob Charlton, Lonely Planet Images
Ralph Hopkins, Lonely Planet Images
Premaphotos, Nature Picture Library

JULY WEEK 2
William Leaman, Photolibrary
Mark Newman, Lonely Planet Images
Rob Broek, iStock
Tim Rock, Lonely Planet Images

JULY WEEK 3
Adrian Bailey, Lonely Planet Images
John Hay, Lonely Planet Images
Sunheyy, Dreamstime
Laurent Geslin, Nature Picture Library

JULY WEEK 4
MG Therin Weise, Getty Images
Dan Burton, Nature Picture Library
James Warwick, Getty Images
Omar Ariff Kamarul Ariffin, Dreamstime

AUGUST WEEK 1
Alain Dragesco-Joffe, Photolibrary
Rolf Nussbaumer, Nature Picture Library
Ariadne Van, Lonely Planet Images
Christer Fredriksson, Lonely Planet Images

AUGUST WEEK 2
Igor Shpilenok, Nature Picture Library
Andy Rouse, Getty Images
Ingo Arndt, Nature Picture Library
Doug Allan & Sue Flood, Getty Images

AUGUST WEEK 3
Dick Durrance II, National Geographic Stock
Hira Punjabi, Lonely Planet Images
Ralph Hopkins, Lonely Planet Images
Michael Lawrence, Lonely Planet Images

AUGUST WEEK 4
Chrystite Licenced, Photolibrary
Ariadne Van, Lonely Planet Images
António Nunes, Dreamstime
Ralph Hopkins, Lonely Planet Images

SEPTEMBER WEEK 1
Dengyinchai, Dreamstime
Craig Pershouse, Lonely Planet Images
Casey Mahaney, Lonely Planet Images
Morten Strange, NHPA

SEPTEMBER WEEK 2
Yoshio Tomii Photo Studio, Photolibrary
Jeff Foott, Getty Images
David Kjaer, Nature Picture Library
Dave Hamman, Lonely Planet Images

SEPTEMBER WEEK 3
tbkmedia.de, Photolibrary
Tom Brakefield, Getty
Zepherwind, Dreamstime
Konrad Wothe/Minden Pictures, National Geographic Stock

SEPTEMBER WEEK 4
L. Kennedy, Photolibrary
Tim Laman, National Geographic Stock
Frances Linzee Gordon, Lonely Planet Images
David Doubilet, National Geographic Stock

OCTOBER WEEK 1
David Tipling, Lonely Planet Images
David Wall, Lonely Planet Images
Hira Punjabi, Lonely Planet Images
Jason Bazzano, Photolibrary

OCTOBER WEEK 2
Ariadne Van, Lonely Planet Images
David Shaw, Photolibrary
Luke Hunter, Lonely Planet Images
David McLain, Getty Images

OCTOBER WEEK 3
Karl Lehmann, Lonely Planet Images
David Tipling, Lonely Planet Images
Mark Bowler Amazon Images, Photolibrary
Adrian Bailey, Lonely Planet Images

OCTOBER WEEK 4
Dennis Jones, Lonely Planet Images
Lee Foster, Lonely Planet Images
Casey Mahaney, Lonely Planet Images
Paul Kennedy, Lonely Planet Images

NOVEMBER WEEK 1
Michael Aw, Lonely Planet Images
David Tipling, Lonely Planet Images
Steve Simonsen, Lonely Planet Images
Vladimir Mucibabic, Dreamstime

NOVEMBER WEEK 2
Karl Lehmann, Lonely Planet Images
Paul Kennedy, Lonely Planet Images
David Tipling, Lonely Planet Images
Joe Blossom, NHPA

NOVEMBER WEEK 3
Andrew Parkinson, Lonely Planet Images
Jurgen Freund, Nature Picture Library
Mark Carwardine, Nature Picture Library
John Hay, Lonely Planet Images

NOVEMBER WEEK 4
Alexander Hafemann, iStock
franzfoto.com, Photolibrary
AccuSoft Inc, NHPA
Paul Sawer, Natural Visions

DECEMBER WEEK 1
Joseph J. Scherschel, Getty Images
Anders Blomqvist, Lonely Planet Images
Alexander Safonov
Kevin Levesque, Lonely Planet Images

DECEMBER WEEK 2
Eric Gevaert, Dreamstime
Dave Adalian, iStock
Greg Brzezinski, iStock
H. Lansdown, Photolibrary

DECEMBER WEEK 3
Kevin Schafer, iStock
Alfredo Maiquez, Lonely Planet Images
Drimi, Dreamstime
Elliot Daniel, Lonely Planet Images

DECEMBER WEEK 4
Martin Shields, Getty Images
John Borthwick, Lonely Planet Images
Dennis Jones, Lonely Planet Images
Warwick Lister-Kaye, iStock

HIGHLIGHTS
Alexander Safonov
Mattias Klum, Getty Images
Bobby Haas, Getty Images
Anatoly Ustinenko, iStock
Eastcott Momatiuk, Getty Images

A YEAR OF WATCHING WILDLIFE
August 2009

PUBLISHED BY
LONELY PLANET PUBLICATIONS PTY LTD
ABN 36 005 607 983
90 Maribyrnong St, Footscray,
Victoria, 3011, Australia
WWW.LONELYPLANET.COM

Printed by Hang Tai Printing Company
Printed in China

Cover image Siberian tiger, Tom Brakefield/Photolibrary
Many of the images in this book are available for licensing from
Lonely Planet Images (LPI). www.lonelyplanetimages.com

ISBN 978 1 74179 279 9

LONELY PLANET OFFICES
AUSTRALIA Locked Bag 1, Footscray, Victoria, 3011
Phone 03 8379 8000 Fax 03 8379 8111
Email talk2us@lonelyplanet.com.au

USA 150 Linden St, Oakland, CA 94607
Phone 510 893 8556 Toll free 800 275 8555 Fax 510 893 8572
Email info@lonelyplanet.com

UK 2nd Floor, 186 City Rd, London, ECV1 2NT
Phone 020 7106 2100 Fax 020 7106 2101
Email go@lonelyplanet.co.uk

PUBLISHER Chris Rennie
ASSOCIATE PUBLISHER Ben Handicott
COMMISSIONING EDITOR Janine Eberle
PROJECT MANAGER Jane Atkin
IMAGE RESEARCHER Rebecca Dandens
ART DIRECTOR Nic Lehman
COVER DESIGNER Mark Adams
COVER ARTWORK James Hardy
EDITORS Averil Robertson, Martine Power
LAYOUT Cara Smith
PRE-PRESS PRODUCTION Ryan Evans
PRINT PRODUCTION Graham Imeson

THE AUTHOR
DAVID LUKAS
David has been a naturalist from the tender age of 5, when he began
memorising field guides before he could even read. He later dropped out of
college in order to travel the world working on field research projects for
15 years, including a year-long stint in Borneo and a project in the Amazon.
For over 20 years he has worked as a professional natural history tour
leader, leading numerous trips to Central America and around his home
base in California's Sierra Nevada mountains. Writing for Lonely Planet has
given him a fantastic opportunity to research and think about many of the
world's great ecosystems, and at last count he has written environment
and wildlife chapters for over 25 Lonely Planet travel guides, from British
Columbia to Namibia.

THANKS FROM THE AUTHOR
This book would not have been possible without countless suggestions
from wildlife experts, biologists, professional tour leaders, photographers,
and authors all over the world. I wish there were space to thank all of you,
especially those who took time to provide extensive details and advice on
some really obscure and fascinating places. Above all else, I am deeply
indebted to the exhaustive research skills of May Chen and Nancy Falk, who
generously donated their time to hunt down high-quality information for
many of the topics that went into this book. Thank you to May and Nancy,
and to the many people who care enough about the natural world to help
make a book like this possible.

A YEAR OF
WATCHING
WILDLIFE